Queer Compulsions

Queer Compulsions

Race, Nation, and Sexuality in the Affairs of Yone Noguchi

Amy Sueyoshi

University of Hawai'i Press
Honolulu

Paperback edition 2023

Printed in the United States of America

Library of Congress Cataloging-in-Publication Data

Sueyoshi, Amy Haruko.
Queer compulsions : race, nation, and sexuality in the affairs of Yone Noguchi / Amy Sueyoshi.
p. cm.
Includes bibliographical references and index.
ISBN 978-0-8248-3497-5 (hard cover : alk. paper)
1. Noguchi, Yoné, 1875–1947. 2. Poets, Japanese—Biography. I. Title.
PL812.O3Z86 2012
895.6'142—dc23
2011034715

ISBN 978-0-8248-9788-8 (paperback)

University of Hawai'i Press books are printed on acid-free paper and meet the guidelines for permanence and durability of the Council on Library Resources.

Designed by Publishers' Design and Production Services, Inc.

To all those who came before me and enabled a project such as this one to take shape

CONTENTS

Individuals and institutions outside of SFSU have also played a critical role in my research. Madeline Hsu, Greg Robinson, Mark McLelland, Horacio Roque Ramírez, Don Romesburg, Scott Kurashige, Eiichiro Azuma, and Susan Johnson have all supported this project in meaningful ways. Susan Stone provided detailed copy edits to improve my writing. Russell Sueyoshi over the years has given me hundreds of dollars in coffee shop gift cards to fuel the immense number of hours I have spent in solitude writing and rewriting the manuscript. I thank Tina Takemoto for her critical feedback on the eve of submitting my final copy to the press. Her careful comments pushed me to improve my manuscript even as my brain cramped in the last stage of revisions.

During my research residency in Japan, Akihiko Noda, Kazuhiro Iwazawa, and Yasuko Bessho went out of their way to teach me about Japanese culture and language. Invaluable assistance from Yoshio Suzuki and Miyako Sueyoshi enabled me to translate difficult-to-read Japanese texts. Chieko Suzuki generously provided sushi and Western desserts during long sessions of poring over articles on sodomy. Chiyo Honda saved me when I often felt like a helpless five-year-old, and Keiko Shinohara took me on lavish daylong excursions. Eliane Yamamoto, Nicole Restrick, and Joanne Quimby provided much-needed companionship when I became unbearably lonely. I thank Osaka Ichiritsu Daigaku's Research Center for Human Rights for sponsoring my one-year postdoctoral fellowship. In particular, I am grateful to Sakura Furukubo, who selflessly shared her office with me and exposed me to a radical community of Japanese intellectuals invested in feminism and social justice. The Osaka Ichiritsu Daigaku Judo Club, in particular Mayuko Yoshida, magnanimously tolerated an old woman such as myself joining in their practice. Additionally, I am indebted to all the Japanese gays and lesbians who befriended me. I refrain from mentioning their names here only because I worry what consequences "outing" them might have. They provided me with laughter, warmth, and opportunities for activism in San Francisco's sister city Osaka. The Kansai Queer Film Festival and the Physique Bar in Doyamacho served as my queer refuge while I was living in Japan. Finally, Kyuya Suzuki and Kyoko Suzuki were absolutely amazing in their hospitality. They introduced me to breakfast treats at the all-convenient *konbini*, put up with my incessant questions about living in Japan, drew pages of detailed maps to the "nearest" train station, fed me on countless occasions, spoiled me with weekend trips to various *onsen*, and most importantly embraced my queer partnerships. Through the Suzukis I learned what it meant to have family in Japan.

Back in the United States, those who generously shared their friendship and love with me at various times in their life—Sheree Wong, Bobby Cheung, Jennifer Kanenaga, Nancy Kim, Holly Bennett—have all been indispensable in the progress of this manuscript. I thank also my mother who has grown with me through the difficulties of my heart condition, my "smart" mouth, my coming out, and my queer activism. I know that it has been a rough road for her, a life that she hardly expected when she boarded the airplane to come to the United States in the early 1960s. She is without a doubt relieved that I have found a "stable" job. Though she is embarrassed by my work in sexuality, I dedicate this book in part to her.

Numerous grants have generously supported *Queer Compulsions*. I am indebted to the Japan Foundation, Japan Society for the Promotion of Sciences, Kansai Kokusai Koryu Kikin, Social Science Research Council, UCLA Institute of American Cultures, and UCLA Asian American Studies Center and Department. And I thank University of Hawai'i Press for giving this project a chance.

Furthermore, this book would never have materialized without the expert assistance of staff at the Bancroft Library, Huntington Library, Kansai Kokusai Senta Library, Isamu Noguchi Museum, and Keio University Library. Yuki Yamauchi took particular care in copying an immense number of articles I had previously searched and found when I suddenly had to return to the United States because of the looming death of my father. Gary Dobbs graciously shared his private collection of Ethel Armes letters. Ikuko Atsumi took the time to answer e-mails from a complete stranger to refer me to other Yone Noguchi experts. Seiji Itoh also shared his personal library of Yone Noguchi publications and took me on a tour of Noguchi's hometown, Tsushima City. Without the assistance of the above individuals and institutions this project could never have come this far.

In December 2008 I attended the opening reception for the GLBT Historical Society's Passionate Struggle exhibit, their first exhibit located in the famously gay Castro District of San Francisco. As co-curator, I felt proud of the final product that more than twelve historians had pulled together, and I invited my mom to the opening celebration. As she watched the running home videos of gay filmmaker Harold T. O'Neal, she focused particularly on the segment on white men gathering in a wooded area for relaxation. My mother then told me about my father's youngest brother, who labored for a fraternal organization in Muir Woods one summer during the 1960s. My uncle had returned from his summer job telling stories of how these odd men dressed up as women in the middle of the woods. He had likely worked for the Bohemian Club during their summer getaways in Muir Woods, where they donned women's clothes.

Suddenly, my family history converged unexpectedly with my research since *Queer Compulsions* examines the intimate life of Japanese immigrant Yone Noguchi, who provided domestic work for the Western writer Joaquin Miller and socialized extensively with Bohemian Club members. While my uncle would not go on to become a famous poet or a scholar of American literature as did Noguchi, he had walked a similar trail of immigrant work, a traveler—this time from Okinawa and more than fifty years later—who came in contact with this broadly queer all-male community.[1] Just a month previously a white colleague of mine had told me she was having Thanksgiving Dinner with her father and her partner at another private San Francisco association for the moneyed, the exclusive Olympic Club. As my colleague's father dined at one of the city's "Big Four" among other elites, my uncle in Muir Woods stood transiently at its margins washing dishes. Under the track lighting at the GLBT Historical Society exhibit as my mother told me about my uncle—the one uncle whom I often imagined as gay—the irony and inequality of these chance connections became almost too much to bear.

Perhaps I should have felt grateful for the opportunities I had been able to grasp in America despite the hurdles of racism, xenophobia, misogyny, and gender normativity. Instead, I felt exhausted not just by the class differences often dictated by race and immigrant status, but also by the struggle to be "normal" and "respectable" that faced my own Asian American family and kept them from overcoming their discomfort around things queer. The situation seems worse for my imagined gay uncle who still resides in Okinawa. My father once told me that, though he lived in close physical proximity to his siblings, only one out of six knew his home address. Apparently my uncle felt comfortable sharing the location of his refuge with only his immediately older sister. I hope that the romantic life of the more famous Yone Noguchi reminds us of the larger forces that shape our most private lives in painfully personal ways. In this respect, *Queer Compulsions* implicitly underlines the courage and strength of those who strive to live healthfully and happily despite sociocultural pressures that frequently force those more marginalized into toxic situations.

Noguchi will not appear to be the "ideal" protagonist of a historical work. He was neither heroically noble nor infamously criminal. Many will find him downright despicable owing to a series of overlapping relationships that he developed deceptively rather than consensually. Yet, as problematic as Noguchi will appear to social conservatives for his multiple lovers or his fathering a child out of wedlock, the real problem lay in his deliberate deception of his lovers into thinking that he was monogamous when in fact he was not. Social norms that touted monogamy, heterosexuality, and finally marriage as symbols of success informed his decision not to be open and honest about his intimate life. Additionally, as troubling as Noguchi will appear for "selling out" by pitching an exotic Japan for financial stability, the true trouble lay in the literary culture that drove him to believe that buying into Japonisme was the best way to sell his writing. U.S. racial realities had pushed him to produce exotic images of Japan with complete disregard as to their implication for Asian America. His struggles become historically significant as they poignantly inform us of the often intense negotiations of race, culture, and sexuality.

In 2003 I traveled to Japan on a postdoctoral fellowship funded by the Japan Foundation. When I presented my research on Yone to an academic research center for human rights, the director inquired, "Do you like Yone?" For the director, it was an important issue. He pressed on about whether I worried that I was further pathologizing "homosexuals" in my work. That year the center, according to the faculty, was the only academic program in Japan dedicated to justice for ethnic minorities and women. For them the primary goal was to legitimize marginalized communities by fighting pejorative perceptions and stereotypes. Work that might be in the least bit critical of such a community would likely become unacceptable. At a dinner with the center affiliates, when I joked about my Okinawan father frequently lying on the floor in only his boxers as he watched television, the faculty, none of them Okinawan, reprimanded me: "Don't say that. These are the very stereotypes about Okinawans that are damaging." Okinawans, perceived as lazy, uncultured, and hypersexual, are one among many ethnic minorities in Japan that have faced discrimination and ostracism. I was stunned with their scolding, and for a moment I wished for my community of color back home

The love triangles and quadrangles that formed among Noguchi, Stoddard, Gilmour, and Armes demonstrate how "separate spheres" were in fact intimately connected through love, sex, and betrayal.

Queer Compulsions locates itself within the rapidly growing field of U.S. history of sexuality and owes its viability to the vast amount of previously published works in queer studies. It fits into "homosexual" history as defined by Martin Duberman, Martha Vicinus, George Chauncey, and David Halperin in its focus on "intimate friendship" and builds on critical developments in queer theory by examining same-sex and otherwise not-usual desires whether based in personal identity or not.[14] Yet *Queer Compulsions* is also distinguished from many of the current U.S. histories of same-sex sexualities in four ways: in its span over multiple cities and regions of America as well as across the Pacific; in its weaving a narrative without the availability of oral histories, a crucial source in documenting silenced histories of the "dispossessed" for whom few print materials exist; in its focus on queer desires rather than identities built around same-sex sexual activities; and finally in its placement of race and one particular man of color at center stage in the midst of his overwhelming interactions with whites.[15]

Perhaps most important, *Queer Compulsions* reminds us of the significance of race as it traces Noguchi's same-sex affairs with Stoddard. Not only would Noguchi's intimacies demonstrate how racial difference charged "friendships" in the seemingly all-white world of bohemian America, they also point to how one Japanese in America stretched moral and racial boundaries of turn-of-the-century American sexual ideology. Noguchi articulated same-sex love and interracial marriage during times of increasing animosity toward both and carved out romantic fulfillment even within supposedly debilitating Asian American "bachelor" communities. Newspaper reports and court cases from the first quarter of the twentieth century reveal that Noguchi would not be the only Asian immigrant forging romantic and sexual connections in unconventional ways.[16]

Queer Compulsions additionally builds upon debates about queer cultures and Western imperialism. Theorists Inderpal Grewal and Caren Kaplan have noted how, in many works on sexuality, the "global" is seen as "homogenizing," rendering all gay culture to be similar around the world or as a "neo-colonial movement of ideas and capital from West to non-West."[17] If we imagine turn-of-the-century bohemians as a precursor of more contemporary "gay culture," we can see how Noguchi's own assertions and manipulations of language, culture, and desire echo an increasing number of theoretical works published more recently that propose that non-Western people construct more hybrid sexual identities and actions rather than simply replicating Western mores.[18]

Queer Compulsions may remind those interested in queer and Japanese American histories of John Howard's work on Japanese American internment camps in the American South in which he argues for the liberatory possibilities of internment for "homosexuals" as well as women. Our works run along parallel tracks in uncovering same-sex intimacy in Japanese American history. In Howard's work as in mine there additionally appears a white man inclined toward men from the Asia Pacific region; he appears as Earl Finch in Howard's book and Charles Warren Stoddard in mine. Yet my work diverges significantly from Howard's in centering on one particular queer Japanese American in Japanese American history and in its sustained focus on sexuality throughout the text.[19]

My work may most closely mirror historian Judy Wu's work on Margaret Chung, surgeon and founder of the Chinese Hospital in San Francisco. Wu traced a likely lesbian connection between Margaret and writer Elsa Gidlow and later actor Sophie Tucker during the 1930s and 1940s, when menacing lesbian identity rather than romantic female friendships undergirded passionate relationships between women. Armed with only what others thought of Chung's sexual orientation, Wu could merely speculate on the nature of her intimacies.[20] In contrast, *Queer Compulsions* uses Noguchi's and his lovers' very words to more aggressively engage in and thus make more definitive claims regarding his intimate life. Whereas the contribution of Wu's work lies in her ability to hint at the possibility of same-sex intimacy in earlier Asian American history, the significance of *Queer Compulsions* lays in its explicit exposure and detailed narrative of how one Japanese immigrant found love and affection with another man over a century ago.

Sources

Correspondence to and from Noguchi composes much of the evidence of his intimate affairs. I include in this book all of the recovered correspondence that sheds light on Noguchi's intimate life either in paraphrased or in its original form. Notably, a large number of these letters have languished unpublished because of their seemingly "trivial" content.[21] During certain years, letters from Noguchi to Stoddard appeared with more frequency. However, I found Stoddard's responses only sporadically through their long correspondence. Letters between Noguchi and Gilmour remain available only in a published collection of edited letters by Ikuko Atsumi. Finally, I recovered only one letter from Armes to Noguchi and found no letters from Noguchi to Armes. Thus passages that may appear uneven in voice, illuminating only one perspective, reflect the reality of unrecovered or missing letters.

I use over eight hundred letters from the Bancroft Library, Huntington Library, Samford University Special Collections, Birmingham Public Library, Isamu Noguchi Museum and Library, Keio University Special Collections, the personal collection of Gary Hobson Dobbs, Jr., and Ikuko Atsumi's published *Collected English Letters of Yone Noguchi*. Letters from both the Huntington Library and Gary Dobbs' personal collection have not been previously cited in recounting Noguchi's life. When citing Noguchi's letters, I have corrected some minor grammatical errors for clarity and ease in reading. While leaving passages in their original form might have more accurately projected Noguchi's actual voice, I deliberately did not do so to avoid fetishizing the nonnative English speaker's idiosyncrasies in language.[22] I hope to highlight Noguchi's experiences of being alienated and racialized in America rather than his linguistic peculiarities as an alien in America. More important, as an immigrant hoping to become a successful English-language poet, Noguchi preferred to present himself in grammatically correct English and hired editorial assistants to do so for each of his publications.

Furthermore, I incorporate additional sources written in both English and Japanese for further context. Noguchi's own published poems and prose offer important insight, illustrating his philosophies of love and life in over thirty publications. Journal and newspaper articles from the *San Francisco Chronicle*, *National Magazine*, *The Nation*, and *Yomiuri Shimbun* provided additional context on ideologies of sexuality and race in both America and Japan. Few works on Yone Noguchi, bohemian American history, or Japanese American history have used both English- and Japanese-language sources in such an extensive manner.[23]

Taken individually, the above sources can be interpreted any number of ways with little certainty of their implications. Indeed, the significance of a single letter might be highlighted or downplayed to countless degrees. A metaphor in a single poem could be understood in innumerable ways. One article in a newspaper might merely be an anomalous occurrence. Yet by analyzing correspondence in the context of hundreds of other letters and by juxtaposing poetry and prose with personal accounts and additional publications, one finds that these sources begin to take on more definitive meaning. Although Noguchi interacted with educated individuals historically recognized as passionate and swooning in their correspondence, I argue that he held an intensely moving intimacy with one particular man, Charles Warren Stoddard. It was an intimacy not necessarily made obvious by sex acts, but by what the two men themselves called "love." This love then testified to the power of passion even during more romantic times and illuminated how "friendships" could be deeply sexual, if not completely homosexual.

On Names

To minimize confusion I cite all names in the text with the first name first followed by the surname, using the usual Western order. In the early twentieth century, Japanese with some connection to the West varied the order of their first and last names based on their personal preference. While some Japanese maintained the more traditional order of listing the surname first, many more living in the United States began citing their first name first. Noguchi himself used "Yone Noguchi" as well as "Noguchi Yone" in his publications from Japan. Later, as his American life grew distant, Noguchi increasingly began using "Noguchi Yonejiro." Moreover, when referring to individuals, I use either first names or last names to reflect their evolving intimacy to Noguchi. Thus while Stoddard's name appears as "Stoddard" in Chapter 1, he becomes "Charlie" in Chapter 2 to mark a shift in Noguchi's form of address as the two grew closer. Though the spelling of Stoddard's name varies from "Charlie" to "Charley" in the sources, I use the more standard spelling of "Charlie" for consistency and ease in reading.

CHAPTER OUTLINE

Five chapters and an epilogue arranged chronologically trace Noguchi's intimate affairs with Stoddard, Gilmour, and Armes. As *Queer Compulsions* asserts the significance of Noguchi's relationship with Stoddard, it simultaneously underscores how race inextricably infused these bicultural affairs. Not only would Noguchi become racialized by whites fascinated by the East, he himself would come to use his imaginings of the "Oriental" to promote his professional and personal life. For Noguchi, a Japanese immigrant to the United States, social acceptance may have held as much if not more importance than sexual excitement and romantic possibility. Noguchi thus becomes neither particularly heroic nor hopelessly victimized as he struggles with the usual pressures of culture, desire, and later family in his intimate life. As unique as his relationships may have been, his negotiations ultimately become as mundane as those of any Asian immigrant who simultaneously feels tied to and alienated from both his natal and his adopted country.

Chapter 1, titled "An Ocean Apart," begins by tracing the lives of Yone Noguchi and Charles Warren Stoddard before they met in 1897 in order to highlight differences and similarities they brought to their relationship. The two hailed from starkly different backgrounds and thirty-two years separated them in age. Yet Noguchi's eagerness to write in English would lead him to America and later to writer Joaquin Miller's home in Oakland. Here, Miller would initiate Noguchi into San Francisco's Bohemian Club, introducing him to various artists and writers who drew inspiration from the Japanese Noguchi. Stoddard was one of these writers drawn not only to Japan, but also to the Pacific Islands. By 1900 he had established himself as an expert on the "South Seas," having published essays and books on his travels through various islands. In these narratives, Stoddard unabashedly logged his attraction for brown boys from the Pacific. While Noguchi blazed his own trail to forge interactions with Western poets and writers, Stoddard directed his attention across the Pacific. The duo's common love of poetry would then spark their immediate affection for one another.

Chapter 2, titled "Two Shy Stars," recounts the beginning of Noguchi and Stoddard's correspondence in 1897, when Noguchi declared his affections toward Stoddard, and traces their growing intimacy in the context of their bohemian circle of artist and writer friends until 1900. Noguchi's writing to Stoddard proved unique as compared to correspondence with his other literary colleagues, specifically to correspondence with Blanche Partington, his editorial assistant in San Francisco and arguably the closest colleague Noguchi had in the closing years of the nineteenth century. While past scholarship has attributed Noguchi and Stoddard's intimacy to a culture of late Victorian bohemian melodrama in which passion among men proved typical rather than exceptional, Chapter 2 argues that in fact their relationship was unique even in this particularly emotionally effusive context.

Chapter 3, titled "To the Bungalow and Beyond," then traces Noguchi's journey to meet Stoddard in his Washington, DC, home in 1900 and the intimacies that would evolve from his move east up until 1904, namely, those with Léonie Gilmour and Ethel Armes. Though he declares he is married to Gilmour and proposes marriage to Armes, continued correspondence with Stoddard even in its ebbs and flows suggests infinitely more emotional connection with Stoddard than with the two women to whom Noguchi considered marriage. Their affairs are almost immediately charged by Noguchi's race, as his white lovers articulate their attraction to Noguchi using metaphors that evoke an exotic and mysterious Japan. Noguchi's treatment of his own race then also takes a distinct turn as he more explicitly evokes the "Orient" in both his personal and his professional life.

Chapter 4, titled "Queer Intimacies," outlines Noguchi's tumultuous engagement to Armes as well as Stoddard's not-so-silent disapproval of the engagement. Noguchi and Armes become embroiled in an emotionally volatile relationship of epic proportions. As the two careened toward their marriage date, Armes proclaimed love to her close companion Alice Wiggins and declared that she found women more fulfilling than men. Armes' very involvement in intimate female "friendships" additionally illuminates how seemingly separate worlds of male and female "romantic friendships" intertwined with confessions of subdued love as well as high drama.

Chapter 5, titled "Double Crossings," follows Noguchi's return to Japan, his career ascent as an expert on the Occident, his crumbling affairs with Gilmour and Armes, and his renewed affection for Stoddard between 1904 and 1909. Armes breaks her engagement with Noguchi, and though Gilmour sails to Japan to join Noguchi, she struggles financially to raise her son and later her daughter as a single parent. Noguchi remained largely absent not just because of his prolonged retreats at a Buddhist temple, but also because, even before Gilmour's arrival, he had married and maintained a separate household with a Japanese woman, Matsuko Takeda. In the midst of these heterosexual entanglements, Noguchi's relationship with Stoddard once again warms. Noguchi made references to Stoddard's gayest works as a source of continual inspiration in lonely Japan and invited him to live with him. Despite his renewed same-sex affections, however, Noguchi's Japanese-language publications begin to proclaim his heterosexuality more explicitly than in his previous writings. Though the shift might seem to point plainly to the social realities of living in a more "backwards" Japan as opposed to the more "advanced" West in terms of attitudes toward same-sex sexuality, this chapter resists this easy conclusion.[24] In fact, Japan had a long legacy of embracing same-sex affection between men before its later move to pathologize male-male love as the nation sought to "modernize" following Western moral codes. Noguchi in an increasingly homophobic society likely felt pressure to maintain respectability and thus heterosexuality as he enjoyed his new-found status as an internationally acclaimed poet. Chapter 5 not only challenges assumptions that necessarily attribute more sexual freedom to the West, but also suggests how individuals considered "normal" rather than "alien" may find their personal lives more circumscribed for fear of losing their privilege.

The epilogue traces the lives of Noguchi, Gilmour, and Armes after Stoddard's death and highlights Noguchi's personal rather than literary significance in bohemian America. While Noguchi dodged racial epithets in the streets of San Francisco, he seemed to have found a haven in California's bohemian community. Yet as inclusive as the group of cosmopolitan writers and artists appeared, their embrace would ultimately be more exploitative than empathetic. Not only would things Asian serve largely as amusing trinkets, same-sex affection that grew too passionate was implicitly taboo. Indeed the terms of Noguchi's acceptable inclusion into bohemia stunted the radical potential of Noguchi and Stoddard's love. While current representations and depictions of Noguchi have largely erased his intimate life, his affairs shed light on how individuals assert themselves in forthright as well as deceptive ways to find romantic fulfillment during desperate times. Though Noguchi loved and lost more than a century ago, his story may not be so different from the issues of xenophobia, racism, and homophobia that continue to inform intimacies today.

Conclusion

In summary, Noguchi's intimate life holds multiple implications in illuminating lived realities of sexuality and race among early-twentieth-century Japanese in the United States. This project suggests how Asian male immigrants could engage in unexpected sexual practices and intimacies. Indeed, Kosen Takahashi and Issio Kuge have also left evidence of their same-sex affections in early Japanese American history. Not only did Noguchi disregard social norms against interracial intimacy in his relationship with two white American women, his public relationship with Stoddard also pushed acceptable boundaries of increasingly scrutinized "romantic friendships" in early-twentieth-century America. Noguchi's life reveals how Asians in America embraced and proactively sought out romantic if not sexual fulfillment in unconventional ways.

While his affairs exhibit romantic self-determination, the engagements came with limitations. As a vibrant homosocial world swirled about, Noguchi ultimately remained an outsider constrained by perceptions of racial, cultural, and linguistic difference. Even in the comforting embrace of Stoddard's affections, Noguchi came to realize that his race and all that it signified would always remain central in his American relationships. After he returned to Japan, familial and professional obligations shaped his domestic life. Still, he forged ahead, at times selfishly, to express his most intimate love within the confines of acceptability. *Queer Compulsions* illuminates not only how people of color could negotiate America's sexual terrain, but also how those sexually marginalized might mediate competing cultural mores.

ONE

An Ocean Apart

1875–1897

In a small town called Tsushima ten miles west of Nagoya City in Japan, Okuwa Noguchi gave birth to her fourth son, Yonejiro, on December 8, 1875. Okuwa's husband Denbei worked as a merchant selling paper, umbrellas, and *geta*, or wooden slippers. While the couple appeared typical of commoners, or *heimin*, they may in fact have proved a bit different from other small merchant families who just seven years previously occupied the lower rungs of Japan's four-tiered social structure.[1] Okuwa's brother was the famous Buddhist scholar Shaku Taishun, and Denbei's father at one point owned a small plot of land.[2] Yet for Okuwa and Denbei, life for the most part was relatively modest without national prestige or noteworthy wealth. The birth of Yonejiro likely proved eventful in their otherwise quiet rural life.

Meanwhile, halfway around the world in Paris, thirty-two-year-old Charles Warren Stoddard spent his days cavorting with young male art students in the Latin Quarter. On evenings when he felt bold, he frequented dance halls to see cross-dressing performers. Though he had recently received a threatening letter from his former lover Frank Millet condemning his flitting about like a butterfly, the socially active Charles appeared unaffected.[3] Stoddard had established himself in both his professional and personal life. He had recently published his first book, *South Sea Idyls*, and he had long figured out how to find other sexual fulfillment with men such as himself. Coded language such as declaring an unfaltering admiration of Walt Whitman signaled to others that you were a literary man inclined toward intimacy with other men. In Paris, Stoddard freely found same-sex affection despite warnings from one close friend to "avoid any appearance of eccentricity" while in Europe.[4] He had not lived his earlier years with as much self-confidence or ease.

Stoddard was born in Rochester, New York, in 1843 to a once-prominent family in decline.[5] After failing in the paper-manufacturing business, Stoddard's father, Samuel Burr Stoddard, declared bankruptcy in the 1850s and relocated his family to San Francisco. At home, Stoddard's mother raised the children as "god-fearing Presbyterians."[6] Outside of the home, the diversity on the city streets mesmerized the young Stoddard as he explored various neighborhoods.[7] Chinatown in particular fascinated him, so much so that he decorated his room with "Oriental mementoes." Yet even as Stoddard appeared engaged with all the city had to offer, he felt notably disengaged from his male peers. He saw himself as "timid" and "sensitive," disliking games and preferring to lounge about and "build dreams." Other boys would comment on his frailty and paleness, and Stoddard's inability to do well in school only contributed to his sense of alienation.[8]

In 1859 fifteen-year-old Stoddard declined attending San Francisco High School to instead pursue a literary career and become the "Boy Poet of San Francisco." He began as a clerk selling books in a book store on Montgomery Street and wrote poetry in his spare time. Later, publication in a new monthly magazine called *Golden Era* brought him into contact with literary types, such as Ina Coolbrith, Bret Harte, and Mark Twain. Through the 1860s Stoddard took on odd jobs and increasingly published more poetry, which often met with unfavorable reviews. As he reached out for mentorship among established writers, he found little support. In 1864 after a year at the Brayton Academy—an attempt to return to school—Stoddard found himself afflicted with a nervous disorder. He traveled to Hawai'i to restore his equilibrium. Four years later, his sister Sarah would marry Parker Makee, the son of a wealthy Maui plantation owner, and another opportunity to visit Hawai'i presented itself.[9] Not until 1869, when Stoddard began writing of his Hawaiian travels, did he begin to win recognition as an accomplished western writer.[10] For Stoddard the Pacific Islands reflected not merely material for his writing career, but more profoundly a refuge from the sexual "hypocrisy" of civilization and "frigid manners of Christians." Pacific Islanders, unafraid of "instincts," would serve as his haven for his same-sex affections. In a letter to Walt Whitman, Stoddard wrote of his motivations to return to the "South Seas." "Barbarism has given me the fullest joy of my life and I long to return to it and be satisified."[11] The Pacific Islands served as a sexual utopia that not even "California where men are tolerably bold" could provide.[12] Stoddard was hardly alone in his imperial same-sex predilections. In the late 1800s many European "explorers" who sought same-sex sexual fulfillment found refuge in colonial outposts in Africa and Southeast Asia as well as the Pacific and Caribbean islands.[13]

For Stoddard, Asia, as a neighbor to the islands of the Pacific Ocean, also held similar value in its exotic attraction. In his travel logs such as *Hawaiian Life*, he shifted easily between references to Japan, Hawai'i, Australia, China, and Tahiti in narrating a mystical tale of wonder and romance.[14] Young brown men, whether Native Hawaiian or Japanese, tantalized Stoddard with their exotic appearance. His attraction could also extend to white men if they exhibited characteristics of his racial preference such as "Oriental, almond eyes."[15] Moreover, Stoddard confessed to being lonely by nature, consoled only by intense and absorbing love.[16] His fetish for the young men from the Pacific Rim combined with his dire need for affection set him along a course toward an individual such as Yone.

When Stoddard returned to San Francisco from Hawai'i in November 1872, friends called him to England to boost his literary career. With the completion of the transcontinental railroad, San Francisco no longer appeared to be an outpost ripe with stories of the frontier. Many bohemians in search of new adventure had left San Francisco just as Stoddard returned. Thus Stoddard joined the exodus and traveled across Europe and the Mediterranean through the 1870s, detailing his adventures in a column for the *San Francisco Chronicle*.[17] Yet, eight months after Noguchi's birth, Stoddard began his voyage home, as money had become scarce. As he returned to San Francisco in 1878, Stoddard appeared to be in good spirits, spending most of his time at the city's Bohemian Club. In 1881 he again traveled to Hawai'i to write editorials for Honolulu's *Saturday Press* and lived there for four years until the University of Notre Dame offered him a position teaching English and American literature. A year later, Stoddard left his academic post because of a scandal involving an intimate relationship with one of his male students and again traveled through Europe before accepting a second academic position in 1892 at Catholic

University in Washington, DC. During the first year of his appointment, Stoddard met fifteen-year-old Kenneth O'Conner, who approached him one fall Saturday afternoon as Stoddard read the playbills downtown. By November 1895 the two were living together in a red brick building on M Street that Stoddard affectionately called the "Bungalow."[18] Yet all would not end happily for Stoddard.

From the very first evening in the Bungalow, Stoddard's expectations for a happy home life had begun to fray. Stoddard in a "honeymoon mood" prepared for sleep in his bed chamber. Two twin beds adorned with "virgin" sheets awaited Kenneth's arrival. Midnight came and Stoddard dozed, awoke, fretted, and tried to read. Not until after 2:30 in the morning did Kenneth finally arrive with his "show-business" brother Eddie and his dog. With muddy paws, the dog boisterously jumped onto Stoddard's sacred sheets. All four would spend this first night together. A disappointed Stoddard consoled himself by keeping in mind that many other nights lay ahead. Though Stoddard sent glowing reports of domestic life with Kenneth, those who visited him at the Bungalow recalled Stoddard as deeply troubled and depressed.[19] At the university, the situation fared no better. In 1895 a new professor of English, Maurice Francis Egan, would stir Stoddard's insecurity and later move to oust Stoddard from his university position.[20]

For young Yonejiro, life in the Nagoya area in the 1880s proved more mundane. In 1885 excitement came to the ten-year-old in the form of his first Wilson's spelling book. He slept with it every night, hoping to repeat that day's lesson if he awoke in the middle of the night. The smell of the foreign book charmed, mystified, and possessed the young boy. Yone immediately fell into what he believed at the time would be a lifelong romance with the English language.[21] So intense would his fever to learn English become that in the evenings he would stand against the fence of one missionary's house to hear the foreign tongue uttered by a native speaker. On another occasion he followed a woman and her child in hopes of "testing" his comprehension until the girl turned around and shouted "Mamma, what does this fellow want?"[22] At thirteen, Noguchi began attending the recently opened Otani School, sponsored by Otani Buddhists in Nagoya, and soon after he matriculated into Nagoya Prefectural High School. Yet small-town Nagoya soon felt constraining for Yone, who hoped for more.[23]

He left for Tokyo since he found intellectual life in Nagoya "far too easy for [his] mind." He hoped to pass the Tokyo University entrance examination. The mathematics section of the exam, however, proved too difficult, and Noguchi set his sights lower, enrolling in 1891 at Keio Gijuku, a private school dedicated to Westernism in Japanese education. As he began reading Longfellow, he grew to despise the spoken English language and took up literature as his new love. Yone would often skip his conversation class and instead spend long hours poring over Washington Irving's *The Sketch-Book of Geoffrey Crayon, Gentleman*. After reading Irving, Yone yearned to go abroad, specifically to England.[24]

While in Tokyo, Yone lived with Shigetaka Shiga doing domestic chores. Shiga introduced Yone to Den Sugawara, who wove seductive tales of America. After receiving further encouragement to travel from the principal at Keio, Yukichi Fukuzawa, Yone boarded a ship bound for San Francisco on November 3, 1893.[25] As he stood alone by an iron rail on the deck with less than $100 in his pocket, eighteen-year-old Yone felt a painful uneasiness. He recalled, "I immediately grew conscious of the fact that I had to face unknown America, a land of angels or devils." The uncertainty of the future, the "darkness" he called it, suddenly clawed at his insecurity.[26]

When Yone arrived in San Francisco one month later in December of 1893, he was aghast at the poor reception he received. Upon descending the plank, he felt as though America had rudely greeted him at the back rather than the front door. Dragonlike smoke invaded the sky and stifled his ability to breathe. And when the polluted air was not clogging his lungs, the irrepressible scent of body odor assaulted him. Wagon drivers and pedestrians alike emitted a repulsive smell that Yone could never have imagined. He wondered if his American dream was a complete failure.[27]

The very first night Yone checked into the modest Cosmopolitan Hotel on Fifth Street, which appeared like a "wonderful palace." The American room with its soft pillows and sheets all seemed strange to Yone, who was accustomed to sleeping on a futon or thin mattress on the floor. As he and his fellow passengers settled into their room, they placed their recently purchased fresh fruit inadvertently in the basin used to collect urine and feces, mistook the salt for sugar, declared the cheese as something rotten, and used a tablespoon to sip the coffee. As they stumbled over which hand to hold the knife and fork with at dinner, Yone resolved that he had much to learn in this new country.[28]

After dinner, Yone stepped out for a walk. He walked up and down the block, turning right and then left. He found himself in front of a store window on Market Street. The beauty of the display had mesmerized him when a hard hand struck him from behind. A red-faced white man, smiling with scorn, retorted, "Hello Jap!" and spat in his face. Not even twelve hours had passed in his new home when Yone experienced his first of what would become many encounters with American racism. Gripped with fear, Yone felt anxiety rush through his body. Indeed one friend had warned him before his departure that he would be entering a den of wolves by immigrating to America. Surrounded by enemies, Yone would need indefatigable determination to survive.[29]

As Yone tried to make his way back to the hotel, sadness began to overwhelm him. All the buildings began appearing identical, and passersby he approached to find his way back coldly rebuffed his attempts to speak English. Disoriented and on the verge of tears, Yone found the hotel only after a Japanese man approached him and pointed out that he was in fact standing right in front of the Cosmopolitan. As he lay down to sleep, his soft mattress gave way uncomfortably to his tired body. For much of this first night, Yone sat alone on his sagging bed through the silence of the night and wondered how he should begin his new life in America.[30]

Over the next few days as he made more connections with Japanese in San Francisco, he grew increasingly aware of the impoverished plight of Japanese immigrants in America. To make matters worse, no one appeared to understand his English. As Yone traveled around town with a pencil and a pad of paper to write down what he wanted to say, many mistook him for a "deaf mute." It proved to be a great disappointment for Yone, who had been studying the language from the age of eight or nine and had great confidence in his ability.[31] Yone blamed his incompetent Japanese teachers for his shortcomings. With anger he cursed them for not giving him "the right pronunciation of even one word."[32] Deep in his heart, a part of him acknowledged that he had made a mistake in coming to the United States.[33]

Similar to other young Japanese men who arrived in the United States around the same time, Yone worked as a domestic. Many Issei, or first-generation Japanese, in the late nineteenth century could only find work doing menial labor in a private home for free room and board. During their free time they hoped to attend school. These immigrants called "schoolboys" came from middling class backgrounds. They sought to improve their position through education and opportunities different from those available in Japan. The work, however, did not prove easy. Cultural and class differences set the stage for countless conflicts between employer and employed. Japanese who found the work in private homes intolerable took up jobs at hotels and restaurants. These young men now had to pay for their own lodging and board. As they put in additional hours, it became impossible to attend school.[34]

When the work became frustrating for Yone, he retreated to the city's Japanese-language daily *Soko Shimbun*, where he first delivered newspapers and later began translating.[35] Yone additionally took on odd jobs peddling knickknacks to improve his conversational skills and overcome his shyness as he made money. When he could not find a position that would provide room and board, Yone with a handful of other Japanese worked, ate, and slept in a three-story "tumble-down affair" infested with rats owned by railroad millionaire Charles Crocker on O'Farrell Street. Yone slept on a bed made out of newspapers and used an encyclopedia for a pillow, the very materials from which he once again began studying English.[36] Yet all was not hapless for the young Yone. When he attempted to shoplift a Dora Thorne book in a used bookstore, the owner decided to befriend him. So desperate did Yone's desire to read appear that the owner generously furnished him additional materials to peruse. Here, Yone gained access to publications by writer Edgar Allen Poe, poet John Keats, and artist William Blake.[37] Later, Yone would discover that he could read books for free at the city library. Despite these small victories, he felt constantly exhausted in his earliest years in America. Trapped in a cycle of menial work to stay financially afloat, Yone had little time for himself to even think, let alone read.[38]

When Yone grew tired of working as a schoolboy, he moved to Palo Alto in hopes of acquiring knowledge by being close to Stanford University. In exchange for cleaning classrooms and waiting on student-boarders in Manzanita Hall, the university allowed him to attend classes. He received no payment for his labor, and Yone grew increasingly uncomfortable being on the wealthy campus in his dirty coat and shoes so worn that they no longer had heels. He decided to work at the Menlo Park Hotel until he could put himself in respectable shape. Looking back on his time at Stanford, Yone could not remember a single thing he had acquired in the classroom.

It was while working as a dishwasher at the Menlo Park Hotel that he first heard about Joaquin Miller, the western writer with whom he would later live. Yone's hands had turned blue-white and become swollen from washing dishes from four in the afternoon to ten at night. As he quietly stared at his disfigured hands, a Japanese student from Stanford dropped into the kitchen to sneak a bit of pie. He told Yone about the poet Miller, an American hermit who cursed at the city across the bay as he watered his roses in Oakland. For Yone who had just begun reading American poetry, thoughts of Miller stirred his heart.[39]

Then in 1894 as war broke out between Japan and China, Yone began translating updates for the Japanese cook at the hotel. Soon he felt restless for his San Francisco friends with whom he could discuss politics. He hurried back to the city in hopes of contributing to the war effort and once again began translating for *Soko Shimbun*.[40] At the office of the Japanese daily, Yone again heard of Joaquin Miller when a fellow Japanese mentioned his visit to the Miller home called affectionately "the Hights."[41] As Yone complained about his fitful nights of sleep and lack of leisure time to read since coming to the United States, his friend suggested he call on Miller. "He is extremely fond of Japanese. . . . You can sleep and read as much as you want. There have been Japanese who have lived with him before, so if you ask him if you can stay, he will undoubtedly agree."[42]

Indeed Miller's home seemed to serve as a haven for many Asian immigrants. As a child, the daughter of writer Herman Whitaker, Elsie Whitaker Martinez, visited Miller's home two to three times a month at the turn of the century and distinctly remembered meeting "a great many interesting Orientals." According to Whitaker Martinez, many Japanese and Chinese artists lived on the Hights, though Japanese dominated in number. She recalled Japanese paper houses built throughout the woods and a meandering little stream "Japanese style" beautifully arranged with gardens and rocks.[43] In 1919, when Noguchi traveled back to California to pay respects to the deceased Miller, he gathered other Issei men at the Oakland office of the Japanese American daily *Nichibei Times*, bought flowers, and drove up to the Hights in two full carloads.[44] Miller's home

Famed San Francisco publisher Edward Mitchell featured Joaquin Miller in front of his home in this postcard, c. 1895. Mitchell is said to have popularized the postcard at the turn of the century. Courtesy of Huntington Library, San Marino, California.

had played a significant role in sheltering many Issei men even as they cooked, cleaned, and ran household errands without pay.

In 1894, as Yone grew increasingly frustrated with his situation, Miller's home presented itself as an attractive escape. Yone desired no pay, but simply a place to live for an hour's worth of his labor in the morning and in the evening. The Hights seemed ideal. Yone sold several books to raise money for his trip and crossed the bay as he rehearsed lines of English to greet Miller. As he approached Miller's home in 1895, however, his courage suddenly slipped. He came upon a narrow wooden path in the form of a low bridge that led directly to the entrance of a ridiculously small cottage.[45] Rose bowers and citrus trees enclosed the front of the house.[46] At the moment he thought he would run away, Alice Oliver, a young woman of African and Mexican descent who according to Yone had been hired to do domestic chores, found him dilly dallying in front of the house and encouraged him to enter with her friendly smile. "If you want to meet Miller, don't be shy and come in," she coaxed. In Miller's tiny cabin, Yone found him still in bed, where he liked to remain when writing. When

Yone met the "red-faced" man with a "tall nose," he could not help but feel frightened. Miller resembled a *tengu*, a Japanese long-nosed goblin. He ate dinner with the Miller family and returned to San Francisco that same day.[47]

The next morning Yone said good-bye to thirty-four friends, packed three books into a small bag, and climbed the mountain to live a poet's life. He quickly settled into his new one-room cottage down a sloping hill. He planted potatoes in a garden alongside a ravine, and from his cabin Yone reflected on the beauty of the canyon full of California cypress "more so pictaresque" than any he had seen.[48] The first night on the Hights proved unforgettable, a moment of unprecedented beauty that Yone would never again witness during his entire tenure on the west coast. Towns at the foot of the hill as well as the stars above appeared within hand's reach. As the dense fog slowly enveloped the houses dotting the landscape below, street lights shimmered through. Yone noted, "It was the first time in my life that I had seen such beauty at night. I felt grateful for all of nature's wonderful writing materials that began to open up to me."[49]

For Miller, Yone's arrival marked a momentous visit of good fortune. When Miller first met Yone, he described him as a "beautiful Japanese flower"—"the most lovely . . . [he] ever saw in the human flesh of either sex." Yone with the "profound bow" had followed the path of the "Nippon" butterfly to arrive at Miller's front door.[50] Miller welcomed Yone with open arms, declaring "why I love Japs," and suggested he stay as long as ten years. He believed all Japanese to be "gentlemen" thirsty for knowledge.[51] Though Miller availed his hillside huts to all who might come of whatever color or country, the Japanese or "the homesick little brownies" appeared to appreciate his hospitality the most. According to Miller, the open little houses and the meditative life among the flowers and birds reminded them of "beautiful, beautiful Japan."[52] Notably, Miller's interest in Japan appeared to be more than just an aesthetic or Orientalist fetish. He, in fact, made it a point to speak against anti-Japanese sentiment in increasingly Japan-phobic California. Additionally, Miller ambitiously sought to refute Rudyard Kipling's poetry, which declared "East and West, never the twain shall meet," by deliberately encouraging and arranging marriages between Asian men and white American women.[53]

With Yone, Miller felt a special kinship. He believed Yone and himself to be "cut from the same cloth" and imagined himself as Yone's guide and friend. "He's one of my class," Miller told the *San Francisco Chronicle* in November of 1896. "I like queer folks—the queer are always good. This boy is the right sort; he does just as he pleases." On occasion Yone would join Miller and talk of men and books. According to Miller, Yone came from the "best blood in the kingdom." In 1896 he stated in the *San Francisco Chronicle*, "Yone is an avowed admirer of Whitman."[54] In a literary world where declared affinity for Walt Whitman served as one code for singling out men who enjoyed same-sex affection, Miller's statement in the city's daily likely aroused the interest of San Francisco men who enjoyed intimacy with other men.

Yone also appreciated how Miller respectfully never entered Yone's separate living quarters and on their initial meeting called him "Mr. Noguchi" rather than the more anonymous "Charlie" or "Frank," names often doled out without consultation to Asians in America at the time.[55] Yone recalled this as the first time in the United States that he was addressed as a "gentleman."[56]

Despite Miller's usually respectful attitude, he had his fair share of presumptions that he projected not just upon Yone but on Japanese people as a whole. When Miller first welcomed Yone into his home and introduced him to his mother, he noted, "This is Mr. Noguchi, a guest from Japan. And since all Japanese are poets, so too is Mr. Noguchi."[57] As they ate together, Yone grew silent since he had forgotten his English. Miller, however, interpreted Yone's quiet as a deliberate act rather than a disability in language. He declared, "Japanese silence is precious like gold." When Miller's elderly mom tried to chat, Miller reprimanded her and again referenced this gift of few words from the East. "Mother, look at this Japanese: there is no waste. That's how Japanese are different. Eating is a sacred ritual. You shouldn't be talking incessantly. Eat quietly, quietly. The silence helps digestion. Eat quietly, think loftily, and be content. This is the word from God."[58] Yone's English-as-a-second-language moment had become to Miller a provocative reflection of Japanese cultural moderation and restraint. To Yone this misinterpretation could only have positive benefits. He felt satisfied that his ethnicity would be such a source of admiration and relished the sweetness of that first meal with Miller even thirty years later.[59]

Notably, as much as Miller thought that Yone desired silence, Yone himself considered the extent to which the two did not converse to be odd.

Yone noted, "I lived with Miller for four long years, however, during that time we never talked. We seemed to communicate through silence. When we went to chop down trees, build a bridge, plant a sapling in the rain or fog, all these tasks were done in his philosophy of silence"—a principle Yone believed to be as the law of Miller's mountain, not of Japan. The two never even once discussed Miller's writing, which Yone read diligently for one to two hours each night before going to bed.[60] What Miller assumed to be Yone's commendable and cultural code of silence in fact was foreign to Yone.

For four years Yone fulfilled assorted household tasks for Miller. Each morning and evening he made coffee for Miller with delight. On fair-weathered days Yone would cook outdoors to the sound of a nearby babbling brook.[61] In "camp fashion," Yone threw lumps of beef, potatoes, onions, and carrots into an iron pot and boiled the stew over a fire for at least two hours.[62] Miller would then spread a linen cloth over a large dinner table that sat beneath a rose bush. If the mood suited him, he would pick and scatter red and white roses over the table and exclaim, "God bless you!" Miller would then open a bottle of wine and linger over meals for hours.[63]

Yone additionally tended to artists and writers who sought refuge on the Hights. When artist Joseph Strong visited Miller in 1896, Yone directed him to his cottage, woke him up in the mornings, served him breakfast, and washed the dishes after meals.[64] In the effective implementation of Miller's pranks on his visitors as well, Yone played a critical role. When Miller performed the Indian rain prayer song, Yone turned on the hidden faucet to spray the awed guests. Yone saw his contributions on the Hights as "volunteer[ing]."[65] So immersed in Miller's life did Yone appear to have become that visitors reported that Yone even grew his hair out "just like Miller."[66]

Yet Yone steadfastly denied accusations that he deliberately began to dress and act like Miller. Poverty rather than admiration for Miller had forced him to avoid trips to the barber and grow out his hair into a long mane akin to Miller's.[67] Despite his insistence that he was not mimicking Miller's style, Yone did initially express some interest in adopting Miller's aesthetic. After his very first visit to the Hights when Yone met the imposing Miller in his top boots and bearskin, he confessed in his memoir that he hoped to save money to buy a pair of top boots for himself though the bearskin was completely out of his reach.[68]

The move to the Hights proved critical for Yone's career. Miller's home enjoyed nationwide fame as a retreat for literary and artistic types.[69] Bohemians flocked to the Hights, where the view dramatically changed from hour to hour and even minute to minute. At dawn the Millers' home sat perched above a layer of clouds, and only the higher streets of San Francisco surged above the rolling mist. The large cross of Lone Mountain Cemetery would rise solemnly above the fog. As mist enveloped the San Francisco Bay, the sea became transformed into a moving floor of silver. When the clouds reached Oakland, only church spires poked through the sea of undulating snow. By noon, however, not a single cloud rested where it had been in the morning, and a peaceful Alameda could be seen below. At night the heavens and the earth appeared aflame as lights from below and stars from above illuminated the evening. Yone became a part of the community of artists and writers who found peace and inspiration in the magnificent beauty that surrounded the Hights. From Miller's home, Yone saw limitless possibilities as he made inroads into California's literary community.[70]

He had entered a dream land that even he had not been able to imagine previously, a place Yone described as "fit for dancing waltzes." Romance and poetry bombarded him. During the day he watched patches of clouds move in and out of the bay. Yone noted, "I felt as though I was living half in the clouds, and that is not an exaggeration." As Yone watched the golden sun sink heavily down through the gate of the bay, he thought to himself how fitting it was that the mouth of the San Francisco Bay be called the Golden Gate. As summer approached, he found flowers bursting, "singing and laughing" all over the surrounding hills. As he lay at the top of the poppy-covered hill, he thought that if he could have such a burial place over looking the bay, death certainly would be sweeter than life. For the first time he felt free to develop as a poet.[71]

After a year of living on the Hights, Yone began writing seriously.[72] In 1896 his poems appeared for the first time in *The Lark*, a short-lived irreverent literary journal considered to be one of the signifiers of west coast bohemianism founded by Gelett Burgess.[73] Burgess prefaced "Seen and Unseen" and "The Song of Yone Noguchi" by introducing Yone as an "exile from his native land" who sat alone in his cabin on the Hights writing poetry. For Burgess, Yone's difference as a foreigner and therefore an outsider to American culture played a key role in his unique style. Yone proved to be "a mystic by temperament, race, and religion." His poetry flowed like "nocturnes set to words of a half-learned, foreign tongue; in form vague as his vague dreams." Burgess could only believe these works to be sincere precisely because the poems "lack art (in its technical sense) in their construction." Though many of the passages seemed to make little sense in relation to one another, Burgess cherished "the vigor of Yone's unworn metaphors, unfettered by tradition of expression."[74]

As critics reviewed his work, Yone's literary debut appeared inextricably intertwined with his race. At an evening banquet Burgess introduced Yone as a budding poet from the Orient. The Boston newspaper *Transcript* complimented Yone's work by noting, "It is always more fascinating to see the thoughts of a man from the Far East expressed in our Occidental speech than to read beginner's poetry in native English."[75] The more critical noted: "His composition is a queer, baffling Japano-English, but has some strong phrases. It is like Stephen Crane with all the affection, but more like an Oriental Walt Whitman, yet not so universal as much as personal."[76] For Yone, the "Eastern child," his Japanese nationality played a central role in his success as a rising poet.[77] While the above comments hold truth in referring to Yone's awkward use of English and his nationality, references to the Orient would ultimately signal more than just idiosyncratic language usage or geographic origin. They took on more loaded meanings pointing to his exotic as well as marginalized position. Yone proved unique as a specifically ethnic writer rather than as a promising newcomer with potential that rivaled all existing poets.

As critics pointed to "Japan" or the "Orient" in discussing the young poet, Yone himself disliked the racialized attention in the early years of his American career. In 1896, as Yone answered requests for his picture, he made it a point not to be photographed in his "native dress." Joaquin Miller explained to the *San Francisco Chronicle*, "He objects to that sort of interest, saying that he wants to write for America, and depend solely on the value of his work."[78] As Yone wrote diligently, he hoped his work would receive merit as exceptional poetry, rather than poetry exceptional for its Japanese origin.

One month after his debut, scandal gripped Yone's promising career. In December of 1896 as Yone recited his poetry at a reception, "unkind ones" rose up and accused Yone of using Edgar Allen Poe's lines as his own.[79] The literary world was "thrown into a frenzy of excitement and indignation," creating a "furor" in the United States and England.[80] Passages in Yone's poems "Lines" and "On the Hights—Two Moods" had surprising similarities to Poe's poem "The Sleeper." Yone had used identical pairings of words such as "curtain canopy," "opiate vapors," "exhaling from," and "BEAUTY" in all capitals. The *San Francisco Chronicle* sarcastically noted that perhaps Yone as an "Oriental" might be unfamiliar with "Occidental criterions of literary honor."[81] Such a topic of discussion did Yone become that various papers and weeklies began publishing poems on Yone's alleged plagiarism.[82]

As Yone's name gained notoriety, prominent members of the California literary community came to his defense.[83] Miller insisted that even if Yone had not read Poe, it could be entirely possible for Yone to produce the same words and expressions. "I do not believe there is any reason to doubt that two minds, in consonance as to points of view, may voice the same thought in exactly the same words."[84] Gelett Burgess noted that as Yone learned English from reading other writers' works, he might naturally borrow words in his own poetry.[85] Porter Garnett similarly defended Yone in the *San Francisco Call*.[86]

Ironically, in a later Japanese-language publication Yone admitted that he had used several lines from Poe in his own poetry after what he may have believed at the time was sufficient alteration.[87] He had been studying Poe's work intently to learn about American poetry. So saturated did Yone become with Poe's work that at one point he believed he had become Poe himself. Yone remained overjoyed that he had produced work similar to Poe. In an open letter to a San Francisco newspaper, Yone wrote that he was happy for having felt the same thoughts as Poe. He could not understand why he was prohibited from articulating the same sentiments if he desired to do so.[88] He declared, "Let critics say [what] they please! . . . I am not sorry a bit if there be an exact correspondence in shape. I am thankful to God for giving me the moment when I felt the same things [as] Poe. I could not understand why you couldn't feel the same thing as Poe if you wanted to."[89] Yone refused to concede that he had committed a wrong.[90]

Despite the initial infamy, Yone overcame his affliction that he himself called "Poe Mania" and went on to publish his first book, *Seen and Unseen*.[91] Yone's collected poems dripped with sadness and loneliness even as he voiced his admiration for nature. He described himself as "wrapped in warm darkness," "lonely, lonely," and "motherless." His soul lived with "darkness" and "silence" as "dark weights" of loneliness immobilized him. In the poem "Alone" he dedicated an entire page to his lonely "withered soul" housed in a body that had grown rusty from the drippings of his own tears. Mother Nature also appeared depressed. The "universe . . . grows . . . frozen-hearted . . . alone, friendless"; the "cricket-songs" seemed "sad" and wrapped in tears; a banana tree slept "broken hearted"; and the sun shined as if "dying" in its glory. Indeed, out of fifty total poems, nearly half explicitly articulated loneliness in the text using the words "alone," "lonely," "loneliness," or "lonesome."[92] As Gelett Burgess wrote in the introduction to *Seen and Unseen*, Yone indeed appeared "in love with sadness."[93] Gloomy works dominated his earliest works, though a few poems of exaltation and optimism also appeared. Yone "the homeless snail" lamented his solitude and alienation.[94]

These works would not just highlight his depression, but they would also reveal how little Yone initially pandered to the West's interest in the East. In his publications through the 1890s, predictable images of the "Orient" did not exist. In Yone's first book of poetry, *Seen and Unseen*, published in 1897, not one out of fifty poems made explicit reference to Japan or evoked metaphors easily associated with Japan. One poem titled "Paper Lantern" peripherally used the paper lantern common in Japan to describe Yone's loneliness as akin to paper drenched wet from a rainy night. This use of the Japanese paper lantern in its drippy disintegrating mass hardly proved complicit with exotic, aesthetic images of Japan. Additionally, in referencing a higher spiritual power, Yone used the Western-based term "God" or "Goddess" rather than articulating "Buddha" as he would in later works.[95] In *Voice of the Valley* as well, Yone evoked minimal Japanese imagery or metaphors. In fifty-one pages he used Orientalist language just twice, referring to himself as a "muse from the orient" in one poem and as "a heathen idol" in another.[96] In 1898, when Yone embarked on his own journal titled *Twilight* with illustrator Kosen Takahashi, no Orientalist content appeared. Illustrations and text in the two recovered issues lacked any stereotypically Japanese imagery. In an illustration likely portraying Yone and Kosen in the June 1898 issue, the subjects appeared dressed in suits with chin-length black hair. The cover of an additional issue from the same year featured a likely Japanese woman in kimono with large yet closed eyes, unbridled wavy hair, and an angled nose. Both illustrations diverged from the usual markers of slanted, slitlike eyes and traditional up-do hairstyles. Prose and poetry in these issues also built on topics not particularly "Oriental" such as life in an American prison and fantastic "moonlit" adventures.[97] As Yone resisted racialization in his own work and persona, he more aggressively countered unjust portrayals of Japan in popular culture.

Two musical productions, *The Mikado* and *The Geisha*, and one novel titled *Madame Butterfly* particularly enraged Yone in their misrepresentation of Japan. When *The Mikado* arrived in San Francisco in the early 1890s, theatergoers enjoyed white actors' enactment of a Japanese love triangle between Nanki-poo, Ko-ko, and Yum-yum. Englishman W. S. Gilbert, the author of *The Mikado*, seemed to poke fun at Japan with his silly names and outlandish story line.[98] A "pleasing opera," *The Geisha*, opened later at San Francisco's Tivoli Theater in fall 1897. The musical presented white women in yellow-face portraying dainty, girlish Japanese women enjoying the romantic overtures of English men. As the opera house filled to capacity nightly, critics predicted a long run for the "sparkling musical comedy."[99] Finally, the novel *Madame Butterfly* reflected pervasive views of Japanese culture and femininity in its romantic tragedy between an American naval officer stationed in Nagasaki and a self-sacrificing Japanese maiden who kills herself after suffering from a broken heart. This Orientalist classic articulated unequal power relationships between East and West through the dynamics of gender.[100] To San Francisco audiences, Japanese femininity as depicted in the American imagination grew especially attractive in its old-fashioned innocence particularly in contrast to what some social critics saw as the rising threat of masculinized women in America. Frequently called the "New Woman," these individuals asserted themselves in sports, leisure, education, and employment in spheres previously believed to be places of men exclusively.[101]

Yone noted, "The vogue of *The Mikado* or *The Geisha*, a comic opera, made my true Japanese heart pained, as I thought it was a blasphemy against Japan; how often I wished to shout from the pit or gallery on its absurdity."[102] He noted how "ridiculously" "Miss What's-her-name" acted in *The Geisha* and commented on her "absurd" appearance akin to a "smiling puppet." Indeed some white Americans blurted out the nonsensical theme song of the musical to Yone in a goodwill effort to connect with his Japaneseness. Yone found the practice annoying and vocalized the musical's grave injustice toward Japan.[103] Notably, Yone was not alone in his protest over the two productions. Outside of San Francisco, reviewers and audiences alike reviled both *The Mikado* and *The Geisha* as insulting and not representative of Japan in the least.[104]

Yone even more scathingly criticized *Madame Butterfly*, warning people against the mistake of buying the popular book. He sardonically called the author of the book, John Luther Long, "Mr. Wrong" to highlight his inaccurate depiction of Japan, a work "full of lies" and "craziness." Long would be better off sweeping streets than writing such "a completely sad affair." The female protagonist, a "Nippon character," hardly proved Japanese. Yone imagined jettisoning the book from a transcontinental train ride for the Nevada mountain lions to cherish.[105] Nearly all the major creative works on Japan at the time infuriated Yone. Even the play *A Japanese Nightingale* by Onoto Watanna, a woman whom Yone initially believed to be of Japanese descent, did not escape his scrutiny. Yone reported to Charlie: "Onoto Watanna's Japanese play made such a mess. I wouldn't go at all."[106] To Yone, *The Mikado*, *The Geisha*, *Madame Butterfly*, as well as *A Japanese Nightingale* misrepresented and insulted Japan. Yone rejected American interest in things Japanese as cheap if not utterly insincere. He equated American Japanophilia as merely "curiosity" for a "dime museum" spectacle rather than any real appreciation of culture.[107]

In 1897 Yone had already endured much by living in America. As a Japanese male living in patriarchal Japan, he had left a nation in which he faced few obstacles outside of his control. In his home country, even if his youth detracted from his social position in the 1890s, it would be a position that he would soon enough outgrow. On his arrival in San Francisco, however, Yone realized that he would face hardships by virtue of his race, an indelible characteristic that he would carry with him forever in America. In a social space where Yone not only felt lonely, but also constantly bombarded by California's less than hospitable reception of Japanese immigrants, Stoddard's warmth and affection for Yone would shine even more brightly.

Stoddard in his early fifties likewise felt tired and unloved in his twilight years. Though in 1895 he was already well-established as a "California humorist" akin to Bret Harte and Mark Twain through his numerous publications on his Pacific travels, Stoddard faced difficulties at work and at home. At the university, an increasingly formidable rival sought to take Stoddard's place and have him terminated. In his home, creating a domestic life with Kenneth had not proved as fulfilling as he had envisioned. Stoddard was "crazy with love" for Kenneth and wanted him "always within arm's reach." Kenneth, however, would not oblige the older Stoddard.[108] While Stoddard had built an impressive reputation as a "western writer," he missed the warm sun and affectionate brown bodies of his more youthful Pacific Island days.

Yet, on the eve of their introduction, their potential affection for one another took on greater significance beyond simply an attraction between two people. Japan and America had just sparked a romance of their own as the two nations struggled to satisfy their deepest desires through each other. A modernizing Japan that had long feared foreign imperialism sought to make ties with the West in its realization that it could no longer maintain its isolationism. Many Japanese, in hopes of adopting the "progress" of the West, embraced American technology, styles, and values. For Americans, Japan offered a cure to a cultural malaise brought on by industrialization. Despite "progress" or economic growth, Victorian intellectuals felt that the quality of life had somehow declined. The United States then turned to Japan to regain a more spiritual and pure civilization. Art historian William Hosley noted, "Like lovers, Japan and the West were eventually drawn to one another by a yearning for wholeness and fulfillment."[109]

Thus Yone's and Stoddard's individual situations as well as their social context would take on a formative role in setting the stage for their attraction to one another. While their common love for poetry would bring them together, their mutual need for love and affection as well as ideological presumptions of the United States as civilized and Japan as savage would set aflame a correspondence of unparalleled intensity. And in these letters a relationship of passionate intimacy unfolded with little inhibition.

TWO

Two Shy Stars

1897–1900

In September of 1897 as Yone Noguchi slept, he dreamt of his new "love" Charles Warren Stoddard. He had long been pondering a poem for his "dearest Charlie," and in the stillness of the night, verses came to him as if a gift from God. "It is our fate that we drift away from each other? Thou and I, O Charles, sit alone like two shy stars, east and west!"[1] Yone, a recent immigrant from Japan and an aspiring poet, had just met Charles, an established western writer, and the two had begun a passionate correspondence. Still, their relationship appeared doomed according to Yone—not by the scandal of their same-sex affections, but rather by their introverted dispositions and their difference in background, Japan versus America. As melodramatic as Yone proved in depicting his ill-fated affair with Charles, their affection for one another grew into an undeniable love that endured until Charlie's death. Moreover, Yone's race passionately charged Stoddard's desire for the Japanese immigrant, since Stoddard had previously found a sexual haven among brown men in the Pacific. Yone more sparingly evoked Japan as he grew intimate with the older western writer. While their exchanges might appear mundane in the context of a community of men who effusively expressed affection to one another, Yone and Charlie's affair was different from typical relationships between bohemian men of the time. Their romance more poignantly suggests how fiery same-sex and interracial affairs could ignite between Asians and whites even in the context of a racially segregated America rife with moralistic movements.

In the final years of the nineteenth century, the United States was hardly a utopia of racial harmony and sexual diversity. For Japanese in particular, the late 1890s signaled the beginning of mounting animosity. Since the passage of the 1882 Chinese Exclusion Act, which banned Chinese laborers from entering the United States, the Chinese population had dropped dramatically, rendering them less threatening in relation to the increasing Japanese immigrant population. By 1900 the brunt of anti-Asian sentiment had shifted its focus to the Japanese. Moreover, with rising Japanese military aggression and success as an imperial power, depictions of Japanese masculinity as aggressive, threatening, and martial dominated the popular presses. Increasing anti-Japanese sentiment spurred the California Alien Land Laws during the 1910s that restricted the ability of Japanese immigrants to own land and culminated in the federal Immigration Act of 1924, which prohibited the entry of Japanese immigrants entirely.[2]

Furthermore, a web of federal and state laws as well as popular ideas of race inhibited formal unions between people of color and whites in the United States. When Yone arrived in the United States, California increasingly sought to prohibit whites from marrying Asians. At the federal level, American women who married Asian immigrants lost their U.S. citizenship.[3] From a Japanese cultural context as well, interracial pairings garnered suspicion and disapproval. Yone, who developed intimate ties with at least one white woman, would not necessarily have found support among his Japanese peers if he had chosen to formally marry one of them. While white women embodied all the trappings of an ideal sex symbol within the Japanese American community, they drew less approval as wives.[4] The board of directors for Dalney Association retracted their offer to Japanese consulate member Torao Kawasaki to return to Japan and assume the position of general secretary when they discovered his wife was "American" or white.[5] While Japan did not legally ban marriage with whites or demonize whites as Americans did to Asians, sociocultural pressures and norms discouraged unions between Japanese and whites.

Unlike antimiscegenation literature, discourse condemning homosexuality appeared less frequently in the 1890s. Moralists at the turn of the century did not necessarily perceive same-sex sexuality as an urgent social problem compared to more pressing issues of sexuality such as "miscegenation" and "prostitution."[6] Historian Peter Gay has described how in the late nineteenth century homosexuals derived certain advantages from reticent, bordering on oblivious, bourgeois culture. He notes, "Homosexual lovers . . . were safer in the earlier days of tight-lipped equivocations than in the later days of clinical inquisitiveness." Literary scholar Roger Austen asserts that the decades before 1920, in fact, tolerated homoerotic if not homosexual material in literature and theater without causing alarm.[7]

Bohemian networks across the United States and Europe appear to have been particularly conducive breeding grounds for innocuous yet intense "romantic friendships." Men who found love with other men could maintain long-term commitments in their private lives. These friendships often grew from late Victorian homosocial environments, where individuals with more financial means often congregated for camaraderie, common intellectual interests, or a civic purpose.[8] Historian Carroll Smith-Rosenberg has also traced the acceptability of late-nineteenth-century romantic friendships among white educated women. Thus, Stoddard and many others who may or may not have had sexual relations with members of the same sex certainly could express ardent feelings of tenderness and love for one another without social ostracism. With references to the "dangers" of passionate same-sex relationships relatively invisible, "romantic friendships" between individuals of the same sex proliferated in certain socioeconomic circles.

While the press may have embraced homosociability, social norms and legal restrictions forbade explicit homosexuality. The city's daily the *San Francisco Chronicle* decried the "revolting" acts of a preacher, W. E. Golding, an Oakland resident who had been found guilty in Nevada of "offenses similar to Oscar Wilde."[9] In 1899 a tragic novel titled *Marriage below Zero* attracted attention for explicitly addressing same-sex sexuality. The novel warned women not to be tricked into marrying a homosexual. From 1900 to 1902, city officials arrested ten men for the "crime against nature." In nearby Alameda County, William Day received ten years in San Quentin prison for sodomy. When he hoped to formally challenge the decision in 1902, the courts promptly rejected the appeal.[10] Stoddard well understood the existing limits of acceptability. Though in his travels through the South Pacific he acted as "his nature prompted him," engaging in physically intimate acts with the native male population, he noted that "it would not answer in America, not even in California where men are tolerably bold."[11] On the Hights, as Yone cooked beef stew and played pranks with Miller, he interacted in notably intimate ways with many white male bohemians who passed through Miller's home. They appeared to be a community welcoming of homosocial affection even across racial lines.

By the time Yone arrived at the port of San Francisco, the city's bohemians had enjoyed over two decades of fraternity.[12] Writers and artists formed networks in which men openly expressed warmth and tenderness for one another without the stigma of homosexuality and enthusiastically experienced cultures not their own. They gathered in each other's rented rooms in the Latin Quarter of the city, where the odor of sour wine and a cacophony of Italian and Spanish floated in and out of the dark streets. The proximity of San Francisco's sexually illicit red-light district, the Barbary Coast, added adventure to these social events.[13] Bohemians also ventured to subterranean bars, where an orchestra or vocalist enlivened the patrons. After midnight, journalists who had just finished submitting their last copy would join already inebriated painters and musicians. Together they ate sandwiches bursting with bologna sausage and cheese, quenched their thirst with large schooners of beer, shared stories, and sang boisterously. In addition to their nocturnal adventures, bohemians also gathered for late breakfasts and picnics. At Sunday brunch events, Stoddard played the piano while artists doodled on the tablecloth.[14]

More formalized club events took place on the last Saturday of each month in the form of "jinks" both "high" and "low." An appointed member designated as the conductor of the festivities selected a theme and invited members at large to address the topic through art, poetry, essays, orations, song, or music. These jinks that could last until the following sunrise served as an intellectual, artistic, musical celebration.[15] At these events, Stoddard among other bohemians openly exalted bachelorhood, the value of an all-male community, and love. Orators at the jinks notably encouraged the avoidance of women and frequently painted marriage as a relationship of doom.[16]

Networks forged out of this bohemian culture promoted an intimate culture of brotherly love. With open emotion and communication, men felt free to express care and affection toward one another. William Dean Howells and William Markham both addressed Stoddard as "sweet" or "sweetest" in their correspondence in the late 1890s. Artist Joseph Strong, considered one of the founders of the San Francisco Bohemian Club, frequently sent his "love" to close friend Stoddard in letters that detailed his painful separation from his wife.[17] When Joaquin Miller tersely chased away one of his houseguests early in the morning while he was writing from his bed, he quickly apologized by gathering a beautiful bouquet of flowers from his garden and declaring, "If you can read what the flowers say, you will see that I am sorry for not greeting you more hospitably this morning. I love you and am glad to see you."[18] At the turn of the century, bohemians held few reservations about declaring affection for other men if their emotions so moved them.

As Yone settled into his new home on the Hights, Stoddard began to hear stories about the young Japanese poet who now resided with Joaquin Miller. He craved to meet Yone but could not bring himself to ask explicitly for an introduction. Instead, he carefully studied Yone's face in a photograph in the literary journal *Bookman*, sent him warm messages of love and sympathy through his soul, rehearsed many a letter to him in his thoughts, and waited impatiently for the day they might meet.

From Miller's home in the Oakland Hills in March of 1897, Yone first wrote Stoddard in Washington, DC. He felt confident that he knew Stoddard well from reports from Miller and Strong. In a polite letter of self-introduction, Yone enclosed his poem titled "The Song of Song's Which is the Mikado" and several pressed flowers in hopes of receiving a response.[19] For Yone, sending a poem to Stoddard was merely one solicitation out of many that he sent out to other literary figures such as poets Richard Hovey, Julian Hawthorne, and Francis Sherman to promote his work.[20] Indeed those in the literary community frequently shared written work with each other to grow as writers. While the enclosed flowers may have signaled something more to Stoddard, for Yone it was simply a customary inclusion. In the same month he wrote to Stoddard, Yone sent wild fern blooms to writer Henry van Dyke and other seasonable flowers to poet Edith M. Thomas.[21] A more or less unremarkable greeting, Yone's first letter could hardly have forecasted the passion to come.

Stoddard responded to the introductory note with excitement. After all, he had already called out to Yone in spirit. Yone must have heard Stoddard's plaintive entreaties of companionship as he slept at night. Explicitly addressing Yone's race, Stoddard wrote, "Dear friend who has come to me out of the Orient! Long I have waited to hear from you: always, from the first knowledge of you, I have wanted to know you, to meet you, to be you in closest sympathy. . . . the Muse has at best brought us face to face and heart to heart. Now we must abide together." Though he barely knew Yone, he longed to grow more intimate with him. "How I wish you were here: I have so much to say to you; I so long to see you, to understand you better and know you more and more."[22]

Stoddard requested a copy of Yone's book of poems. He commanded Yone to include a message on the fly leaf so that he might treasure it always. He additionally enclosed a photograph of himself for Yone's judgment and then begged for Yone's picture as well. He hoped to write both his and Yone's names upon the photograph, frame the image, and place it in his study. Stoddard thanked Yone profusely for the cluster of dried flowers. "I would bask with you in the rare garden where they were gathered," he elaborated. "Write to me often and at length," Stoddard demanded as he closed, "Your loving friend."[23] Charlie's warm embrace indeed contrasted sharply with the harsh treatment that Yone received at the hands of less loving San Francisco whites.

While the exchange of written work and photographs was typical among turn-of-the-century bohemians, studying someone's image in a journal and sending soulful messages of the heart even before meeting was more unusual. Indeed, other literati who responded to Yone's solicitous letters wrote with less affection than Stoddard's heated response. When Yone sent wild fern blooms to Henry van Dyke he responded with passion directed at the flowers themselves rather than Yone personally. "My dear Sir:" he addressed Yone, " . . . thank you for sending these wild fern blooms. Flowers spring around the earth. Their beauty is as the Divine Sun which passeth knowledge, and yet we know it." "Sincerely yours," closed van Dyke. Edith M. Thomas also answered Yone's letters with less intimacy than Stoddard: "To Yone Noguchi—A 'Son of The Island'—I have received your springtime greeting, with many lovely and seasonable things it contains." Thomas closed her letter "Yours truly."[24] Indeed the very beginnings of Yone's correspondence with Stoddard diverged notably from letters he exchanged with poetic men as well as women.

Yet even if Stoddard had responded with premature passion, Yone quickly matched his ardent sentiments. He declared to Stoddard how much his note had touched his heart. So joyous was Yone upon receipt of Stoddard's thoughts that he kissed the cherished letter. To Yone, the letter arrived like "moonbeams" lighting his "lonely walks" at night. He

Portrait of Charles Warren Stoddard, c. 1890. Courtesy of Bancroft Library, Berkeley, California.

more than simply enjoyed the notes. "Alas I like it, I love them. That's all I know!" Yone looked forward to seeing what he anticipated as Stoddard's serene face and responded exuberantly to his invitation to visit him. "I like you, I love you, I like to be some day in your study sitting all day by you indeed." He hoped to leave California soon. Yone thanked Stoddard for showing him his lovely heart and looked forward to future advice. Even in this early stage of friendship, Charlie and Yone seemed to grow easily passionate toward one another.[25]

From the earliest days of their correspondence, Yone appealed to "lovely man" Stoddard's experience, highlighting their difference in stature, gender, as well as nationality. "Oh my dear Stoddard[,] [I] being such a Japanese youth I have no experience, I want always certain good advice." He envisioned Stoddard as the "honest sweet gentleman" to whom he wanted to be the "most feminine dove." Yone hoped to become true friends.[26] By evoking his youth, Yone underscored the age difference that critically informed their relationship. Since Yone had "no experience" and hoped for "good advice" from Stoddard, the older writer's experience and wisdom made him particularly attractive to Yone. Additionally, by referring to himself as the feminine dove, Yone marked himself as distinctly female to the more masculine Stoddard, underlining a gendered relationship in notably heterosexual terms. At the very least the metaphor would signal a "friendship" charged with gender difference, diverging markedly from the more typical expressions of same-sex friendships among bohemians at the time. Two men writing letters of love to one another typically highlighted their sameness in gender—as well as rank, status, and sentiment—rather than difference in the forging of their important "fraternal" bond.[27] At the most, Yone's letter revealed the seeds of an intense "Daddy/boy" relationship that would develop—an interaction not strictly familial between a father and a son but rather an affair erotically charged through role play abetted by age difference.[28]

This letter in spring 1897 also marked the beginning of what initially appears as Yone's innocent use of his nationality. By referring to himself as youthful and feminine, Yone also bolstered stereotypes of the Japanese in the U.S. literary and art world as always childlike and female. Yone, who had resisted racialization five months earlier by not taking photographs in his native dress, may have been less concerned about what race would mean in his personal interactions with Stoddard. His early declaration of his nationality less likely served as a deliberate tool of self-Orientalization.[29] Still, to bohemians such as Stoddard, these explicit references to Japan compellingly drew them into the exotic world that Yone embodied. If his skin tone, hair color, and racial features did not serve as enough of a reminder, Yone's declaration of Japan and Japanese culture would send bohemians reeling back into a mystical realm of cherry blossoms and wind chimes, an area of increasing interest for artists and writers of the time.

By 1891 several members of the Bohemian Club had traveled to Japan and published on Japanese culture and aestheticism. Japanese décor such as rice paper lanterns enlivened bohemian life. At that year's Christmas Jinks, the theme song of the Orientalist musical *The Mikado* by W. S. Gilbert and Arthur Sullivan opened the event. Moreover, in 1892 at the Midsummer Jinks, club members rallied to the theme of "Buddha." North of San Francisco Bay in Mill Valley, sculptor Marion Wells and his assistants erected an enormous statue of the Buddha modeled after the famous Daibutsu in Kamakura, Japan. Surrounded by redwood trees, the plaster Buddha stood seventy feet tall at the foot of Mount Tamalpais in a grove called Sequoia Canyon now known as Muir Woods. More than two hundred bohemians enrobed in white and red kimonos wound their way to the sacred spot to worship the surrounding trees and find a higher spiritual consciousness.[30] For San Francisco bohemians, Japanese culture thus served as a familiar and useful tool to further their intellectual and artistic development. As they appropriated what they believed to be authentic Japanese culture to enhance their spiritual lives, these "cultured" white men would embrace Japan and its people as a conveyer of leisure and exotic titillation.

As Yone's affection for Stoddard grew, Yone seemed aware and approving of the older western writer's romantic predilections toward other men. Yone expressed sympathy for *South Sea Idyls*, Stoddard's first book, which detailed his travels through the Pacific Islands and more provocatively revealed his "unabashed delight in seeing, touching, and being touched by handsome naked males." Writing of petting and hugging, growing excited as he slept with young Pacific Islander men, Stoddard made obvious his own sexual preference for men. In late May 1897 Yone prayed that he would be friends with his "tender-hearted poet" forever. He declared, "Let us love each other as heavenly twain!"[31]

Yone soon began addressing Stoddard by his first name, Charles, as their relationship deepened. He appealed to the Charles by painting himself in diminutive terms in direct contrast to the older western writer. "My dearest friend, you are such a lovely man as I am such a lovely boy!" Yone closed his letter with hopes to grow closer. "Pray let us be a friend truthful! Let us be able to understand each other! I like very much to see you, I long so much to sit by you. When I may have such a fate to go to your Washington?" On days when loneliness weighed heavily on Yone, thoughts of Charles saved him. From the "airy nothing" Yone would conjure Charles' figure to keep him company. Yone declared himself an "Oriental youth" who came to "drink the love from the well of Charles' heart." Charles' affection was a gift from God, as refreshing and life-giving as shade on a hot summer day. "Good bye, my love," Yone closed.[32]

Charles likewise appeared hypnotized by the "boy" from the "Orient." His affection for Yone and his work took on racial tones as he portrayed the young poet as an untouched part of the wilderness. Yone, an "unconventional child of nature" with his "exalted muse," bore his heart and soul "naked and bare." Charles noted that the "sensuous imagination of the Oriental had lost nothing of its fire and splendor." Using the most literal English ever uttered, Yone's lines were charged with "primitive eloquence . . . a spontaneous song of heart . . . over flowing with melody." As an "unspoiled poet" from the Far East, Yone appeared appealingly pure and primal.[33]

During the summer months of 1897, Yone more affectionately began to call the older poet "Charlie," as he lavished him with tender sentiments of intimacy and affection. Charlie's notes blew in like a summer breeze and stole Yone's heart like the steps of a gentle lover.[34] His love literally saved Yone's life on days when he felt irrepressibly gloomy, boosting him with youth and love when he no longer wanted to live. He implored, "You don't stop your writing for me as I wait [and] live to hear from you." With Charlie's affections giving him "spirit," he could face growing old without fear or regret.[35] From June to the end of August, Yone at times could barely wait even a day before writing his next letter to Charlie. Though he remained acutely self-conscious about their frequency and worried that Charlie must surely get tired of his letters, Yone continued to write incessantly, often without even giving Charlie a chance to write back.[36]

During the summer of 1897, Yone believed in the inspiration of love and its importance in life. Charlie generously showered Yone with kisses of love with each arriving letter. Yone felt blessed.[37] He could never find words that would adequately represent Charlie's sweet and noble heart.[38] Indeed, in a world of countless beautiful people, Charlie proved to be unique, one of a few that Yone would come to love.[39] Perched atop Telegraph Hill in a room he had rented temporarily to write, Yone stared down at the distant people scurrying about and dreamt of Charlie.

In August, Charlie invited Yone to visit him at his Bungalow. Yone answered ecstatically, "Of course I like to see you—how I long to see you, how I long to see you!—I must go to Washington to enjoy with you!" While he had made friends and managed to earn his keep, nothing meaningful tied him to California. If nothing else, the east held the promise of Charlie's companionship. He wrote frankly to Charlie, "I will tell you that if I . . . start [for] . . . the eastern city, there's no reason and any purpose but to see you and to have a new life of love." For Yone, who had given little thought to what he might do in the east, Charlie's wish to have him by his side proved to be worthy enough reason to move. "If you command me that I must be with you I will come to you—That's all!—That's all!—That's all indeed!" Though Yone had only become acquainted with Charlie less than four months ago, he determined with great faith to follow Charlie wherever he called. "Command me, Command me!" Yone demanded.[40] Though he realized his own foolishness, the promise of pursuing a more intimate relationship with Charlie was something he could not forsake. Yone's mind overflowed with all the possibilities of what the move might mean for their relationship. "To see you, to understand you more, to love you, to live in perfect poetry with you—and—and—and—what must I say when they come at once?"[41]

As summer months rolled into fall, difficulty to make ends meet and homesickness moved Yone to seriously consider whether he should remain in California, return to Japan, or accept Charlie's invitation to join him on the east coast. While he adored the Pacific Ocean and the glory of the "Golden Gate," Yone described California as not suiting him.[42] He found the people cold-hearted, unhelpful, and lacking sweetness. Indeed, Americans as a whole did not appear to appeal to Yone. "I dare say that the Americans are not romantic people—just like a stone-built mansion, not like a Japanese garden!"[43] In such a land where people appeared barren of romantic sentimentality, Yone believed that he would have more opportunity to improve his poetry if he returned to Japan. In his mother country, Yone imagined every mountain and river hailing his return and inspiring him to write. Still, he wished to go to Washington, DC. He grew envious of Charlie's home and the haven away from city life that it offered. "I have heard that you command a most quiet place where you may dream and write as a heavenly king."[44] If only he had more money Yone would remain in the United States.[45]

When Yone's requests to his father for money went unanswered, he called on Charlie for assistance. Yone showered Charlie with affection, expounding on how he wished to be with him, and then called upon his generosity. "Oh, my dearest Charlie, are you not rich enough to provide me a ticket across the continent?" He promised to repay him in five months after his money arrived. He could no longer bear to stay in "rude California!" Impatiently, he inquired about the money, "Have you or not? Am I not right asking such a matter?" He declared, "Let me have a ticket—I will say goodbye to California!"[46]

Ultimately, it would not be a cadre of warm-hearted Californians or a large gift of money that would persuade Yone to remain in America. Between September and October the Japanese government reminded Yone of his obligation to serve as a soldier in the Imperial Army on his return. By late October he had decided to avoid his military service. "So I must be here in America a little more time," decided Yone.[47]

During these cooler fall months when Yone believed he would be returning to Japan, his letters to Charlie only intensified. Yone's own lines comparing himself and Charles to "two shy stars" inspired him as he slept one September night.[48] He considered asking Joseph Strong to make a sketch of himself to send to Charlie. And through October Yone imagined Charlie every moment he felt alone. Thoughts of Charlie always cheered Yone, and Charlie's letters had become necessary for Yone's life. "Pray, write me often!" he pleaded on October 8. "Oh love! I love you," he declared on October 30. "You write me always will you?" he worried. Charlie's letters brought Yone "unspeakable pleasure" that Yone himself could not explain.[49] He sent off responses to Charlie's letters on the very same day he received them. Though it upset Yone when Charlie did not write, he wrote to Charlie regardless of whether he received a response. "But you don't forget about me," he admonished when Charlie could not keep up. Yone's passion in writing to Charlie escalated from the summer months. Still, Yone remained patient about the day they could finally be together. "I am so sure that when I think of you, you are thinking of me. We need not hurry to take a short walk arm by arm and I believe the time may come soon where we may have a happy day and night. Pray let us wait."[50]

Then in November Yone expressed greater affection by articulating "kisses." From his room on Montgomery Street, Yone sent "juicy kisses" to Charlie. On December 11, after complaining of his exhaustion with California, Yone emphatically gave Charlie "<u>many more kisses</u>" in his postscript, highlighting their import with an underline. Again in the same month, he toasted Charlie: "Here are many kisses to you! Love and kisses are the sweetest things. Let us enjoy them." In the following January of 1898 he sent Charlie "boundless love and kisses." Three months later from a room on Eddy Street, Yone added "Yone and kisses" in a postscript before sending his letter.[51]

In between these osculatory expressions, Yone continued to expound on Charlie's many virtues and their remarkable love for one another. As

View of Telegraph Hill, 1896. Immersed in love for Charles Warren Stoddard, Yone Noguchi imagined Stoddard's footprints in the earth when he walked up Telegraph Hill. Courtesy of San Francisco Public Library, San Francisco, California.

1897 came to a close, Yone reflected on the past nine months of correspondence. To Yone, he and Charlie seemed to have met by accident. Remarkably, they understood each other immediately as if they had known each other for an eternity. So long ago did the beginning of their correspondence appear that its memory seemed to be fading as a "gossamer by sunshine." Yet it was not a sad fate. "Be so as it is. Thank god, I find myself in love with you!" Yone, full of "boyish love," felt fortunate merely to have met Charlie.[52]

Indeed the letters had forged a remarkable emotional tie between the two. Yone's relationship with Charlie made the world joyous. Charlie appeared in Yone's dreams often. On walks up Telegraph Hill, Yone hunted for footprints that Charlie might have left when he lived in San Francisco many years ago. The shoe marks were visible only to Yone's hopeful eyes.

Though Yone's impoverished state left him depressed and with little status in what he perceived as a pecuniary world, he found happiness in his fantasies of Charlie. Living a life without Charlie's sympathy each day could only be one of deprivation. "Man can never live with only bread and butter," declared Yone. "How glad am I to have you loving me with your truthful soul!" So powerfully did Charlie begin to disrupt Yone's thoughts that he felt unable to complete his own work when he thought of Charlie. As much as he tried to complete the nocturnally inspired poem for Charlie titled "Two Shy Stars," Yone could not in the state of unrest that thoughts of Charlie provoked.[53] As Yone wrote to his "sweetest love," he demanded a response to each of his letters. Only a serious illness, so debilitating that it rendered Yone too weak to write, would prevent him from connecting with Charlie. Even in his feverish delirium, though, Yone in ecstasy would dream of Charlie.[54]

Through the summer months of 1898, Yone felt further impassioned regarding his love for Charlie. Letters from Charlie thrilled Yone to tears. "Have my love and kisses to thee!" Yone declared. Elated, he would kiss each letter with excitement. His bosom trembled with delight with the mere sight of Charlie's handwriting. Charlie's letters touched Yone like the brilliance of a star shining upon him. Yone showered compliments upon Charlie, a truthful man as sweet as "honey." He called him his best friend and thanked God for their divine relationship—an interaction so beautiful that it would make the entire world warm and kind in its radiance. Yone suspected that even the angels must be jealous of their relationship. No matter that they had never grasped each other's hands, their correspondence full of soul and sincerity reflected the heart of God. Letters without soul were after all "worthless sods." According to Yone their connection must last forever.[55]

Yone envisioned himself and Charlie interchangeably as two bodies lapping up against one another—the sea and the land—two entities that at times took each other for granted but would be connected forever. While Charlie's letters brought Yone great comfort, even saving him from suicide, he could no longer live apart from Charlie. "How I wish to be with you, how I pray for the time coming upon me—when I may stay with you! I can not be alone any more. I am too sad to be alone. I think only you make me happy with your most sympathetic soul.—Can you not my dearest friend?" He continued, "Tell me when we may be together, bring together each other with sweet love! Tell me when!" Yone wished to study English with Charlie to improve his writing and complained bitterly of not finding someone willing to help him. Yet Yone himself remained unwilling to take on just any tutor. He commented on the availability of many "pretty ladies" but did not wish to work with them. "I want you to help me!" he declared. "May I fly to you—to your Washington? Sometimes I wish to die—but not yet, not yet!" Indeed it would be his hope of meeting Charlie that kept life meaningful.[56]

Even as he spent his days with Joaquin Miller on the Hights, he thought of Charlie and longed for his company. He wished that they could together share in the gentle pleasing breezes that caressed the Hights. On August 13 after a walk in a nearby canyon, Yone returned home tired and drank a glass of wine in Charlie's honor. Indeed, Yone had few pleasures, of which reading Charlie's letters remained chief. His letters, far too sweet, would be too much of an indulgence to be read too often. "I love thee and thy sweetest of letters!" Yone declared. Charlie's sweet letters beguiled Yone into the "gate of love."[57]

Then, in the winter of 1898, Yone's passion for Charlie decreased significantly as his affection for San Francisco grew.[58] Though he had hated the city just months earlier, he now spoke of "making love" to it. He particularly enjoyed walking the city's evening streets when fog crept over the city as streetcars charged through the darkening streets and stars began to sparkle through the misty veil. Yone marveled at Chinese, Japanese, French, Dutch, and Italians rushing to their homes after work.[59] Trips to the Cliff House, a restaurant perched at Land's End, where the San Francisco Bay meets the Pacific Ocean, aided in Yone's recuperation from afflictions of "brain fever." Here, barking sea lions lifted his spirits.[60] No doubt his newly acquired appreciation for the city left him less depressed and thus less reliant on his correspondence with Charlie to make life meaningful. Moreover, in October Yone had decided after all to pursue one of the many "pretty ladies" that offered editorial assistance in the city and solicited writer Blanche Partington to edit his works. Through a network of writers, Yone, now twenty-three years old, met Partington, who at the time was thirty-eight.

Partington came from one of San Francisco's "most distinguished families."[61] Blanche's father, J. H. E. Partington, was a successful British artist who founded the Partington School of Illustration when the family moved from Manchester, England, to Oakland, California, in 1890. Three out of her six siblings went on to occupy prominent positions in music and the arts in New York as well as California. Though her passion lay in drama and music criticism, Blanche freelanced as a personal editor for additional income, as did other women writers of the time.[62] Though the late twentieth century had offered more possibilities for women than ever before, job opportunities still remained limited for the increasing number of women with college degrees. While settlement house work proved to be one sphere in which educated women could pursue professions, more literary women became personal editors for aspiring male writers to earn income in between publications of their own work. Yone knew of these women as an important resource for more than a year before he chose to hire an editor. Partington was well suited if not overqualified for the job. Through the 1890s Partington and acclaimed essayist Ambrose Bierce had corresponded extensively about their thoughts on writing and literature. In 1892 Bierce called Partington a "formidable critic, whom I fear more than all the others."[63] Ironically, white women writers, whom Yone initially eschewed, would come to play a central role in his intimate life.

In August of 1898, when Partington lingered for three weeks on the Hights, she spent a considerable amount of time getting to know Yone. In his room, on a donkey ride through a nearby canyon, as he cooked dinner in the kitchen, and as he ran errands for the Millers, Partington chatted with Yone about his dream to become a poet and travel to London. Partington described Yone as a "charming boy." His appearance and demeanor seduced Partington in a distinctly racialized manner. She could not resist Yone's "clear olive skin," "straight black hair of his country," and "haunting brown eyes." His "tender frolicsome side-glance" charmed Partington to no end. As she jotted down her thoughts on Yone, the words that spilled from her pen—"old ivory," "olive," "orchid-like," "elfin," "mystic," and "fanstasia"—demonstrated how impressions of Yone could never be separated from Western imaginations of the "exotic" East. Within two months she would return to Miller's home determined to write a paper on the "Japanese poet."[64]

Blanche Partington was among a large number of writers within the bohemian community who embraced racial diversity as a tool to enliven their experience or bring more meaning to their lives.[65] Essayists and artists not only wrote about or drew "exotic" cultures, they also regularly employed racialized or culturally laden words to evoke passion, humor, and adventure in their correspondence to one another. Various correspondents addressed Stoddard as "my beloved Buddha" or "Carlos." Countless letters between Stoddard and other white bohemians opened and closed with "Aloha."[66] Ina Coolbrith signed off her letter to Blanche Partington, "Yo tea mo." Ambrose Bierce had more "Indian antiquities" to show off to fellow bohemians than did Native American friends with whom he corresponded.[67] Also, bohemian friends frequently gave each other foreign-themed items when giving gifts to one another such as "Chinese balls," "Japanese prints," and "kimono."[68] In the 1890s, when Miller referred to Japan as a "laden little pear tree at our very gate" ready to be picked, the metaphor depicted how U.S. self-interest ultimately motivated interaction with the East. Miller warned, "If we do not hold our hats and shake it others will."[69] Not only did Blanche Partington value going to lectures sponsored by the Japan Society, she also enjoyed visiting Chinatown with Noguchi since it gave her new insights into understanding Asian culture broadly.[70]

Cultures not American thus became an arena of entertainment particularly for individuals passionate about literature and the arts. The Bohemian Club of San Francisco used ethnic themes to enact "art" from a variety of countries. The midsummer performances by white men called "jinks" carried appropriately titled themes such as "Montezuma," "The Quest of Gorgon," "The Atonement of Pan," "The Fall of Ug," and "Rajvara," in addition to their erection of a large Daibutsu in 1892, when they paraded around in kimonos.[71] In September of 1890, Stoddard had read a poem titled "The Daughter of Pharoah" at a gathering where members inaugurated a newly acquired mummy to the Bohemian Club. One stanza animated the mummy and addressed its very displacement to San Francisco. "Where be ye now? And where am I at last? / With gay Bohemia is my portion cast: / Born of the oldest East, I seek my rest / In the fair city of the youngest West."[72] For club members, the corpse's new location seemed a willing move on the mummy's part, bringing history and hope to San Francisco. For twenty-first-century activists the acquisition would likely signal a violation of the most sacred aspects of indigenous culture—the right for the dead to rest peacefully in their ancestral home.[73] For members of this turn-of-the-century fraternity of white men, however, this mummy had become a decorative home accessory for the amusement of "gay bohemia."

Yone would also become a spectacle around which whites would congregate, similar to a world's fair exhibit or a cabinet of curiosities. As much as a decade or more after he had come to the United States, white women continued to covet experiencing Japan through Yone. In April 1904, after spending an evening with Noguchi the previous week, writer

Helen Bridyman invited herself and her husband to Noguchi's home in New York for a Japanese dinner. To Helen, "all things Japanese" were "so intensely interesting." She intended to bring another woman "wild to see [Noguchi's] place." She detailed the exact items she wanted served including tea and bean paste "as before," pickled and spiced raw fish "in square[s]," a steamed custard, raw oysters, and salad. Zona Gale evidently had previously come over for a similar course, and Helen insisted that she have several of the exact same dishes. Helen additionally requested "saki" to accompany the "more substantial courses" and inquired if Yone might be able to drum up a "Japanese sweet" when closing the meal with a second serving of tea. She even dictated the placement of his appliances. "The gas stove by your elbow," she noted. Helen advised Yone in the postscript to "keep this letter on account of the menu" and added, "I want spoons served with that steamed bowl" since it "was far too good to lose between the chopsticks." To Helen's credit, she admitted that the demands appeared condescending—a to-do list from the mistress of the house to her servant. Still, it did not inhibit her from commanding Yone to host dinner along her specific guidelines. "This is a veritable housekeeper's letter, but some things must be attended to, and you will forgive me I know," concluded Helen. One week later in a further move of boldness, Helen took the liberty to invite two other guests to dinner and merely informed Yone about it after the fact.[74] "Thank you so much for making it possible for me to have another glimpse into Japan," Helen declared.[75]

Though Yone enjoyed entertaining when he lived in New York, he preferred cozy dinners of two to four as opposed to the meal for six that Helen outlined. He also more often cooked "American-style" rather than Japanese meals. Yone additionally refused to meet people in kimono since he disliked performing Japaneseness. He avoided it as if it were the "Bubonic plague." No doubt, the dinner with Helen grated on Yone's nerves.[76]

On October 4, 1898, as Blanche Partington approached the Hights in hopes of interviewing Yone, she joined the growing wave of America's fascination with Japan. Partington bumped into Yone as he attempted to board the same car from which she had just disembarked. The two settled underneath a nearby tree, and Yone unfastened his bundle to share his recent work. Partington found Yone's confidence in her judgment curious and amused herself thinking about how the two of them together might appear to passersby. She wrote in her diary, "It was a delicately comic and charming little ensemble that we made sitting there chanting his poems in a strange high voice and intonation." Partington saw clearly the "very faulty" constructions of his poetic expressions yet believed strongly in the "wonderful beauty" of his phrases that had "a hanging together that is felt rather than seen." She committed herself to providing "sympathetic editing." Though she brought a large parcel of mutton to share with the Millers, Partington decided to devour it promptly underneath the tree with Yone. She concluded, "I think the gentle Jap—one of the most poetic souls I ever met."[77]

In their early correspondence he revealed his sentimental side, appeared playful, and appropriately flattered her. "My dear Miss Blanche," he began. "I think you were beautiful last night." He then flirtatiously inquired about her age and shared that he hated to write letters because he felt afraid to engage in such an intimate act. In fact, letter writing seemed to hold the same risks as love. He explained, "Love is too sweet, so we fear to love: it is the same with letter-writing. How sweetly beautiful to write a sweet letter!" Still, as he proclaimed his dislike and fear of letters, he simultaneously wrote of their pleasures. "I have a friend who writes me very beautiful letters once a week; his letters always bring me new light and freshest beautifulness." His "friend" was likely Charlie, and as much as he expounded on his fear of letter writing and thus love, he seemed able to love Charlie immediately and boundlessly. As he complimented Partington's good "womanly" judgment and wisdom, he prayed that she would become a friend as well as a professional colleague.[78]

In October they philosophized on the meaning of friendship as they exchanged poems. "Yes, many people are hunting each other, but so rarely meeting well," Yone agreed. As he praised Partington's ability to encircle herself with so many friends, he mourned his own friendless state. He wrote, "I have only a few friends, or have no friend." Notably for Partington, Yone made a distinct difference between friendship and love, two concepts that he appeared to conflate more easily with his dear Charlie. He explained to Partington, "Friendship must be pure and truthful as Love must be, and Friendship is different with Love."[79]

For the most part, the discussion of recent publications and edits in progress dominated Yone's exchanges with Partington. Warm sentiments for Partington appeared only once per letter usually near the opening. In October of 1898, Yone opened, "Dear Blanche Partington: Glad to receive your letter, and now eager to write you again. I am very much pleased with you and your sympathies." In an additional letter written in the same month, he began, "Your letter came bringing me another delight," and closed with "Your bright voice refreshes me as the sea-voices brighten me all the time." In early November Yone's only compliment to Partington was describing her command, "Work!" as coming from "the voice of a queen." Even as Yone's letters to Partington became more familiar in their address, evolving from "Dear Blanche Partington" to "Dear Blanche," toward the end of December he wrote only of himself, his health, and his writing. Not until January 10, 1899, would he again comment on Blanche's beauty as he had three months earlier in his most effusive letter of October 11. "I was intending to see you on coming Sunday—Alas, Alas, I can not see your beautiful rather stern face." Yone's comment on her appearance remained a qualified compliment.[80]

Conversely, Blanche more clearly appeared smitten with Yone. She surprised even herself when in one meeting with Yone she began fantasizing about the young poet. In her notebook she wrote to herself in the third person, "Was she really unfeminine and hard hearted? And she caught herself wondering if this cold, handsome boy were wishing to kiss her now, and her cheeks flamed afresh at the thought." And just as if he could read her mind, Yone then looked at Blanche's blushing face with a compelling gaze.[81]

Blanche would not be the last American to find Yone notably attractive. Countless women meeting Yone for the first time commented on his stunning beauty. Yone stood as did "other Japanese" on the small side, but with unusually broad shoulders and exquisite facial features. A publication titled *Human Life* noted his "finely moulded" "brown face" was "not too brown." To "enthusiasts," Yone would appear "Italian looking—dreaming—beautiful—spirituelle." In 1905 a woman journalist declared with a caveat Yone's attractive force on behalf of women everywhere. "Yes, there are some dozen layers under a pretty stiff and salty icing of reserve to cut through before one tastes sweetness. On the word of women of the world—a perfectly charming man."[82]

Among all the recovered letters from Yone to Blanche, the one on June 7 expressed the most affection. Yone appeared mired in his usual depression as an "Oriental poet" and had not corresponded in over a month.

To make amends for his silence, he wrote to Blanche, "I will see you after one month with all the love and health. I am thinking of you all the time—say, day and night; I can not forget you. There are many reasons why I don't write to you." "Good-bye, my dearest Blanche, till I will see you again!" he closed his letter.[83]

However, even in these most passionate passages to Blanche, Yone's affections still diverged significantly from those he expressed to Charlie. While he flattered Blanche in a limited manner and never wrote explicitly of loving her, Yone generously extolled love upon Charlie. While Yone wrote of his isolation to Blanche and asked her to be a friend in a city where he only had one or two friends, to Charlie he declared that he was his "best friend," and he spoke of Charlie as his "lover." Even Yone's more muted fall and winter letters to Charlie remained markedly different from those that he wrote to Blanche. As Yone wrote to Blanche of her "beautiful" yet "stern" appearance, he expounded on the "precious odor and bliss" of Charlie's letters. In December of 1898, he wrote to Charlie, "How I wish to see you and be with you, how I wish to learn good English and to interchange thoughts and love each other! O that time must surely come to me." And in anticipation of Charlie's new book, Yone inquired if Charlie might send it after writing "some love in it." Yone gushed, "Yes, you are so sweet as a summer night dream. I thought of you as a great comfort." He closed, "With love and kisses, Yone"[84]

In late April 1899 Yone considered traveling the American continent by foot to experience the "tramp life" in "poetical fashion." He would chop wood for meals and sleep in barns. He packed a few dollars in his pocket in case of emergency and set out for Los Angeles. One night early on in his journey, Yone was sleeping in an empty wagon car when it suddenly began moving. As he stumbled to put on his trousers in the middle of the night, his coins spilled out of his pockets. Yone continued to hitchhike or walk toward Los Angeles with literally no money. To his relief he encountered Japanese people keeping a bamboo store, running a laundry shop, or working on a farm in nearly every town along the coast. His well-known name within the Japanese American community gained him immediate trust from his countrymen. They accommodated Yone with welcome arms when he begged to stay in their homes for a few nights. He would take the opportunity to wash his dirty clothes with hot water prepared by the generous host. In exchange for their hospitality, Yone often helped them write an English letter or interpret a business transaction. In Monterey, he inscribed his name in Japanese on the wall of the Carmel Mission.[85]

After nearly starving, suffocating, and falling to his death on numerous occasions, Yone finally arrived in Los Angeles in July 1899. On a visit to an American church, he found the women talking about everything but religion. The odor of sweaty armpits clung to the air, the sermon proved sleep inducing, and the bishop hardly seemed impressive because he "ate meat like anybody else" unlike Buddhist monks who subsisted on a crust of bread and three spoonfuls of tea. Additionally, the women seemed to be attending church primarily to find a husband. Yone returned to Northern California after a two-week stay. While many of the dreams and plans that he had for his tramp remained unfulfilled, he found his journey a satisfying learning experience. During his travels Yone had begun writing the *American Diary of a Japanese Girl*, initially titled *Ocho-san*. On his return to San Francisco, he wrote to Blanche from his room on Powell Street, eager to meet with her and begin revising.[86]

Even though Yone's notes to Charlie were less heated after fall 1898, he still expressed notably warm sentiments. In August 1899 he apologized for not writing during his travels. Thoughts of Charlie had come to him every day and night, Yone stressed, yet day-to-day living was too sad to write even a single line. Yone assured Charlie, "You are the best of all my friends—How can I forget you!" Charlie's letters "full of sincere love" never failed to cheer Yone like a "shower on [a] hot summer day." He closed, "Pray, excuse me and be a good friend forever! If I will be with you, I will make you happy and comfort you. With the same love, your devoted friend, Yone Noguchi." In September 1899 he again expounded on Charlie's sweet letters that filled him with love, power, and poetry. "I love you very much!" he declared. In January of 1900, Yone proclaimed himself Charlie's greatest admirer, more so than even Joaquin Miller, who often gushed with compliments for Charlie. These letters continued to differ starkly from the letters of task he wrote to Blanche, the only other person to whom Yone appeared to write consistently in the final months of 1899 as he began to write what would later become *American Diary of a Japanese Girl*.[87]

Notably, Yone and Charlie's correspondence point to how men cultivated passionate romantic relationships based on emotional love rather than sex—an interpersonal style typically assigned to female rather than male friendship. Scholars such as Alan Bray, Eve Sedgwick, and Alan Sinfield have more explicitly articulated sexuality among men by such words as "homosexuality" rather than the more ambiguous "friendship" and referred to homosocial "desire" and "passion" rather than "love" to emphasize its erotic nature. Literary critic Valerie Traub aptly summarizes the difference between early male and female friendships studies when she notes, "The boys had sodomy and the girls had romantic friendship."[88] Yet Yone and Charlie expressed great romantic affection for one another even before meeting in person. For these two "boys," emotional connection rather than sex would drive their passion for one another.

In the final years of the nineteenth century, Yone had found an intense love affair with western writer Charles Warren Stoddard. In spring of 1897, when Yone first began writing to Charlie, their letters quickly grew to surpass usual literary affection. As they wrote of their delight in corresponding with one another, a torrid exchange unfolded. While Charlie focused on Yone's race and ethnic difference, Yone hoped to be recognized as more than just an "Oriental" even though he also emphasized his youth and nationality. For Yone, the gestures perhaps grew from his own ethnic pride as well as his humility as an English-language poet in training. Yet differences of race and age were apparent to Stoddard without Yone's articulations. While these evocations may have appeared as no more than innocuous markers of difference for Yone, for Charlie they more potently coalesced to reinforce Yone's identity as an "Oriental" morsel. In 1900 Charlie recorded his private thoughts about Yone in his journal under the title "Notes, Wise, Unwise, and Otherwise." Charlie wrote, "Yone—Is Dream Child—as clear as glass—as pure as water—as sweet as milk."[89] While Yone proclaimed undying devotion to Charlie, his intimate life would become more rather than less convoluted as he arrived at the Bungalow to finally meet his most important love.

THREE

To the Bungalow and Beyond

1900–1904

In May of 1900, Yone Noguchi's long-awaited visit to Charles Warren Stoddard finally materialized. As he prepared for his departure, he exclaimed, "At last! At last! The time has arrived! . . . I suppose you will welcome me with your heartfelt words of delight and love. At last the time has come!!"[1] He reminded Charlie of his love and declared his impatience to see him this very minute.[2] In the ensuing months their relationship would reach new heights of intensity as the two finally embraced in person. Charlie, however, was not the sole object of Yone's affection. Within three years after arriving at the Bungalow, Charlie's home in Washington, DC, Yone would impregnate his newly hired English language editor, Léonie Gilmour, and propose marriage to journalist Ethel Armes. Still, as Yone maneuvered through his increasingly complicated heterosexual affairs, he appeared most intimately connected to Charlie. Yone's race played a critical role in his white admirers' attraction to him. By the early 1900s Yone, in turn, would slowly reverse his earlier stance opposing America's insulting fascination for Japan.

Even as Yone privately revealed a pressing desire to see Charlie as motivating his journey east, publicly he described his move to New York as a stepping stone to his final destination, the more literary London.[3] On the first leg of his cross-country journey, he traveled for three days and three nights by train across two hundred miles to Chicago. Yone found the city humid, filthy, and disgusting. More specifically, he described Chicago as "crazy," "stupid," "noisy," and "the most vulgar town in the world."[4] A blur of ceaseless activity greeted Yone as hordes of people got on and off clanging street cars crisscrossing everywhere both above and below ground. Dust, smoke, and litter permeated the streets as ragged, barefoot boys ran in and out of crowded lanes of street vendors. At night Yone lamented that he could not see a single star and complained of the water, in which a horrible mixture of sand or sediment settled to the bottom of every glass that he poured. "Surely, Chicago must be hell," declared Yone.[5]

Yone nonetheless survived what he described as the "nasty" midwestern metropolis to arrive in New York City in early July.[6] Immediately, Yone fell victim to a pickpocket, who took all of his money save for a few dollars in his trouser pocket. Realizing that he would not be able to pay for lodging, he immediately vacated his hotel room and found refuge in a Brooklyn boarding house run by a fellow Japanese. Nearly penniless, Yone felt lonely and desperate, begging Charlie for assistance. When Charlie responded generously to Yone's request, Yone thanked the older western writer, "the most kindest soul in the world!"[7] Exhausted, Yone stared pensively at the flattened ten-dollar bill from Charlie. For Yone, the trek across country proved arduous, full of unexpected disappointments and mishaps.

In his first month in New York City in July 1900, Yone additionally reached out to Edwin Markham for support, visiting his home in Brooklyn. Edwin and Anna Catherine Markham lived only forty-five minutes from the beach and near a park that the Markhams described as "a lush retreat of the muses." They found the weather endurable if not pleasant. Yet, when Yone arrived, he complained bitterly of the heat and refused a second invitation to visit. His recent encounter with a pickpocket likely contributed to his sour disposition toward New York. Anna Catherine speculated that he was dressed inappropriately for the weather. Edwin found Yone pretentious, prematurely believing he was a skilled poet. Edwin suggested Yone find work. Yone, who did in fact believe himself to be a poetic genius, found the interaction utterly demoralizing. Edwin was clearly a changed man. The "devil" of capitalism now possessed him and had chased out the last remaining shred of poetry that may have lingered within him. "Go to Hell," thought Yone. Edwin Markham was now "dead." As Yone parted from the Markhams for perhaps the last time, Anna Catherine felt sad for "poor little Yone," who would likely have to go find a job. She had such sympathy for Yone since he was "such a beautiful boy."[8]

In September 1900 Yone finally arrived at Charlie's home in Washington, DC, affectionately called the Bungalow. From the front, the narrow two-story red brick building stood indistinguishable from all the others that lined the street. Yet its corner location and its eastward facing windows covered in ivy gave the house a distinctive flair. Inside Charlie had furnished the house with collectibles from his various travels, mostly through the Pacific Islands. Coconuts from Fiji, fans and feathers from Hawai'i, and weapons and dancing skirts from Tahiti adorned his home. Endless volumes of books and tributes to Catholicism also lined his walls. Housewarming gifts from friends, such as Persian pillows and a cut-glass punch bowl, brought additional character.[9]

On their meeting, Charlie seemed even more perfect to Yone, a saint from one hundred years ago who had renounced all worldly possessions despite all the obvious clutter. He was Yone's "ideal person," filled with goddesslike tenderness. Yone declared, "You are a rare china, which I am afraid, might go to pieces."[10] Charlie, in contrast, expressed disappointment. He had hoped that Yone would appear more Japanese and condemned him for being "far too Americanized." Yone knew with certainty that Charlie would have found him more "natural" if he had come to him barefoot in a Japanese kimono. Yone incredulously noted, "Did he expect me to be another Kana Ana—a little sea god of his South Sea, shaking the spray from his forehead like a porpoise?"[11] Despite his annoyance, Yone still revered the older writer.

As they settled into the Bungalow, the two chatted endlessly and shared each other's most trivial secrets. They spent afternoons dozing comfortably together in a single arm chair. In the evenings they slept in the same bed. Yone reveled in Charlie's sweet magnetism—a quality he had rarely come upon. Charlie's breath, so soft and impressive, reminded him of autumn rain.[12] After many years of passionate correspondence across long distances, they had finally consummated their affection for one another in person.

Yet, according to Noguchi scholars such as Ikuko Atsumi, visiting the Bungalow more significantly signaled the beginning of Yone's love for journalist Ethel Armes, a reporter at the time who later became famous as

Photograph of Ethel Armes published in National Magazine *in 1905. Courtesy of Bancroft Library, Berkeley, California.*

Alabama's "first historian." She approached Yone for an interview for the *Washington Post* and arranged a meeting at the Bungalow. Yone initially worried a bit about the propriety of an unchaperoned meeting between a man and woman but ultimately reassured himself in the fact that both he and Ethel called Stoddard "Dad." With the same "Dad," Yone and Ethel were akin to brother and sister. On the day of Ethel's visit, Yone descended from his upstairs room to find Ethel playing the piano in the reception room. "Awfully glad to see you, Yone," she greeted him.[13]

A charming woman with a long, slender face and bold, defiant eyes, Ethel drew Yone in with her beauty and soon after her intelligence. Ethel came from a prominent southern family. She was the daughter of Lucy Hamilton Kerr and George Augustus Armes. Her mother's side of the family boasted a number of senators and congressmen. Her father had served as a colonel in the Union Army and an aide to General Ulysses S. Grant during the Civil War.[14]

Yone's racialized physical features immediately drew in the young journalist. To Ethel, Yone appeared "small, slender, brown; quick and agile in movement, spontaneous and responsive; delicate and refined in features, with wonderful eyes." Yone's personality also intrigued Ethel. She observed, "Like his books he is full of odd fancies, heavy and weighted with drama."[15] Two years later, Yone and Ethel would become engaged to marry. According to Noguchi scholar Ikuko Atsumi, Yone "fell in love at first sight" with Ethel at the Bungalow.[16]

In the midst of Yone's allegedly instantaneous connection with Ethel, he began cultivating a relationship with an additional woman with whom he would soon after consider marriage. In February 1901, just five months after Yone's first visit to the Bungalow, Léonie Gilmour responded to Yone's advertisement in the *New York Herald* for an editorial assistant.[17] Yone had returned to New York City after his visit with Charlie and promptly began to prepare to write. Gilmour, similar to Blanche Partington and Ethel Armes, belonged to a cadre of white educated women who sought out careers as writers. Born in 1874, just a year before Yone, Gilmour had always done well in school, winning scholarships to attend Bryn Mawr College and study French literature at the Sorbonne. Gilmour's mother, Albiana Smith, worked as a nurse and raised Léonie and her sister as a single parent, though she remained legally married to the absent father Andrew Gilmour, an immigrant from Ireland. Upon graduating from Bryn Mawr, Léonie began teaching Latin and French at a Catholic girls' school in Jersey City during the day and wrote at night.[18]

When Yone met Gilmour; she may have appeared very much like a schoolmarm. Hazel-colored eyes peered through rimless glasses. With delicate facial features and neat dress, Gilmour conducted herself in a refined manner. She stood at five feet three inches, a half inch shorter than Yone, and appeared shy to the point of unsociability. Gilmour was a reticent and serious young woman, dedicated to producing her own work and intent on taking care of her mother.[19] As Yone decided to hire Gilmour to edit his English, the two initially embarked on a professional relationship.

The recovered letters from 1901 until 1925 expressed little tenderness for the woman with whom Yone would father a child within three years after their first meeting. Over seventy pieces of correspondence to

Gilmour consisted almost entirely of brief messages of editorial direction.[20] After first apologizing for not being able to pay her more, Yone met with Gilmour regularly, as often as three times a week, to discuss his writings.[21] Together they eliminated repeated words and banal lines while still retaining Yone's unique style. Yone wrote and rewrote, submitting each new version for Gilmour to read, and notified her with updates on the status of articles submitted for publication. As Yone worked on one particular project, what would later become *American Diary of a Japanese Girl*, he declared to Gilmour, "I think the girl's diary is getting [on] nicely. Don't [be] surprise[d] when you see it!"[22] He asked her to make his writing more clear, to condense paragraphs accordingly, and to take liberties to make his writing "perfect."[23] Indeed the only sentimental compliments he wrote were directed toward his writing rather than toward Gilmour. "Diary! Diary! Charming isn't it? I think that it is very clever."[24] Even as Yone's salutations grew more familiar in late April, switching from "Miss Gilmour" to "Léonie," the content of the letters remained work related. On May 31, 1901, Yone wrote, "Léonie Boh! I wish you will typewrite . . . all you have."[25] Moreover, Yone closed his letters with little affection, particularly in comparison to his ardent partings from Charlie. When he took more care, Yone wrote, "With my best regard," "Yours," "So long," "Good Bye," or "Bye-bye" before signing his name. Most days, however, he abruptly ended his letters with simply "Yone," "Yone Noguchi," "Yone N." or merely "Y. N."[26]

In the months that Yone began corresponding with Léonie, he crafted more passionate notes for Charlie. "O dear Charlie: I hardly know how to open this letter. Oh, how many months since I wrote last! Pardon me! Pardon me, dear Charlie!" On July 26, 1901, Yone again wrote: "My dearest Charlie: You are ever so kind and sweet. You don't know how much I am thinking of you. It was delightful to read your letter again. World will be all right, I fancy. Thank God!" On October 7, 1901, Yone wrote, "I don't know when I will be again with you face to face in Washington! Dear Charlie, I like to see you so much! I am lonely,—Oh, well, everyone cannot be allowed to be happy always. I suppose."[27]

In 1901, a little over a year after Yone's first visit to the Bungalow, Yone moved into Charlie's home with some expectation of living with Charlie as one of his "kids." Charlie welcomed Yone's company as a respite from the loneliness that had long hung over him as if an unshakable dark cloud. Two months earlier, Charlie had realized that Kenneth had outgrown him and was running with a set that had no connection with the older writer. Charlie felt unsettled in both mind and body and yearned for rest and nurturance. He needed "a great deal of cuddling," of which he had none of late. Charlie declared, "The melancholy days have come—the sadness of these years. I feel greatly depressed."[28]

On the mid-December day that Yone moved in, Charlie succumbed to "the grippe." In a small room with barred windows to prevent delirious patients from throwing themselves out, Charlie spent a gloomy Christmas week with another patient overhead who yelled and moaned all through the night.[29] For sure, Yone grew despondent over Charlie's illness. He declared, "Oh well, this world isn't the place of laughter I fancy." Still, Yone made the best of the cards life dealt him. "Let it go!" he reminded himself.[30] Yone then visited the infirm Charlie every day for the following eight days, bringing letters, a copy of the *New York Journal*, or other little gifts. On Christmas Eve, Yone with Ethel brought candy and mistletoe to Charlie's bedside. The three finished the candy and hung the bough under the chandelier over Charlie's head.

Despite Yone's care and attention, Charlie focused on how his live-in companion Kenneth neglected him. Charlie grew anxious wondering if Kenneth had spent all the money that he had given him. On Christmas Day he resisted going to Benediction in the chapel, in case he might miss Kenneth if he came to visit. As Charlie waited with anticipation in his hospital bed, Yone reported that Kenneth was in fact sleeping with a "stranger," a man from the "streets" that he had brought into the Bungalow at around 4:00 a.m. Charlie cried to himself, ""What a blow to my 'Merry Christmas.' . . . Oh my God! No more kids for me, save as playthings . . . it's broken my heart often enough over this most unworthy one." After Charlie returned from the hospital, Yone slept with Charlie at night while Kenneth slept downstairs. So depressed was Charlie that Yone's efforts to cheer him up were without success. When Yone bought tickets for him and Charlie to see Chases-Vaudeville on New Year's Eve, Charlie reported the event as "not too much fun."[31] The sorrowful loss of Kenneth weighed heavier than the reward of enjoying Yone in person. Even as Charlie lavished affection on Yone, ultimately Charlie's longing lay with Kenneth.

In these difficult first few weeks, the two managed to find some comfort in their mutual misery even if they remained unable to lift each other's spirits. As Charlie wallowed in his heartbreak over Kenneth, Yone remained as others had already perceived him, "in love with sadness."[32] In the afternoons Charlie enjoyed Madeira wine, while Yone puffed on cigarettes. The two lounged about a living room table littered with holiday gifts and pillows of pine needles. As they bantered back and forth, Charlie from time to time passed his fingers through Yone's blue-black hair. When a reporter from the *Washington Post* dropped in at the Bungalow to write about "the brown poet" Yone, Charlie did much of the talking. Yone's quietness hardly reflected passivity on his part. With each sentence Charlie spoke for Yone, Yone exhaled smoke directly into Charlie's face, to his displeasure. When Charlie called Yone a "fiend" about cigarettes, Yone laughed merrily and blew more smoke into Charlie's gray beard, causing him to cough and shake.[33]

As a witness to Charlie's pained relationship with Kenneth, Yone felt relieved to leave the Bungalow shortly after the holidays. He had grown exhausted from meeting new people and caring for Charlie. He decided that it was better to be alone and do what he pleased. Sometimes, he "dislike[d] companions." He told Charlie that he would rent a room so he could finish some writing. Charlie agreed it was the best course to follow. When Yone returned to New York, his report to editor Frank Putnam of his largely "unsuccessful" stay at the Bungalow not only revealed his disappointment that he had not been able to live with Charlie, but also his need to hide any excitement that he likely still felt for Charlie.[34]

In October 1901 Yone griped about Charlie to Léonie. "My old friend at Washington wrote me inviting me to come up. But I don't like such a sentimental fool. Yes, Stoddard is an old fool! I like to go to Washington, however; the place is nice and quiet, a genteel town. I think I will go there, if he promise[s] me to act less fantastically. Truly I would go there next month if he would promise me that. He has such a great library—thousand[s] and thousand[s] of books."[35] Calling Charlie an "old fool," referring to him less affectionately as "Stoddard," and commenting on the impressiveness of his library rather than his personal character placed Yone on less intimate terms with Charlie than their actual correspondence from the same time implies. These remarks may have signaled

Yone's diminishing affection for Charlie. Yet, they could also have pointed to a more careful Yone. He may have overtly attempted to downplay his intimacy with Charlie in full knowledge that the passion he held for him might appear inappropriately unique.

Notably, one month later, when Yone sought comfort from Charlie after being evicted from a New Jersey lodging house, he sounded like a different person from the young man who complained to Léonie about the "old fool." Forced to find a new home after the owner of the lodging house decided to move, Yone sought refuge at Charlie's. "So many troubles gathered on me; I am almost sick. I must come to you and try to be happy. Do you welcome me? Oh pray. . . ."[36] The affection that Yone showered on Charlie seemed to be something he preferred not to share with Léonie or Frank.

In the year after November 1901, intimacy between Yone and Charlie deepened as Yone began to address Charlie as "Dad." Previous scholars suggest that Yone and Charlie's frequent use of "Dad" and "kid" indicated a relationship more akin to that of father and son.[37] Indeed, with men younger than him, Charlie developed mentoring ties where he became "Dad" or "Master" and his admirers became "kid," "child," or "little one." Yone, however, did not necessarily see Charlie as a father figure even though he called him "Dad." He explicitly stated that he never saw Charlie as a mentor. For those with whom he did feel a parent-child kinship, Yone expressed it in a forthcoming manner. When Yone shared lodging with several Japanese men, he claimed one individual in particular, "a man called Watari," acted "fatherly" toward him. When referring to Miller as well, Yone noted how he often looked out for his welfare "as if a mother lion after a baby lion."[38] Even more than the lack of an explicit description of Charlie taking a fatherly role in Yone's life, interactions between him and Charlie ultimately proved different from those between father and son, or even mentor and mentee. In fact, Charlie and his associates' use of "Dad" and "kid" likely pointed to a relationship of "love" and "intimacy" in a fraternal and potentially erotic context. In the late nineteenth century heterosexual couples frequently used terms such as "Daddy" or "papa" and "baby" in their expressions of romantic affection.[39]

For a childless bachelor such as Charlie, his "Dad" and "kid" relationships may have additionally provided a cover for an otherwise "curious" lifestyle. According to historian Judy Wu, Margaret Chung, founder of the Chinese Hospital in San Francisco, also affectionately known as "Mom Chung" in the 1940s, similarly adopted a mother persona for herself to quell rumors that she might be a lesbian.[40] While "Mom" provided weekly dinners with her surrogate family members, Charlie would more deliberately avoid "family" gatherings. When Yone suggested a reunion for all of Stoddard's "kids" during the Christmas holidays, "Dad" refused with emphatic despair.

Literary critic John Crowley noted that Charlie, whose "deepest and most sustained love affairs were pedophilic," did not find a "necessary contradiction between paternity and 'homosexuality.' "[41] As Austin Strong, the son of Charlie's good friends Isobel Osbourne Field and Joseph Dwight Miller, matured into manhood, moved to New York, and became a dramatist in his own right, Charlie admired his beauty. "As his 'natural-born' god father . . . when I get East, if I ever do, I shall long to spank him cordially. He used to have alot of that sort of thing when he was a 'tot;' now that he is beautifully developed, I fear his beauty goes to waste?"[42] Another man he referred to as a "charming kid" he described as "ripe" and "luscious."[43] Charlie's biographer Roger Austen recounted how Charlie in fact had sexual relationships with his "kids."[44]

Indeed, as one of Charlie's "kids," Yone occupied a special place in his "Dad's" heart. The two consistently expressed an attachment for one another more passionate than typical between father and son. On November 3, 1902, Charlie declared: "My own Yone! Your dear letter came just now. How I have mourned for you and wondered at your silence. I sometimes thought that you were angry or that you had forgotten me. Alas! That would be saddest of all. We must cling to one another always!"[45] Just two days earlier Yone appeared to have read Charlie's thoughts as he wrote a letter to reaffirm his devotion to Charlie. "Oh, where are you? Are you well? So much silence between us! Are you going to blame me? Pray, don't! Am I forgetting of you? Never!!!!!!!! Oh, believe me Charlie! I love you all the time. How I wish I could see you just this moment!"[46] As they corresponded regularly with one another, they missed each other intensely and hoped to be reunited.

Yet, in the midst of writing effusive letters of love to Charlie, Yone also dedicated time to become more intimately acquainted with the *Washington Post* reporter Ethel Armes whom he had earlier met at the Bungalow. Ethel went to New York City to visit Yone, and they spent every day together during her two-week visit. They explored small, quirky restaurants and scurried forward whenever they passed a church because of Yone's fear of the cross. Ethel became enamored with Yone's idiosyncrasies. Still, soon after her New York trip, Ethel "fell in love" with another and had a "furious affair" with not just one but later an additional individual, as well. She had only "imagined" that she was in love with Yone. Ethel had no time to write to Yone, and he quickly slipped from Ethel's mind.[47]

Yone, bitter at being abandoned, called Ethel a "fish" in addition to "other dreadful things," likely referring to Ethel's seeming flippity-floppity fickleness. Ethel in turn responded by sending a rod, a line, and bait, a sarcastic acknowledgment of her apparently fishlike quality. After another response from Yone, the two curiously became even more committed. Ethel recounted to her friend Alice Wiggins, "So after that—I can't remember how it came about—we got engaged."[48]

In 1902 Yone announced and insisted upon his love for Ethel to "Dad." Charlie, perhaps not surprisingly, responded to Yone's announcement to marry with disapproval. He advised Yone against an "early marriage" adding that it would be the "most exasperating fate that could befall a young man." Yone still had "much to see, much to do" before he "settle[d] down." He must remain "free to come and go as you please." If Yone were to marry now, he would "sorely regret" it, and a baby would "ruin all." Marriage best suited "middle aged" men who had grown out of their "follies" and could afford to be "practical." Only for them would marital partnership be appropriate. Yone would be better off outside of the binding contract of matrimony. As Yone planned for a six-month visit to London to promote his writing, Charlie reassured him that the break would do him "wonders." Charlie encouraged Yone to continue to love, suffer, and long for things unattainable. These experiences served as the seeds of poetry.[49]

Yone, however, insisted upon his and Ethel's love for one another and their commitment to marriage even as their relationship teetered on the brink of dissolution during their two-and-a-half-year engagement. Soon after their first proposal to marry, worries that the two would not have any money gripped Ethel, and she immediately broke off the engagement. Yet after another "make-up," the two reinstated the engagement and all "went along all right" until Ethel wrote a "love letter" to Gelett Burgess, "simply to see what would happen" and to test Yone's jealousy. According to Ethel, then disaster broke loose, a situation that she could only articulate to Alice in a letter as "+\!!!=X>?^!!" Ethel then nearly became afflicted with "nervous prostration." The less fortunate Yone caught "fever" and remained ill for weeks. On November 6, 1902, Ethel reported to Alice that her relationship with Yone was "all broken again," and she doubted that she would ever hear from him again. Their last letters had crossed and Ethel suspected neither of them would answer. "Of course it is all off," she exclaimed.[50]

According to Ethel, both she and Yone remained culpable in the unraveling of their affair. They frequently found dealing with each other "impossible." Even when on the best of terms, they found each other selfish and conceited. They entangled themselves in "mazes of misunderstandings" that left them nearly always "upside down." When their relationship grew more serious, the magic seemed to leave their correspondence. Additional conflicts revolved around expectations of marriage. To Yone's displeasure, Ethel could only promise a one-year commitment since she could not possibly agree to marry any man for more than a year. Yone, in contrast, believed that marriage was for an eternity. Yet, even as Ethel declared, "So that's the end of Yone and me," Ethel continued to hope that something would happen to demonstrate that he in fact "suit[ed]" her and had more "sense" than she.[51]

By late November 1902, Yone had settled in London to further his career as a writer, and Ethel appeared distinctly unhappy about his move.[52] As she wrote to notify Yone of her move from Flushing, New York, to Birmingham, Alabama, she expressed her disapproval of Yone's relocation to England. "Do you know the sun has quite set on our 'love affair'? You aren't my style, Mr. Noguchi (to run away and leave me!) Oh! But that was a silly thing for you to do! I have to laugh at you now." While Yone's departure appeared to signal the end of Ethel and Yone's relationship, it more likely piled just another tiff on the ever-growing mound of altercations between them. In the very same letter, Ethel, whose actions still indicated her investment in their relationship, enclosed a photograph of herself to provide Yone with "sunlight" in gloomy London where there existed "not sufficient attraction" for her to join Yone.[53]

Charlie unrelentingly pressed against Ethel and Yone's impending union. He reminded Yone that despite his fondness for Ethel he should not marry because of his "temperament." A wife would only become a burden, and Yone could easily find companionship. Thus, as a "poet," "dreamer," and "idealist," he should remain "solitary," free to act without "hindrance." Ethel specifically also appeared to be a less than suitable partner. She would only bring unrest and unhappiness if taken seriously. Charlie warned: "Write to her, by all means and tell her of your success. But go no farther—if you love me you will heed me! I know what I am saying!" Charlie went as far as to state explicitly that Ethel did not deserve Yone's love. Charlie warned, "Love her not, my dearest . . . she is a flirt and not worthy of the serious passion of a true heart."[54]

As he advised against the union at the beginning of 1903, Charlie may have felt particularly needy for a more faithful "kid." The University of Notre Dame had fired Charlie in November 1901, and he could no longer financially maintain his Bungalow. Charlie had moved in with the parents of his "kid" Kenneth in 1902.[55] More than the cramped quarters, Charlie found Kenneth's increasing independence "hellish torture." As Charlie watched Kenneth carouse all night and take up "kids" of his own, he longed for the companionship of those who appreciated and loved him.[56] Charlie missed Yone's company. He longed for the days at the Bungalow when his friends would gather. In late January Charlie confessed that he wrote letters to keep his heart from breaking.[57] Still, despite the stresses of his personal life, the older Charlie, who had seen many men fall in and out of love, may have carefully considered Yone's character and imparted the most lucid advice he could on behalf of what he believed to be Yone's best interests.[58]

In London, Yone made contact with various important figures. Upon hearing of Yone's literary success, Charlie became wild with delight and trembled all over. He longed to embrace him in person. As he gazed at the "most beautiful picture" of his Yone, which he had placed on his desk to keep it constantly by his side, Yone's "sweet sad face," "too sensitive mouth," "delicate chin," and "beautiful hands" all called out to Charlie for care and love. And he would willingly oblige.

Charlie craved to see more of Yone, in fact all of him as "God made him—naked and not ashamed." He longed to hold and caress Yone's hands as well as feel their caresses. To Charlie, Yone was "all beautiful" and "all worthy of love." If he had his Bungalow, Charlie would keep Yone by his side forever. Without the Bungalow, they should instead both settle together at the Hights. Charlie needed Yone's "tender and loving spirit" to quiet him and create an atmosphere of tranquility. He declared:

"Once more a thousand embraces! I fold you to my heart with number of kisses."[59] Charlie's love for Yone continued to draw Yone to the western writer despite his lack of support for Ethel.

On February 2, 1903, when Charlie discovered that Yone had dedicated his latest book to him, he became so wild with excitement that he hardly knew what to do with himself. Charlie wrote to Yone, "My love was great that had you been here I must have held you in my lap all day long, fondling you, as my very own." With the darkness of the night, he would have folded Yone in his arms, embraced him, fallen asleep upon one pillow, and held him until morning. Yet, with Yone so far away in London, Charlie felt alone. Kenneth had long become a distant companion, away from the house all day and evening. Charlie would see him at times for breakfast or dinner or when he came in late and greeted Charlie with a "good night" on his way to bed. To comfort himself, Charlie imagined Yone by his side as a loving soul, to pat, caress, and cheer him with affectionate words and deeds. As he longed for Yone often and ardently, he closed his letter, "Come, place your lips to mine in one long rapturous kiss."[60] For Yone, who wrote of lips as the "portal of the human heart" and kisses as a "heavenly" stamp of love, the above yearnings articulated by Charlie must have been very moving indeed. In the five days between January 28 and February 2 in which Charlie wrote these three letters of commendation and congratulations to Yone for his literary accomplishments in London, he revealed an unprecedented level of intimacy.[61]

As Yone wrote to Léonie Gilmour through February, March, and April of 1903, his letters grew increasingly familiar. Still, they did not include any notable expressions of affection. On February 2 he reported on the idiocy of editor Frederick Stokes. On February 19 Yone sympathized with Léonie in a run-in she had with another Japanese man and then detailed directions on publishing his next endeavor, *American Letters of a Japanese Parlor-Maid.* Five days later, he announced his new book and listed the literary acquaintances he had made. Two letters in March notified Léonie about the details of his return to America and the publication of a book of poems. By April 19 Yone had returned to New York and reported on his meeting with Bliss Carman and Gelett Burgess. He signed his letters, "Yours," "Sayonara," "Good luck and strong health," "Good-by," or just simply "Yone."[62] Few might have foreseen that a year later Léonie would be carrying her and Yone's child.

Yone's letters to Charlie, though still affectionate, also had decreased in fervor from April to September of 1903 compared to the notes he wrote in the 1890s. Before he returned to the United States in early April, Yone appeared to answer with tough love, if not cool sympathy, a letter from Charlie complaining about his situation with Kenneth. "I am awfully sorry to hear that you are not peacefully situated and comfortably placed. But don't expect too much from anybody. If you do it will be reason to make you disappointed."[63] On July 16 he again reprimanded his "tender" Charlie on his unstable life, albeit gently and avowedly more poetically than Charlie's other friends. Yone reassured Charlie, "I love you all the same and I always pray for your happiness and health."[64] In September Yone wrote a brief note asking for a picture of Charlie and his Bungalow as he prepared to publish his article on Stoddard. "Dear old bungalow! I dreamed I had been there and had slept with you," Yone reminisced. Still, he signed his letter merely "Yone." After a trip to Brooklyn, Yone wrote to Charlie that he was too tired to visit. He argued, "Undoubtedly your place would be crowded today," as he signed off, "love, Yone."[65] How different did Yone's 1903 letters read from those in the 1890s when he lived to save enough money to see Charlie! In the thirteen additional letters that Yone wrote to Charlie in the same year, there existed not even the briefest articulations of love.[66]

Charlie, however, appeared unfazed if not unaware of the change in Yone's letters. Though their exchanges were no longer ablaze with passion, Yone continued to sporadically insert gestures of "love" into Charlie's letters, writing consistently to Charlie at least twice a month. Interaction with his "dearest Yone" would delight Charlie all the same.[67] On April 2, 1903, with Yone's return from England, Charlie announced his departure from Washington, DC, and with it his final break from Kenneth. He wrote with urgency: "We must see each other as soon as possible. Who knows what plan we may make."[68] On April 14, 1903, when the two reunited in New York, Yone came bounding up three flights of steep stairs, rushed into Charlie's arms, and kissed him "like a young lover." Charlie marveled at what London had done to Yone. He seemed self-possessed, glib, and full of charming anecdotes. Yone carried the air of an accomplished man. When they went to lunch, the other two guests who had come to visit Charlie declined to share in the wine Yone had brought for Charlie. Yone once again charmed Charlie by placing all four wine glasses in a row in front of the older western writer "in the most humorous manner but with Japanese delicacy." Charlie remembered the moment fondly in his journal, "Each was filled and I emptied them all."[69] Additionally, Yone and Charlie regularly met for dinner or the theater and called on people's homes together until early June, when Charlie moved out of New York to Cambridge. On April 22 Charlie looked forward to dining with Yone at the home of Bliss Carman. The following day Charlie had confirmed box seats for himself, Yone, and two others to see *Hamlet.* On April 25, just two days later, Charlie invited Yone to have dinner. In May, Richard le Galliene invited both Yone and Charlie to dine with him. And in June, Edith Thomas heartily accepted Yone's suggestion that he and Charlie might pay her a visit.[70] The two ostensibly appeared to be a pair, if not an inseparable couple, attending nightly social events together.

Notably, when Yone received notice from Charlie about the box seats to *Hamlet,* he discouraged Léonie from coming along, saying that she would feel "very uncomfortable" in the company of Charles Warren Stoddard, Bliss Carman, Percy McKays, and himself. Yet if Léonie wanted to come, he suggested, "I will tell Mr. Stoddard about you." The letter may signal Léonie's exclusion from bohemian and literary circles as well as her compartmentalized existence in Yone's life in April of 1903.[71]

Perhaps Yone's ability to spend time with Charlie no longer necessitated passionate correspondence motivated as much by frustration as by love. Still, their close proximity to one another accounted for only the first two months of a longer period in which their correspondence had largely cooled. By early June, Charlie had moved out of New York to Massachusetts. Though Yone's letters might signal less affection for Charlie, Yone still felt fondly for "Dad," as demonstrated by their numerous New York outings and the short but tender well wishes that he continued to send even after Charlie left the city. In July 1903, after Charlie had settled in Cambridge, he felt appreciative of Yone's "delightful" letters, filled with news and "so loving." While he was happy in his situation, he "longed" to see Yone and wished he were "within reach." Six days later, Charlie responded to Yone's update on his business selling trinkets. He yearned to set up a booth right next to Yone's and be "loving rivals." "O, how I wish I could see you there in the Roof Garden," Charlie declared. "I would kiss you before the whole world!"[72] In the fall months of 1903, Yone dreamed of returning to the Bungalow and sleeping with his "Dad." He made plans to visit Stoddard in Cambridge.[73] Charlie welcomed Yone with love: "I long to see you, my little one. I must hold you in my arms a long time."[74]

Yet Yone's attentions may have drifted to another. One Tuesday morning he sent an urgent plea summoning someone to visit. "Say, Dear, come and I must see you today. You have one hour for your luncheon. Take the elevator and come to see me about half-past eleven, if possible. Tell your MR any sort of excuse for half an hour. One hour and half would be enough to make one trip. I expect you. Don't fail! Come Deary!"[75] With no recipient and date indicated, the letter remains largely a mystery, yet archivists have speculatively dated the letter July 1903. That summer day Yone may have been working at his booth at the Madison Square Rooftop Garden, where he encouraged an individual to take the "elevator" for a quick visit. As inconclusive as the note is, this letter remains the most passionate of all his recovered letters from his first year back from London.

Yone may have been occupied with thoughts of Zona Gale, a former reporter for the *New York Evening World*, who later won a Pulitzer Prize for her novel *Miss Lulu Bett* in 1920. Charlie had introduced her to Yone in 1903 to distract him from his romance with Ethel. Yone indeed found her to be a "blossom," a "rare beauty" and "unattainable star beyond his reach" who could create artful verse. Though Zona had another suitor at the time, Yone continued to visit her every week to discuss his writings.[76]

Then, four months later, on November 18, 1903, Yone sent a brief note to Léonie. He wrote only a single line. "I declare that, Léonie Gilmour is my Lawful wife." Noguchi scholars in Japan have relied on this document to signal marriage between the two. The union seems particularly convincing in light of the birth of their son Isamu in November of 1904. Yet Léonie as Noguchi's "first wife" makes little sense in the context of recovered letters preceding the November 18 letter. No notable affection appears to have passed between the two as they carried on a largely professional correspondence. In the recovered letter closest in date to this November 18 declaration, Yone appears at best playful, yet hardly romantic or affectionate, in his writing to Léonie. On September 17 Yone inquired if Léonie was "deadly tired" of him and indicated that he could make a "graceful exit" in a manner akin to a "jelly fish which has no head and tail." He additionally quipped that it would sound more "romantic" for Léonie to lose a leg than to elope with a "Hindoo Prince" and tried to lift her low spirits by noting it was "awfully foolish to be blue."[77] If the marriage declaration was written in jest, it may have pointed to Yone's continually playful manner perhaps to appease Léonie after a particularly unpleasant disagreement. Yet, even as a prank, it could also have hinted at underlying romantic affection if not sexual tension for one or both parties.

If, however, Yone wrote the note in all seriousness, it likely marked the beginning of their sexual activity in the fall and winter months of 1903, according to historian Masayo Duus. The two had begun living together on East 26th Street. Duus described Yone as deceiving Léonie to facilitate a sexual relationship between the two—"an easy way to satisfy his sexual desires and get on with his work." Léonie believed that they would marry soon, committed herself to him, and then moved in to cut living expenses. Léonie reportedly confessed to one friend that she became pregnant during Yone's last days in New York City, when they spent time together daily and lived as man and wife though they shared separate homes. Yone soon after declared that he did not love Léonie as "a husband should a wife," and the two parted ways. After seven months of living with Yone, Léonie, who could no longer hide her "swelling" pregnancy, joined her mother in California. Yone then found another apartment on West 64th Street.[78]

Both Yone Noguchi and Isamu Noguchi scholars in the United States have been unable to find a marriage license or any legal record of their union and never refer to Isamu's parents as "married" or "husband and wife." Léonie's later letters to her friends suggest that she believed the note to be a declaration of marriage and only realized in later years that the two were never married. While Yone's note did not carry the official seal of a marriage license, Léonie held great faith in Yone's word.[79] As late as 1915, Yone referred to Léonie as "my wife in California" in an autobiography.[80] One thing remains evident in the single-sentence declaration of November 18, 1903. Whatever its motivation and intent on Yone's part, by the time Léonie became pregnant with Isamu in spring of 1904, Léonie had reason to believe that she was married to Yone.

In the months following Yone's note to Léonie, Ethel and Yone's tumultuous engagement once again careened forward as his love letters charmed Ethel in December 1903. He "danced" with her mind as none other had done previously. Ethel anticipated joining Yone when he returned to Japan, as he intended to do. They would live three miles outside Tokyo in a small house with a garden. She imagined their yard filled with one hundred cherry trees. One "maidservant" and a "jinriksha man" would attend to their various needs.[81]

Ethel pointedly attributed Yone's alternative masculinity as a significant source of her attraction to the Japanese immigrant. Additionally, she explicitly referred to Yone as a boy rather than a man in declaring his uniquely attractive characteristics. "Such a man—boy rather—as Yone is rare." In the single recovered letter from Ethel to Yone, she began the letter, "Hello my boy!" In 1904, when Ethel became engaged to Yone for at least the third time, she described him as unlike any man that she had ever met. He had a "wonderful nature." Sometimes she believed he was "too sublime" for her. "The sweetness and gentleness, the exquisite sensitiveness,—I have never met a man like him."[82] Ethel's articulations of Yone's attractive youthfulness, gentility, and sublimity ran parallel with the ways in which bohemians fascinated with Japan characterized its culture and people.

While Yone initially resisted racialization, as outlined in Chapter 1, by the early 1900s he began to employ Japan more actively in his personal letters and professional writing, reinforcing language and images that he had previously avoided. Not only did he appear to encourage his own racialization, but he also contributed to Orientalist works of fiction during the height of America's fascination for Japan.

In 1901 he started using the very term "Jap" that had previously injured him to refer to himself and his Japanese American colleagues. When Yone described his lodgings on Nineteenth Street to Charlie, he called them a "Jap boarding [house], full of prank and noise." In October, when he wrote of loving the hot days of summer when everything appeared "beautifully untidy," he explained, "I am [a] Jap who hates any strict order and severeness, you know." From Riverside Drive in New York, Yone closed his letter to Léonie with "Yours Jap friend, Y. N."[83] Well aware of the scathing nature of the term, his shift to begin using the term around 1901 may have signaled a new attitude toward taking the greatest advantage of his ethnicity. Using the word "Jap" among his intimates in the literary world likely felt safe. For Charlie, Léonie, and Ethel, "Jap" more likely stirred images of sculptured tea gardens than an uncontrollable rage to pummel the nearest "Oriental."

In his correspondence, Yone began pairing his use of "Jap" with additional explicit references to Japan and the "Orient," including the insertion of Japanese words. "So, sayonara, for some days," he wrote to Charlie in November 1901. To Léonie as well, he concluded "Good-bye, Sayonara, Yours, Y. N." in one letter and merely "Sayonara" in another.[84] Moreover, when Yone and Léonie became embroiled in a disagreement over Yone's criticism of Léonie's editorial comments, he suggested that his tactlessness was rooted in his cultural background. "I was truly severe to you. . . . You know I am such a damnful fellow who never speaks well of another. I know that is wrong. Moreover, as long as I keep such heart, I know, I can not be an American gentleman, but [I] can't help it."[85] Yone claimed his abrasive demeanor came from his inescapable Japanese nature, citing his "heart" so unlike that of a specifically American "gentleman." In 1903 as well, Yone began to print "Japanese" deliberately in brackets after his name on the title page of brown-paper pamphlets that he distributed.[86]

In the starkest turnaround in the use of his nationality, Yone also took a new set of photographs sometime around 1901. These pictures, which he hoped to send off to publishers and other literary figures, featured Yone deliberately robed in a kimono. The move proved astutely strategic on Yone's part. In May 1901 the publisher Funk and Wagnalls Company returned Yone's previous photograph in a suit and requested the newer version to keep "on file." They politely inquired, "Would you be so good as to favor us with one of your new photographs, the one you mention in your esteemed favor as being taken in your Japanese kimono?" In 1904 writer Helen Bridyman also coaxed Yone to send his photograph in "Japanese costume" because of its "beauty and individuality." She knew Yone preferred the one in American dress but hoped Yone would make the "right" decision.[87] Requests for enacting and imparting Japanese culture through dress and ceremony no doubt pushed Yone to take a more practical approach in presenting his ethnicity. He may have begun to consider taking better advantage of his Japaneseness as early as 1899, when he was thinking of writing his first book of prose, titled *American Diary of a Japanese Girl.*

Depending on the literary critic, *Diary*, published in 1901, either catered to or critiqued American ideas of Japan.[88] While debates over whether Yone's work bought into or rebelled against American Orientalism may never be definitively settled, the text more decisively illustrates the dilemma Yone faced in producing a work that would be popular among an American readership and simultaneously express his discontent for U.S. attitudes toward Japan. Yone in fact had hoped to render critiques of American life through the palatable voice of a "charming" Japanese maiden.[89] He took up the pen name "Miss Morning Glory" to use the racialized Japanese female form to his advantage as he began to capitalize on his ethnicity.[90] He believed its "girlish quality" would make his work a financial success. As a conscious act, Yone would be a calculating writer in the promotion of his own work.[91] While Yone cringed from the abuses and exclusions that markers of racial difference brought, he maximized what benefits he could reap from Japanese stereotypes to cushion him from the hardships of living as an Asian immigrant in the United States. At his "Japanese bazaar" at the Madison Square Roof Garden in New York City, Yone sold trinkets from Japan and made seven to twelve dollars each night, an effective way to more literally profit from his ethnic identity.[92]

Yone's use of his Japaneseness, however, never meant that he was complicit with the ways in which the West referred to the East diminutively. When Joaquin Miller paired with Yone to publish *Japan of Sword and Love* in 1905, the dissonant juxtaposition of the two writers' works seemed like a sword fight between the paternalistic white man and the angry Asian boy. While Miller expounded on the youthful, small demeanor of Japanese men—calling them by names such as "brownie," "brown child," "boy," and "wee brown man"—whose only passion was cold tea, Yone aggressively promoted a martial, merciless Japanese man. Yone spoke of teaching other nations to "respect another's right," "break[ing]" the "white nation's" race prejudice against and condescension for Japan, and restoring "liberty." Japanese soldiers would "sweep in like a northern tempest" to win the war and restore "morality."[93] Ironically, Yone's hypermasculine depictions of Japan would play right into ideas about Japanese as martial and threatening that were proliferating in the early 1900s.

At the dawn of the twentieth century, as Yone's correspondence with Charlie ebbed and flowed in its passion, their exchanges would remain the most intimate among all of his friends. While finally meeting Charlie in person initially intensified Yone's love for Charlie, his later connection with Ethel appeared to compromise his passion for "Dad." Though Yone remained intimately invested in Charlie, he hoped to embark on a serious relationship with the young journalist from Birmingham. Charlie adamantly stood opposed to the union. Noguchi scholars have claimed that Charlie's jealousy motivated the opposition. However, the older writer may have sincerely believed that marriage to a woman would only spell doom for Yone both spiritually and professionally. Though clearly a sensitive man, Charlie has never been characterized by scholars as a possessively jealous man who would sabotage another man's happiness for his own personal benefit. Charlie for the most part settled for what life afforded him as he delicately lived in a social world that grew more explicitly homophobic. In the midst of these two intensely intimate connections with Charlie and Ethel, Yone declared his marriage to his editor Léonie Gilmour.

Moreover, while Yone initially resisted pandering to imaginations of the Orient that whites foisted upon him, by the early 1900s he had begun to employ Orientalism in furthering his personal and professional affairs. In the face of American racism, his hope for fame and affection pushed him to make decisions about how he could best use his ethnicity while maintaining his own integrity.[94] His decisions regarding the use of his marginalized racial position reveal how individuals might compromise themselves or their community to gain acceptance in white America. Yone's immersion into and later manipulation of race and racialization plainly illustrate the dilemmas Asians in America juggled with the pressures of racism and Orientalism.

FOUR

QUEER INTIMACIES

1899–1904

By December 1903 Yone Noguchi appeared to be married to Léonie Gilmour, even as he reinforced his engagement to Ethel Armes and wrote letters of affection to Charles Warren Stoddard. Yone and Ethel's relationship proved particularly tortured as the two waded through countless disagreements. As they mended their relationship with each tumultuous turn, they insistently avowed that they hoped to marry one another. Yet their most important love may not have been with one another. Charlie remained a key figure in Yone's life, and Ethel herself seemed to prefer long-term romantic relationships with women rather than men. Part of her attraction to Yone stemmed from the fact that he held characteristics atypical of men. Yone and Ethel's engagement became undeniably queer as they promised to take each other's hand in marriage even in the midst of more passionate connections with members of the same sex.[1] In their articulations and enactments of love, Yone and Ethel's affairs would not only demonstrate how seemingly separate spheres of male and female friendship overlapped intimately, but also how these affections within the white bohemian community often took on explicitly racialized tones.

As Ethel and Yone's connection grew, Yone's attention toward Charlie appeared to wane. When Charlie stood at death's door in winter of 1904, Yone responded with uncharacteristic coolness. Doctors at Cambridge Hospital diagnosed him with "brain congestion" after Stoddard was found unconscious. People assumed his end loomed close at hand. Relatives and friends paid their last respects, and a priest delivered last rites. Various newspapers and magazines prepared and even published eulogies.[2] Yone, uncertain of which hospital to send his letter to, wrote to Prescott Hall, where Stoddard resided. "I am awfully sorry that you are not well. I shall come up and see you if you are terribly ill, of course. What's the matter?" He ended his note: "Hoping you are better by this time. Yone" Frank Putnam responded to Yone's inquiry by informing him the trip would be useless since Charlie would not "know" him at all. A letter from Charlie himself would later surprise Yone. Still, Charlie's miraculous recovery did not prompt Yone to visit. On February 15, 1904, he wrote to "Dad" that though he had considered traveling to Boston, the beginning of the war with Russia had caused him to change his mind. Charlie appears to have invited Yone to travel with him to California, where he had recently received a six-month commission from the journal *Sunset.* Yone responded with ambivalence. "I wish I could go with you to California or anywhere. I will be good companion to you, I hope, I will—but—! I don't know just yet." Indeed his 1890s excitement over Charlie seemed to have vanished. Yet Yone had not lost all affection for "Dad." "If Japan wins the game, I will take you to Japan. Then the time for us will come, you know. Just now, everything is compressed in excitement and fight. Write me again, Dad!"[3]

In December 1903 Ethel coveted a life of love that she might lead if she married Yone. For love, she would walk "the earth's length" on "white hot iron." Since she would never find her "dream" man, Ethel would marry Yone because of *his* devoted affection for her. "It is not so much that I am in love with him, but . . . he is crazy—quite crazy about me—and that suits me." As a wife she could then return her husband's undying intense love: "[I] could learn the love that I dream now is the right kind." Her commitment to Yone remained largely a secret, however, except among her most intimate friends. Her family knew nothing of the engagement.[4]

Months later, in May 1904, Ethel again appeared to be on the "out" with Yone, "for good this time it seems." Four days later, Yone wrote to Charlie in an effort to contact Ethel. "Did you hear anything about Ethel? I think our connection has been cut off." Yone regretted falling out of touch with Ethel because of his own neglect in not writing to her for several weeks. Then, three weeks later, in early June of 1904, Ethel once again found herself planning for a May 1 wedding the following year with Yone. Impulses behind this engagement appear to have been much less romantic than previously. Yone had been losing his sight, and Ethel felt responsible for the "thousand" horrible deeds she had committed against him. "I believe I have nearly killed him and I am going to stop it. We shall be married," Ethel declared. If Yone's eyesight grew worse, Ethel planned to move up the wedding date to tend to his needs. She cared for Yone more than she had cared for any man, and she vowed to be present during his time of need. "It took me a right long while to find out how much I did care." Still, Yone's love for Ethel rather than her own love for Yone served as the primary glue that kept her by his side. "He adores me,—and for love, what would I not do?"[5] Ethel's sympathy for Yone, however, would not carry this rebirth of commitment very far.

Two days later, as Yone's vision improved, Ethel once again found Yone unbearable. "I guess I better not mention Yone again,—I am too horribly provoked with him. I don't know whether I will marry him or not. He is very much better these last few days but he is so wretchedly impractical and so am I and I am not sure of anything and I haven't been for all the year and maybe longer. Heaven knows when I will be." Ethel noted, "He makes me very tired." To recuperate from the affair with Yone as well as work-related stress, Ethel planned a getaway to Canada if she could not go to Greece. Still, by the last days of June, Ethel appears once again to have gotten back together with Yone and then quit the relationship again. On June 22, 1904, she reported to her close friend Alice, "I have just broken off again with Yone—he makes me angry—so angry I cannot see sometimes." Though she still cared for Yone, Ethel increasingly came to realize that he would not be able to provide the stability that she sought in a relationship. Yone remained too much the "clinging vine" in a pairing where Ethel had hoped to cling as well. Yet even in her darkest moments when Ethel felt absolutely infuriated with Yone, she distrusted her instincts to separate from him. "I may be imagining everything," she confided to Alice. Her self-doubt rendered a final break-up at this time difficult.[6]

The alternative masculinity that initially attracted Ethel to Yone would create conflict in their relationship. In late June of 1904, Ethel wrote to Alice, "Oh he is not big as I dream nor strong nor bravehearted nor practical nor—how could I say—protecting—if one could [use] that word. I feel so much that is it I who would have to be the husband—that is it—when I want to be the little one—and the wife." "He is nearly all that my heart desires—but is not all because he is not what I think men ought to be." Ethel confronted Yone with her concerns that he "bends like a reed, like a blade of grass and in the wind."[7] While Ethel's description of Yone's shortcomings eerily echoes late-twentieth-century stereotypes of the emasculated Asian male in America, her criticisms diverged sharply from increasingly martial depictions of Japanese men in print at the time.[8]

Ethel's observations mirrored assumptions of a select population of Americans who embraced Japan as the land of Buddhism, bamboo, and beautifully simple objets d'art. Ethel's assessments of Yone's sensitivity and reedlike qualities paralleled how American artists perceived his homeland in the wake of an aesthetic movement that embraced Japan called Japonisme. This fibrous flexibility more negatively associated with indecision would then take on gendered implications in its contrast to more masculine decisiveness. Understandings of race have always been inflected by ideologies of gender and sexuality.

By the turn of the century, Japonisme had swept America and Europe by storm. A perspective similar to Orientalism in which the West produced and perpetuated exotic images of the East, Japonisme more specifically used Japan as inspiration in the visual, decorative, and literary arts. Art historians date the origins of Japonisme at the middle of the nineteenth century, soon after Japan reversed its two-hundred-year policy of isolationism. As Japan opened its doors to outside trade and interaction, artists from the West saw the mysterious nation as having infinite aesthetic wisdom. The French first excitedly embraced Japanese design, and the fascination for Japan quickly spread across Europe and the United States into leisure culture. Curios such as Japanese kites, hats, and fans flooded markets. An explosion of fictional works such as plays, short stories, and poetry with Japanese themes titillated readers and theatergoers. In San Francisco specifically, writers at the turn of the century equated Japanese femininity with gentility and delicate womanhood in local publications such as the *San Francisco Chronicle* and *Overland Monthly*. Advertisements in city newspapers utilized visuals of Japanese kimono-clad women to promote tea, city events, and hair products.[9] As late Victorian Americans felt dissatisfied with their quality of life even in the midst of economic growth, they turned to Japan to satisfy their hunger for a purer, more spiritual civilization rooted in an appreciation for nature. To Americans, Japan still remained untouched by the ravages of industrialization.[10]

Charlie's fascination for Yone took on more explicitly racialized undertones than Ethel's. He described Yone's eyes as "the windows of a temple, filled with the shadow of mystery." Yone's "pernicious little body" seemed to be made of ivory "as an idol that has wakened from a mystical dream." Yone's soul was like a "jewell in the lotus."[11] Charlie's evocation of "idol," "jewell," "mystical dream," and "lotus" signified Asia. Japan appeared to represent only positive traits for those concerned with culture and the arts.

Make no mistake, however, regarding the extent to which Japonisme substantively shaped the daily lives of *nikkei* or Japanese America. While Japanese themes appeared aesthetically pleasing and desirable, San Franciscans rarely treated Japanese immigrants as individuals of delicate artistic value. Physical and verbal assaults as well as open discrimination in housing and employment made life difficult. On city streets white men and women angrily glared at Japanese. The more aggressive hurled fistfuls of pebbles and balls of spit at the new immigrants. When people maliciously called Yone a "heathen," he reminded himself that he was as "good as any Christian."[12] Neighbors also called Yone "George" with little regard to his real name.[13] Renowned artist Yoshio Markino in 1910 noted, "It is a world-known fact that [Californians] hate the Japanese." During his four-year stay Markino never ventured to the park for fear of "savage people" who pummeled him with stones and bricks. Expletives of "Jap!" assaulted not just Markino but Japanese from seemingly every corner of the city.[14] So damaged were the psyches of some *nikkei* that they considered it a compliment when told they did not appear to be Japanese. To Yone his fellow San Francisco comrades seemed to be "dry tree[s]" with "souls dying."[15]

Perhaps it was natural that Yone's early correspondence to Charlie appeared depressed. While in 1902 he confessed to being "born a pessimist," conditions in San Francisco likely aggravated Yone's dark mood. In fact, four years earlier he had told one reporter that he had not always been sad and melancholy. "In school in Tokio I was ever pleasant, but now it is different."[16] Living abroad, particularly in xenophobic and anti-Asian California, could have stirred depression in even the most jolly of Japanese immigrants. By 1904 Yone wrote to Dad, "I am tired in this country."[17]

Yone appeared to have also internalized American ideas of Japanese inferiority. When he began looking for an artist for his publication *Ameri-*

can Diary of a Japanese Girl, he preferred a good "American" artist rather than a Japanese one.[18] In 1900 Yone explicitly articulated Asians' low intelligence and lack of work ethic compared to whites.[19] All the while, however, Yone felt great pride in being Japanese.[20] As contradictory as this might seem, it points tellingly at the complicated dilemmas of self-esteem and cultural pride that colonized casualties of Western imperialism faced. Individuals could hold great pride in their cultural background even as they felt inferior to the more "modern" West.

To soften the hard edges of living in an alien land, Japanese in America banded together and took special care in supporting one another. Not only did Yone receive assistance along the California coast and in New York when he had no money, Yone likewise helped other struggling countrymen. In January 1900 Yone assisted a Japanese friend in San Francisco and also volunteered two to three hours a day for a Japanese newspaper.[21] A few months later he introduced his friend Unosuke Wakamiya to Charlie. "Any favour—what a sweet word favour is!—given to him will be very much appreciated by your dearest friend, Yone."[22] Around 1902 he arranged for the release of a fellow Japanese from a Rochester jail and sent him to New York City with money.[23] During Yone's four-month visit to England, he immediately sought out Yoshio Markino. When he reached Yoshio's residence, he emphatically announced his arrival, shouting from the bottom of the stairs "Bokuda, bokuda!"[24] The two gave each other much comfort in London.[25]

Moreover, Yone appears to have held more intimate ties with at least one Japanese in America. Kosen Takahashi, an illustrator for the Japanese-language newspaper *Shin Sekai* and co-creator of the literary journal *Twilight*, had "wooed" Yone in the late 1890s "as a boy do so for a girl." He had sacrificed his "whole heart," and the two, according to Kosen, had become "lovers." During Yone's tramp to Los Angeles in 1899, Kosen waited anxiously for his "eloping love" to return so their warm lips could join in an eternal kiss. He had nearly drowned in his own tears after having lost Yone to "Naughty Spring" and teetered on the brink of insanity searching for him. Though Kosen found Yone to be the "most queer boy among all Nipponese," the two had much in common, including dreaming "always" of their "sweet" Japan. "I am utmost queer fellow as much as Yone," declared Kosen. Describing Yone as "charming as spring blossoms," he exclaimed, "Yone is my love forever."[26] For Yone the Japanese

Photograph of Kosen Takahashi inserted into letter to Blanche Partington, 1899. Courtesy of Bancroft Library, Berkeley, California.

American "bachelor" community provided financial support as well as romantic affection.

In addition to their own community, Japanese in America could also find some refuge within the literary and arts world in which Japan had come to hold a powerful aesthetic meaning of gentility and exotic culture. Even if Japanese racial inferiority lay in the back of white bohemian minds, ideas of Japonisme largely prevailed to shape bohemian interactions with Japanese. Thus, Yone's notably brown beauty and all that it connoted would mesmerize Ethel as it did Charlie and even Blanche.

However, even as Ethel became increasingly involved with Yone, she continued to cultivate intimacy with others. In December of 1903, she had informed Alice of enjoying "romance" with Daniel Quinn, whom she hoped to visit in Greece in June 1904.[27] Moreover, Ethel's personal correspondence reveals her longstanding preference for meaningful and physically affectionate relationships with women rather than men.

In 1899, just a year before she began her romance with Yone, Ethel saw marrying a "girl" as one of her future goals. Yet she would never ask a woman to marry until she felt able to support her in good style. Her monthly salary of twenty-five dollars at the time made prospects of becoming a "Rockefeller" "not very bright." Still, Ethel had "lots of confidence" in her future success. Furthermore, Ethel expressed ready availability to kiss women, as much if not more so than men. She never could see any "harm" in kissing and enjoyed it "very much." Annie Briggs, a woman Ethel hoped to marry, could testify to Ethel's pleasure in kissing.[28]

In 1899 Annie Briggs held a uniquely intimate relationship with Ethel that evoked the brilliance of romance more than the darkness of shame despite its same-sex twist. However, Annie's parents disapproved of the union. While Annie suggested that Ethel's Catholic religion served as the point of objection, Ethel believed it attributable to her lack of financial wealth. "Mrs. Briggs wants Annie to marry for money," noted Ethel. Interestingly, their same-sex relationship in and of itself seemed to be of little concern. Ethel noted, "If I had $50,000 they (Mrs. + Mr.) would not care what I was." Yet Ethel claimed she did not "care much" about the parental disapproval since she "wanted" only Annie and not the rest of the "tribe." "And I am going to have her too some day," declared Ethel. Annie and Ethel had already discussed their union one Sunday evening when they were "together" from 7:00 p.m. until almost 10:00 p.m. and they "did enjoy ourselves ever so much."[29]

As Ethel proclaimed her love for Annie, she simultaneously invited Alice Wiggins, her confidante when it came to her disastrous affair with Yone, into her fold of intimacy. Ethel wrote to Alice, "I don't think a person knows what it is to love, unless they love and so my dear . . . I earnestly hope that you will try to return some of the love that I give you for Alice I do love you and why shouldn't I?" Alice had given Ethel "many pleasant hours" and assisted in "so many different ways" that Ethel could not "help but love" Alice. She insisted that Alice call on her with any request and that she would do "anything in this world" for her.[30]

Since 1899 Ethel had hoped the two could deepen their intimacy by kissing. As "queer" as it might be construed, Ethel explained, "I tell you dear Alice when one person thinks a good deal of another both can get more genuine satisfaction out of a kiss than if they shook hands and talked all day."[31] Alice appeared more reserved, often not responding to Ethel's overtures, which Ethel then interpreted as consent. Ethel playfully allowed a more reluctant Alice to refrain from kissing. "Of course, if non-kissing is one of your hobbies only I suppose I will have to let you go this time." She looked forward, however, to the next meeting when Annie would join them and "two good big ones" would be consummated. In January of 1899, Alice herself had never yet kissed a "boy." Ethel's osculatory inclination proved rebellious during times when moralists hoped to regulate a kissing craze, even in more liberal cities such as sexually notorious San Francisco.[32]

Ethel's flirtations with Alice signaled her intense love for a woman she felt immediately drawn to "the second" she met her. Though Ethel felt she "knew" Alice that first moment she saw her, she felt "shy" about approaching Alice so boldly. Her "pride" prevented Ethel from pursuing Alice.[33] She further feared that regionalism would come between them. While Ethel considered herself a southerner, Alice was definitely a New Englander. Ethel had no reason in venturing north, except for Alice alone, the "fruit" of her journey. As she realized she had found a "friend" in Alice, she sang "Hosanna" in joy.[34]

By 1902 Alice had eagerly responded to Ethel's romantic overtures. On November 6 Ethel addressed Alice as "Oh my man!" She complimented Alice's ability to court a woman better than any "Southern gentleman." "Oh you are dear," gushed Ethel. "How you could woo a lady if you loved her. And me—even me. Très difficile me." Ethel continued, "Really Alice if you were a man it would be ideal and I know I wouldn't be into such a mess as I do with all of them. You'd manage me. That's what I want!" Ethel's use of "my man" to address Alice appears deliberate, less likely to signal Alice's mannish qualities than to make a statement of the intimacy between them akin to a heterosexual couple. In 1904, when Ethel mistakenly referred to Alice as a "girl," she deliberately corrected herself. "So long my girl, MY MAN, I mean," Ethel wrote as she signed off.[35]

Still, it appears that Alice was unable to explicitly articulate her love for Ethel. While Ethel enjoyed Alice's gifts, she waited for the day when utterances of love for her would pass from Alice's lips. Ethel pleaded, "I wonder when-when-when you would love me enough to write and tell me so. . . . I must be told you know dear over and over and over." By fall of 1902, Ethel had reached some level of mutual understanding of love and intimacy with Alice. After years of deliberate distance in which she had struggled to keep herself from seeing Alice and then kicked herself for it since, she declared, "now—now—now—I can throw my arms around your neck."[36]

In November of 1902, Ethel invited Alice to spend the Christmas holidays with her in Birmingham. "At least the South will be something to see—or there is your girl—. . . surely she is worth going over a thousand miles for?" If money proved to be an obstacle, Ethel suggested that Alice borrow from her parents. Ethel offered to pay it back with proceeds from her first book. More than anything else in the world, Ethel wanted to be loved, petted, and spoiled, and she believed that Alice was just the one to fulfill her needs. Ethel found Alice so intoxicating that she feared that she would make her "lose responsibility." Ethel thanked her for all the photographs though she missed being by her side. "Had I but been with you the entire time—what a delight," lamented Ethel.[37] The photographs of Alice brought such pleasure. "Send me all the pictures you can," she demanded. They would make an impressive gift for Christmas. And what would Ethel give in return? "Perhaps I will have nothing!" she teased. "How sad <u>that</u> would be," Ethel wrote.[38] After five pages of gushing over Alice, Ethel then recounted her trials with the now passé Yone. Yet, even after six pages of Yone, Ethel would ultimately find comfort in her love with Alice. "Really—Oh, I am so glad I know you like me and miss me," she wrote to Alice. In the final two pages Ethel embraced Alice with entreaties of love. "My man. Dear man. Aye—I'll be your Indian bride. When are you coming to court me? Come—woo me—for just sweet wooing's sake. Love me–adore me."[39]

Ethel's use of "Indian bride" to frame her relationship with Alice would infuse their love with romance and innocence as well as passion and taboo. In the late 1800s images and ideas about Native American women had been in circulation for at least two hundred years in Western art and literary works. In these portrayals largely by white men, American Indian women frequently embodied contradictory characteristics—innocence as well as savagery, sexual purity as well as availability. In marriage to white men, particularly fur traders in North America, the beautiful "Indian bride" came to symbolize a shy, submissive women about to embark on a pure marital union of mutual love. Having escaped the tyranny of the Native American husband by whom she would be reduced to a "slave," the pensive, dreamy beauty could now enjoy romance that was more civilized as well as passionate. Even as she appeared as an exotic Other through clearly articulated racial markers, the "Indian bride" became a part of America, appropriated and then packaged together with an Anglo man to symbolize Jeffersonian ideals of racial harmony through intermarriage. The couple would come to represent America. As romantic as this endeavor appeared, most of the nation perceived these unions as problematic for their cross-racial nature. The Indian bride became an icon of harmony even in her transgression of racial order.[40] In this context, by calling herself Alice's "Indian bride," Ethel painted herself as the object of lust and infused distinct meaning into their passionate affair—a pure romance built on companionate love, but also illicit perhaps in its unconventional same-sex pairing. Ethel as the "Indian bride" might also suggest her own role as temptress spinning a web of seduction around the less sexually savvy Alice. In fall 1902 Ethel further pushed Alice to confess her love for her. "I will bet one thing. Of all the girls you ever met in your life, you liked me best—didn't you Alice?" Ethel closed her letter, "Tell me over again you like me for always. Your friend—bride—I should say, Ethel"[41] For Ethel her relationship with Alice proved more intense than mere friendship. It would hold as much significance as the holiest of heterosexual unions.

A little over a year later, Ethel felt dogged by the dilemma of female love that faced her. If only Alice had been a man, their intimacy could be requited in a lifetime commitment. "Again I have to say it—why in the world aren't you a man?" she queried Alice. Alas, it only made sense that only a woman could "know" another woman, yet it proved to be the most exasperating reality for Ethel. Ethel adored Alice for all the characteristics that were uniquely Alice. "I like the bigness of your body even,—a good bigness—and your spirit is quick and slender and flies long and far to the stars." Ethel scribbled sweet-nothings to Alice in the margins of each page of her nine-page December letter. On page 4 she entreated, "Couldn't we talk Alice." "[Y]ou listen so marvelously," she flattered. On page 5 Ethel wrote, "Say something peppery or I might turn you into a litany of sweets." On page 6 she added, "I can't resist the temptation to add talk on the margins before I fold this up! What should I say next? I love you." Finally, on page nine Ethel wrote, "It suits me so to be adored—as you love me Alice. I am so thankful. I think that you are fascinating. I know you better than anybody else does too!"[42] By June 1904, when Ethel notified Alice of her and Yone's engagement, once again she pleaded with Alice, "Please love me forever." In a later letter that outlined Ethel's breaking of her engagement to Yone, Ethel sought solace in the Alice's intimacy. As Ethel concluded her letter, she wrote: "Do please love me lots. That after all is the only thing on earth I want and the one thing I cannot get,—to my heart's desire."[43] Ethel's same-sex intimacies appeared to raise little concern among her friends or even with Annie's parents. Perhaps her connection appeared as merely platonic love, intense romantic female friendships typical of the time. Yet Ethel's desires were more than mere consummation of an intimate female friendship. They proved to be romance articulated by the very heterosexual institution that defined a relationship between man and woman as more than friendship—marriage. Indeed, if Ethel's expression of kissing and love appeared typical among women, then articulations of marriage to a woman, her desire to financially be capable of supporting her spouse, and finally signing her letter "Richard" more powerfully pointed to how Ethel expressed her same-sex love through heterosexual discourse.[44]

If her correspondence did not signal her unique affinity for Alice, then it pointed to how Ethel as well as her intimates did not feel closed off to simultaneous, multiple experiences of "love" at the turn-of-the-century.[45] Ethel believed that she could in fact fall in love with anything, even "a stick, a stone, or a tree," as she would with a person. "I can adore or despise just as I choose according to that which I make or see."[46] She felt unbound about whom or what to love and vocalized such thoughts frequently, though she fully realized that she was unusual in her sentiments. Ethel wrote to Alice, "Maybe I am different from you other people—because as I have often said—all my life I have been recognizing the ideal in women, in men,—in things—in places. I have actually found it—no matter what may be said that it does not exist."[47] Ethel proved to be at best a woman of generous heart and at worst an individual "all mixed," or so she herself worried. Ultimately, however, Ethel only wished to be loved. She confessed to Alice in early November 1902, "How my heart beats wishing for people to like me."[48] Still Ethel declared that she could never imagine herself in a long-term relationship with an individual not of her own sex. She declared, "I could not possibly agree to marry for more than a year—any man."[49]

From their first meeting, Charlie sensed Ethel's limitless capacity to love. For him, the characteristic was negative, particularly in relation to Yone. Ethel was "so excessively feminine" that she could never resist the temptation to flirt. She would be unable to help herself from making any husband feel "uncomfortable."[50] From June to August 1904, Charlie pressed Yone to reconsider the union even as Yone repeatedly proclaimed his devotion to Ethel.[51] Though Charlie's open disapproval of Yone's engagement saddened him, it did not seem to detract from their intimate relationship. Yone continued to send tender phrases and impassioned pleas to Charlie. Yone would go anywhere with Charlie as his "good companion," and he felt "crazy" to see Charlie as he pleaded with him to write more often. Thoughts of Charlie would fill Yone with love, kisses, and happy dreams.[52]

Even so, with each of Ethel's letters Yone felt further bewitched.[53] Though neither of them might be worthy of marriage, he could not help but love her. He admitted that, although as Charlie warned she would undoubtedly make him feel "uncomfortable," marriage seemed very much like "gambling at the horse track." He determined, "I will take the risk and bet—if I win—it would be so much better." If things did turn out "well," that would be his fate. Yone prayed that Charlie would not stand in his way. "Truly determined" to marry Ethel, Yone told Charlie of her confessions of love. "She love[s] me more than any other fellow. I think what she says is true. How can I doubt it?"[54] Indeed among men, Ethel likely cared for Yone the most. Yet if women were to be included, he might barely have made the top three, behind Alice and Annie.

As Yone planned to return to Japan in July of 1904, he decided to stop in Birmingham, Alabama, to see Ethel on his trek back to California. If the visit went well, he would immediately marry her or travel alone to Japan, find a steady job, and then call Ethel to join him.[55] Charlie responded with panic, not because he wouldn't be able to see Yone but rather because of his impending marriage. "I pray you do nothing rashly! How I wish that you were here that we might talk it all over calmly. My heart is in my throat for thinking of you and worrying over this affair." Charlie then closed in perhaps his characteristic style. "I wish I had one of your savory photographs such as I saw in the Age Herald. Do write me! Loving Dad."[56]

No amount of protest from Charlie could change Yone's mind about marrying Ethel. Yone noted that, though she may not have been "perfect," she appeared "strangely wild" and held a certain hypnotic charm. Stoddard's criticisms of marriage appeared only to fuel Yone's insistence that he cared for her. Though he did not know why, Yone could not help "lov[ing] Ethel so" and begged for Charlie's compassion if his judgment proved wrong. He requested that Charlie stop speaking so negatively about Ethel and the union. "Dear Dad, you never took any interest in Ethel, and rather you have had a mean opinion about her. But, Dad, don't say anything displeasing about her." And he hoped for Charlie's blessing: "Pray, say some kind word about Ethel, Dad."[57]

On August 1 Stoddard responded more carefully to Yone. He told him to "fear not" for he would never say or think unkind thoughts of Ethel. Never had Charlie had a bad opinion of Ethel. He in fact had taken an interest in her since their first meeting ten years earlier, finding her "clever," "warm-hearted," "affectionate," and "spontaneous." Indeed it was pleasant to be under the spell of her charm, admitted Stoddard. He worried that neither Yone nor Ethel had "a nature sufficiently practical to manage domestic affairs." He advised Yone: "You should both be free, remain free of encumbrances so long as you live. This is my firm conviction." According to Charlie, it would be best to live a love life that had no greater intimacy than the mutual confessions of two hearts, or even one, though an ocean might be between them.[58]

Charlie's disapproval may be releated to the value he placed on relationships between men as part of the bohemian community. In San Francisco, club members frequented a spaghetti restaurant called Coppa's on Montgomery Street between Clay and Washington, where male homosocial bonds solidified even within the presence of mixed company of both men and women.[59] Inside Coppa's a string of stenciled prowling black cats ringed the perimeter of the dining area immediately below the ceiling. Elaborate murals spanning the length of the restaurant told the history and exhibited the values of the San Francisco Bohemian Club. Artists such as Robert Ingersoll Aitken, Perry Newberry, and Xavier Martinez rendered the drawings in charcoal, chalk, or crayon across several Sundays over free lunch and wine provided by Coppa's.

In this family-owned restaurant local artists and writers felt free to do whatever they pleased. Budget-minded artists usually bought the fifty-cent three-course dinner and wrote and sketched freely on the walls. One year before the ruinous 1906 earthquake and fire, Porter Garnett had borrowed Oscar Wilde's words and scribbled on the wall "Something Terrible Is Going to Happen." Others broke out in French songs and reveled in their irreverence. Many more dressed, ate, made friends, and seduced lovers as they chose. At their regular table in the center of the restaurant, gathered bohemians came to symbolize the nucleus of much of the intellectual thought of the day as Coppa's quickly came to epitomize west coast bohemianism.[60]

As inclusive as Coppa's may have appeared, however, bohemians deliberately carved out a "boy's club" for themselves. If women wanted to join club members at the center table, they did so as marginal participants whose attendance first had to be approved. An unwritten rule stated that only one new girlfriend at a time could be present and that the group would take a vote under the table. When George Sterling brought renowned writer Mary Austin, bohemians gave her a thumb's down, and she was never invited again. Sterling remarked, "She was writing beautiful stuff but she wasn't pretty." Notably, more attractive women tended to receive easier approval with much less accomplishment in writing.[61] Ina Coolbrith also bitterly complained of the exclusively male access to the Bohemian Club. Though Coolbrith spent countless hours contributing to the intellectual community of the Bohemian Club at the turn of the century, club members made it clear that she was of the "abhorred" and "superfluous sex" by confining her movements to only the first floor of the club.[62]

Charlie's discouragement of Yone seemed more than the usual masculinist impulse within the bohemian community. He seemed more personally invested in Yone as an individual, expressing his ultimate support of Yone if he choose to marry after all. He would not make a scene. "You know my dearest, I could not say anything ill of you; I know nothing ill of you; I know only that in my eyes you are sweet and clean and loving and true and wiser than your years and I believe you will make one of the best husbands in the world."[63] Charlie additionally grieved over the thought of never seeing Yone again. He had hoped he would see Yone during the summer.[64] Charlie proclaimed, "How I long to see you; to hold you in my arms again and tell you how dearly I love you or how I shall miss you when you are gone far away. If I had my Bungalow and the money to run it I should implore you to come to me and dwell with me forever."[65] Stoddard's vision of Yone's "unencumbered" or unmarried life would still include "Dad" at his side.

From July to August 1904, Yone and Ethel's renewed relationship likely kept both busy. Ethel had just conceded that indeed both had done "terrible" and "crazy things," yet she in particular may have been a "wretch" in her dealings with Yone.[66] The two embarked on preparations for their wedding, still scheduled for May 1905. Ethel also prepared for Yone's late July visit to her family in Alabama.[67] In August Yone arrived in Birmingham on the afternoon train. He had not seen Ethel for nearly two years, and he looked forward to their reunion. They had kept in touch through letters, and throughout their correspondence she had remained the same beautiful, sharp, and forthright woman he had first met. Yone checked into a hotel, sent a telegram informing Ethel of his arrival, and washed up. When Ethel arrived at Yone's hotel, she appeared more beautiful than ever.[68]

Ethel immediately took Yone to dine with her friend Anne Kendrick Walker, a writer for the *Birmingham Age Herald*, for a taste of the "Old South." Anne's mother made broiled chicken, waffles, and fig preserves. Candles in old brass candlesticks grew dimmer as the evening lengthened. Anne's father shared Civil War stories, and Yone also read his own poems. Anne's mother found Yone "very handsome." Yone would delight Walker's mother by sending her a note of appreciation. After dinner Yone and Ethel linked elbows and walked toward Ethel's home.[69]

As much as Yone enjoyed the "Old South" in the Kendrick Walker home, he without a doubt had arrived in the heart of the "New South." Former states of the Confederacy contending with their own racism hoped to remake their image as modern and industrialized at the dawn of the twentieth century.[70] Hysteria over protecting white womanhood from rapacious African American men had been sweeping over the region. Gangs of angry whites insecure about the solidity of white supremacy used the myth of the black male rapist to terrorize the African American community through home invasions, lynchings, and sexual violence.[71] Interracial unions with a white woman thus became particularly contentious in the American south.

Despite this overwhelming reality of racial abuse and segregation, Birmingham enjoyed some moments of positive racial mixing as it strove to become a center for industry and commerce. The coalfields that enveloped the city when Yone arrived for his visit in 1904 stood out for their racially mixed labor force where African Americans and whites in nearly equal numbers worked together to unionize in notable but still extremely limited ways. Ethel knew of the significance of the coalfields surrounding her home since she had begun work on a book on the coal industry that would be published six years later.[72] Though Ethel did not address issues of race in her book, she undoubtedly had heard of the controversy surrounding white and African American miner families through the early 1900s who gathered for picnics and funerals as well as lived amongst each other in tent cities during strikes. So inflammatory did these events appear to southerners invested in white rule that opponents of the union sought to undermine the coal workers' interracial organizing by declaring that they strove for the "unspeakable crime" of social equality. The union refuted the charges, adamantly insisting that they did not preach or practice the doctrine of social equality.[73] Indeed interracial unionism did not necessarily mean acceptance of racial equality. Sexual relations between African American men and white women both real and imagined stirred extreme violence.[74]

Whether or not Birmingham's racially mixed labor force shaped in some small way racial "toleration" if not tolerance among the Walker and Armes families, the fact that Yone was Asian rather than African American more likely enabled the two southern families to approve of the Ethel's interracial affair.[75] Activists and historians have noted that opposition to and hysteria around African American men interacting with white women powerfully pointed to white fears around political enfranchisement of Blacks rather than any actual sexual intimacy. With citizenship rights tied inextricably to manhood, sexuality would thus become a metaphor for what was really at stake—white socioeconomic privilege. Thus

African American men who had in some measure succeeded financially or made political demands would often face castration or genital mutilation at the hands of angry whites.[76] In the Deep South, where white supremacy could conceivably become displaced by African American rather than Asian American movements for social justice, Yone's engagement to Ethel would elicit little anxiety. To the Walkers as well as the Armeses, Yone more likely appeared as a mystical foreigner from a fascinating culture than a menacing person of color living in the United States.[77] In California, however, where Asians comprised much of the "race problem," fears of maintaining white women's chastity in the face of dangerous Asian masculinity ran parallel to fears of African American men interacting with white women in the south. In California antimiscegenation laws would prohibit "Mongoloids" as well as "Negroes" from joining with white women in marriage, whereas no such law banning Asians from interracial unions existed in Alabama.[78]

Additionally, class inevitably shaped the way whites would receive Yone as a potential mate in marriage. Yone, a published internationally recognized poet claimed to have attended prestigious Keio University as well as Stanford University. Though in fact he had no degree from either institution, Yone appeared as a cultured, educated individual—an appropriately "respectable" member of society.[79] In California, many interracial couples composed of educated Asian men and white women found some refuge from the brutalities of intolerance in their well-to-do status.[80]

In Birmingham Yone lived only in bliss. In the days that followed the first dinner at the Walker home, Yone and Ethel took long walks along with Ethel's younger brothers Edmund and Harvard, ate lunch and dinner at the hotel, discussed marriage, and reread their correspondence from three years past. "What silliness," they agreed as they laughed over their letters. On their last day together, Ethel gave Yone a gold buckle for success, a silver spoon, and a clover-shaped pin. "As a clingy clover, I will always be bound to you," declared Ethel as she gave him the pin. Yone in turn described the life they would share in Japan. They would plant a garden full of cherry blossom trees for the spring, chrysanthemums for the fall, and share a cup of tea as they watched the moon rise high into the sky.[81]

The visit solidified Yone's love for Ethel. He spent a "jolly time" with the Armes family, the "happiest time of his life." Ethel's mother felt relief that Yone was so youthful and decided that she liked him "very much."[82] As they planned for their wedded life together, Yone and Ethel invited Charlie to join them in Japan.[83] He and Ethel would provide a home for "Dad" more comfortable than any of the other "fellows" could provide.[84]

Though the visit to Birmingham went well, Yone and Ethel decided to postpone the wedding until April 1905 in Japan. While Ethel's mother had sincerely liked Yone, she expressed some hesitation about their engagement since she did not know Yone well. She had only literary reviews of Yone's work to assess him as a person. Yone hoped that reassurance from "Dad" regarding his character would bring her peace of mind. It seems a strange request to make of person who so bitterly spoke against their union.[85]

Just a week after Yone's visit, Ethel busily prepared for her departure to join Yone in Tokyo. Her dreams of visiting love interest Daniel Quinn in Athens had flown from her head and heart as she readied herself to depart for Japan by October. Yone would have already prepared their home, and they would be married soon after she arrived in Japan. She also felt no reservation about sharing Alice's affections with another woman as she prepared for her impending departure to meet Yone. Ethel pressed Alice to pay particular attention to Theo, "the most wonderful girl in the world." Ethel assured her, "You two will have delight in knowing one another," and admonished, "and you must treat her as you would your Indian bride my man."[86] In 1904 Ethel seems to have relinquished her position as Alice's Indian maiden.

By November of the same year, the introduction to Theo appeared to have taken new significance in Alice's life. Ethel referred to Theo as Pallas Athena, the goddess of wisdom and justice, and encouraged Alice to allow Theo into her life since they could be "such comrades." "She rarest of women and most sensitive and delicate of spirits—and you a good mate (Sure I will not be for kissing of the blarney stone no more)." Ethel insisted that this time Alice wear her "heart on [her] sleeve" just once. "Among all the hundreds that summer only I did see your spirit and the heart of you—and it is largely your own you know—and you never gave to me—till twenty times over I gave to you. I guess nothing panned out right at all." "At any rate you two ought to hit it up someway or other—and if you don't then may you be damned both of you—I'll wash my hands of you—as a pair. Try it once again, Alice." Ethel encouraged an intimacy that she named "friends" yet with unique ties than merely "friends" or even "sisters." As Ethel gave Alice suggestions on her approach to Theo, she stumbled through awkwardness: "I mean I don't know how to tell you, but I could of course myself—for we have been far more than sisters these twelve or more years." "Oh really I don't know Alice—just simply be to her as you were to me—only more so. Of course if you feel like it." Even as Alice found new opportunities to find "friendship," for Ethel the woman she once hoped to marry was still her "man" to be "friends to the core forever." They would maintain an unbreakable tie where Ethel and Alice both believed they would never "go back" on one another.[87] Ethel's still affectionate words to Alice diverged notably from previous letters in which she pressed Alice to proclaim Ethel as her most intimate woman friend.

The messy love triangles and quadrangles that intimately linked individuals together suggest how seemingly separate worlds of male and female love often converged and overlapped at best in affectionate overtures and at worst in irreparable conflict. Women and men provided each other with support, if not with spouses for heterosexual marriage, as these communities interacted both romantically and intellectually. Alice frequently introduced her circle of friends to Ethel. In fact Ethel had no qualms about demanding introductions not just to Alice's "best books" but also her "best people."[88] Ethel introduced Alice not only to Yone Noguchi, but also to Charles Warren Stoddard, Josephine Preston Peabody, and Theo Potluck. Blanche Partington, rumored to have had a short affair with Ambrose Bierce, also received impassioned letters of affection from Bierce's daughter Helen Ray Bierce. In 1894, when Helen received a portrait of Blanche, she grew excited over her beauty. Helen declared, "I just kissed you over and over in my delight and my only regret was that I had not the original herself." Helen wished that she were a "nice rich man" so that she could marry Blanche, put her on a "throne," and "worship" her. Helen explained, "In return for my devotion you should be made to 'play at me' for hours."[89] In another twist, Charmian London, the wife of Jack London, often asked Blanche to reassure her that they "loved" each other despite Blanche's affair with Jack while he was married to Charmian.[90]

At the Bungalow as well, women appeared as frequent guests. In January of 1902, one woman made herself more than at home as she reclined near the mantelpiece and ate chocolate with both hands. Charlie, disgusted with her gluttony, threw her a scornful look and declared, "Imagine a man sitting like that and eating candy without stopping for half an hour." He turned to Yone, who smoked near him on folded knees, and noted, "Never mind Yone, when we go to Japan and live in a temple, there we shall see no women." Yone confirmed, "No women are allowed in Japanese temples." Irritated with Charlie and Yone, the chocolate-eating guest threw an avalanche of chocolate cremes on Charlie. As much as Charlie appeared to tease affectionately, his jesting also pointed to his dreams of an exclusively male space. Charlie came to view more than a few of his women friends as raiding the Bungalow of his "kids." To his dismay he witnessed a number of ill-matched heterosexual pairings devolve into misery.[91]

Queer intimacies seemed at the nexus of Yone's personal life. Not only would Yone and Ethel's heart-wrenching relationship oddly sustain itself break-up after break-up, affairs between Yone and Charlie, Charlie and Kenneth, Ethel and Annie, Ethel and Alice, Alice and Theo, and Yone and Kosen seem queer in their same-sex affection. Ethel's attraction to Yone's unconventional masculinity and the pair's involvement with both men and women also stands as queer. Race played a critical role in charging desire even in pairings of seemingly raceless individuals. While Charlie and Ethel felt drawn to Yone because of his distinctly "Japanese" characteristics, Ethel would invoke loaded meanings around Native American women in articulating romance with another white woman by calling herself Alice's "Indian bride." White women and men could utilize racialized connotations of gender and sexuality to better articulate romance and therefore infuse more passion into their personal affairs.[92] Finally, Yone's complicated relationship to America and Western imperialism instilled in him both a deep shame and rebellious pride in being Japanese. While this experience of racial and cross-cultural ambivalence may be painfully familiar to many who come from immigrant backgrounds, it might seem disconcertingly odd to others.

For one of his last dinners in America, Yone enjoyed a banquet thrown in his honor by San Francisco Bay Area Japanese. He had returned to the Hights, where he relished spending his last days before his departure. Joaquin Miller stubbornly refused to let him return to Japan. Though they spoke to one another even less than the previous time Yone stayed in

Miller's home, Yone and Joaquin enjoyed simply looking at each other and breaking into laughter now and then. It felt colder to Yone than in previous years. Surrounding clouds and fog chilled his bones, hindering his sleep. Yet chirping crickets and whispering trees eventually brought him peace as well as clarity and focus in thought. "Yes, here is the ideal place, to be sure. But I must leave," concluded Yone.[93]

As Yone sailed through the mouth of the San Francisco Bay to the Pacific Ocean on the steamer Golden Gate, the water appeared seamless and serene. He felt confident about the decisions he had made about his personal life.[94] Yone assured himself of his love for Ethel and pressed Charlie to convey his love to Ethel as well. "Write Ethel lots of love and other things, will you?" He signed his letter to Charlie merely "Yone."[95] Still, on his last day in San Francisco, Yone again invited Charlie to come live with him and his "sweetheart" Ethel forever.[96] As secure as Yone's relationships appeared to him, his personal life would unravel uncontrollably in the years immediately following his homecoming.

FIVE

Double Crossings

1904–1909

When Yone Noguchi arrived home in Japan in September 1904 after thirteen years abroad, he faced an overwhelming welcome. Dinners and receptions in his honor took place every day. While he wrote to Charles Warren Stoddard of the "nuisance" of all the events that left him no time to himself or his writing, he relished his new celebrity status. He was delighted to stay at home with his parents and confessed that "it is not so bad to be treated [well] in the native country. I am a line on the Japanese newspaper."[1] Still, all would not end blissfully for the internationally accomplished poet. His unofficial "wife" Léonie Gilmour seven months pregnant prepared for the birth of her and Yone's son, and his "fiancé" Ethel Armes remained in the United States awaiting Yone's call to join him. As Yone's heterosexual affairs crumbled, letters to his "dearest Charlie" that had previously cooled once again warmed. Moreover, despite the endless engagements in the early weeks of his return, Yone soon found plenty of time to write. As he wrote in Japanese instead of English, he explicitly declared his heterosexuality in his publications like never before, even as his same-sex love for Charlie resurfaced with renewed affection. Yone's public proclamation of his sexual desire for and encounters with women rather than men made sense in the midst of increasing disdain for same-sex sexuality in Japan. As much as Yone might appear to be a casualty of tightening moral codes, his transition signaled his astute maneuvering of shifting sexual mores in Japan, in the United States, and then back in Japan. Indeed, Yone demonstrates how a plurality of intertwined sexual ideologies shaped the way he sought romantic fulfillment in socially acceptable ways.[2]

When Yone arrived at the Tsushima train station, his own father could not recognize him. As Yone approached him, calling out "father," the older Noguchi stood transfixed by surprise. Yone's mother, who greeted him with tears, also thought he looked different—"occidental" around the eyes and nose.[3] Regardless of his Western appearance or perhaps even in part because of it, Yone quickly reached celebrity status as the Japanese who had returned from America. As news of his homecoming spread, neighboring men, women, and children called on his home to visit in groups of at least two. Childhood friends whom he had not seen for more than seventeen years appeared. Admirers commented on his achievements abroad and his Western clothes. Yone's high school principal invited him to give a speech. The townspeople held a banquet in his honor. At home, his mother laid out his bed, heated his pajamas on a furnace, and prepared his childhood favorite dishes. Yone felt loved by both his family and his community. It was better to be liked in Japan than in the United States. He now understood the full meaning of "home sweet home."[4]

As Yone enjoyed the reassuring comforts of home, Léonie spent the final weeks of her pregnancy sewing, reading, and working in her garden on East First Street near the site of the present Los Angeles City Hall, where she lived with her mother.[5] Roses, vegetables, and herbs grew in her yard. Surrounding cottages spread far apart dotted the hillside. Los Angeles, still a small town in 1904, sat on the outer edges of the American frontier. The city attracted the "hopeless and hopeful," as described by historian Masayo Duus, seeking different lives. For Léonie, the anonymity of the expansive West as well as a growing Japanese community in Los Angeles likely appeared to be a relatively hospitable place to raise a fatherless child both Japanese and white.[6]

Léonie lamented Yone's absence. He seemed to be a bird that had flown through her room and vanished. She suspected that she would never see him again. Léonie consoled herself, or rather attempted to, noting that she was more fortunate than other women who must witness their "loves" grow old, indifferent, and commonplace. "Mine will be ever young and ever [the] poet."[7] As she made the most of a lonely situation, one particular friend, Catherine Burnell, became a great source of support. Léonie cherished Catherine's letters, filled with wishes of happiness for Léonie and her soon-to-be-born baby. A blanket of softest wool from Catherine arrived just in time for the arrival of the baby two weeks later.[8]

Léonie and Catherine had long shared a close friendship of love, caring, and affection—a romantic friendship rather than a romance passing as friendship. Through the earliest years of the twentieth century, Catherine's letters brought great happiness into Léonie's life as the two playfully wrote to one another. "Highty, highty, jiggledy, jiggledy jig! The above is the tune to which I danced on my head upon receipt of your note," wrote Léonie to Catherine. They grew particularly close over their common love of poetry since the average person had "nothing but pitying contempt for the race of rhymesters and rhyme mongers." Léonie felt spoiled by Catherine when she sent narcissus with "the most graceful poses." She enjoyed "wagging" her "tongue" to Catherine. A few of Catherine's letters Léonie "kept always."[9]

In 1902, when Léonie had begun working for Yone, no mention of the aspiring poet appeared in her correspondence to Catherine. She wrote only of the latest books she had read and her adventures on the streets of New York. Yet as Léonie faced the final weeks of her pregnancy, Catherine provided great comfort. Léonie hoped that she would be the godmother of her child.[10] Their support and affection for one another demonstrated how same-sex friends in late Victorian times could in fact better provide for one another as life partners than the spouses people might have married.[11]

On November 17, 1904, Léonie gave birth to a baby boy. Léonie chose to call him "Baby" for the first fifteen months of his life.[12] Soon after, Léonie, her mother Albiana, and the newborn moved to a tent village in Pasadena, a town at the foot of the San Gabriel Mountains in Southern California. Here the trio enjoyed dry, warm weather year round. Léonie took up work as a typist at the Los Angeles Chamber of Commerce while Albiana, in her sixties, looked after Baby. Léonie's sister Florence joined them in Pasadena after quitting her job at the Encyclopedia Britannica in New York.[13]

Yone acknowledged the birth with his own letter to Léonie in which he asked her forgiveness, asked about the baby, what she wanted him to do, what he must do, and what he ought to do. He expressed his appreciation for "her kindness as kindness" and wrote of how he deplored his "temperament."[14] Yone's use of the word "temperament" in the early 1900s could have signaled a number of meanings. In the most innocuous use it could point to Yone's personality as a poet and his inability to commit to a single project let alone individual for very long. In its more provocative interpretation it could easily have pointed to his same-sex desires. During a time when same-sex sexuality could be seen as an inclination rather than a biologically rooted fact, the term often served as code in referring to same-sex sexual tendencies.[15] All that remained certain was that Yone "wished to god that he could love her" but remained unable. Ironically, even as Yone reached out to connect with the birth of his baby, he held little fatherly feeling for the boy.[16] A little over a month after his son's birth in December of 1904, Yone continued to direct his monetary commissions from published articles to his "American agent" Ethel in Birmingham.[17]

Meanwhile, Léonie enjoyed her new baby, gazing at the funny expressions he made in the earliest years of his infancy. Baby likewise lived an untroubled and happy life surrounded by the beauty of the Pasadena Hills and the love of three fiercely independent women. Initially, he seemed to resemble Yone. Yet the likeness quickly wore off, leaving what Léonie reported as a "funny little Irish-Japanese" grin. Catherine also continued to send gifts. Shoes that would take time for Baby to grow into, a night gown for Léonie, and a kimono for Léonie's mother arrived for Christmas.[18]

In the same month that Léonie attentively took care of her newborn, Yone in Japan thought of Charlie nearly every day. He had sent him numerous postcards and still had not received a single response. Yone pleaded, "Why don't you write me?" He accused Charlie of having plenty of time and still not writing "at all." "Is it fair?" he queried Charlie. "You are bad, Dad, you must drop me a line or so—saying that I still occupy your mind. Let me know whether you are dead or alive!"[19] As Charlie's body weakened with age, physical exhaustion rather than callous neglect likely prevented him from writing as often. Yone again invited Charlie to come live with him and Ethel. He would build the "ideal home" and then Charlie could come to his "final house." "I would make you as happy as possible," wrote Yone.[20]

As thoughts of Charlie filled his head, Yone sifted through a huge bundle of Charlie's old letters, perusing each one to trace back their relationship. He then crafted an essay exalting their intimacy. In December 1904 his article appeared in *National Magazine*. "Ho, ho . . . in Charley's Bungalow! Til that day we had embraced each other only in letter." He recounted sharing the deep hollow of a single armchair with Charlie, dozing comfortably nestled against one another. "We talked on many things far and near,—things without beginning and apparently without end. We agreed upon every point. We aroused ourselves to such a height of enthusiasm." Yone wrote, "Is there any more delicious thing than to listen to his talk about nothing? Sweet nothing!" The two would fly away from the world together and bury themselves only in each other's company.[21] As Charlie lay asleep beside him like a "tired faun," Yone thought to himself, "Should I cover his head with ivy?"[22] For scholars of gay literature, Yone's passionate declaration of his intimacy with Charlie could easily be interpreted as an unequivocally queer debut.

Yet this 1904 essay served more likely as a conclusion rather than a beginning to Yone's sexually ambiguous and thus potentially queer writing. His earlier writings on love rarely if ever referred to a woman as the object of his desire. In his books of poetry published in 1897, *Seen and Unseen* and *Voice of the Valley*, Yone expressed love for almost everything female but women. Sunlight, spirits in Heaven, and small streams in their remarkable strength and beauty all appeared gendered female, and Yone would kiss and express devotion for all of Mother Nature. Yone's "love-fountain" would be one born out of his love for nature.[23] While Yone's tribute to Charlie appears to be the crowning jewel to Yone's sexually ambiguous writing, it signals a distinct shift in Yone's treatment of sexuality in later writings from Japan.[24]

As ardently as Yone expressed his love for Charlie, the essay in *National Magazine* in its conclusion explicitly describes Charlie as heterosexual. Yone noted, "Doubtless he must have fallen in love with many a woman in his life. He might have married one of them if he had been sure of not getting tired of her after awhile. He often said he could never forget the scar of a wound which he might give her in saying or doing something he ought not to say or do—something that would make her hate him."[25] To readers closed to the thought of the viable existence of same-sex sexuality, Yone's passage affirming Charlie's heterosexuality rendered his love for Charlie as obviously a platonic one between "friends." After highlighting his same-sex affection for Charlie in much of the essay, Yone may have found it necessary to conclude by casting Charlie as a heterosexual for fear that he may have gone too far. As Yone wrote this double-edged essay from Japan, his heterosexual conclusion foreshadowed the tone of Yone's Japanese writings that followed.

In spring 1905 Léonie seemed aware that Yone's attentions lay not with her but elsewhere. She confided in a friend that she accepted without "wail" or "whine" that Yone not only did not love her, but that he also could not love her. Still, Léonie believed in the marital union that allegedly bound her and Yone together. In her thoughts he remained a man of "honor." In October of 1905, when Catherine sent a letter to Léonie and addressed her envelope "Miss Léonie Gilmour," Léonie immediately corrected her. "Kathleen dear, I'm s'posed to be married, tho' I'll admit it don't seem much like it living in this maiden solitude."[26] Though she was fully cognizant of her loveless affair with Yone, the possibility that he might be making plans to marry another woman was probably the last thing that entered Léonie's mind.

As March 18, Ethel's planned date of departure, approached and then passed, the young journalist from Birmingham never boarded the steamer bound for Japan. In the early months of 1905, Ethel received a blow that would finally bring her roller coaster relationship with Yone to a roaring halt. Rumors reported that when the Armes family approached *National Magazine* for a two-hundred-dollar advance on Yone's articles to fund Ethel's fare to Japan, the surprised editor, Frank Putnam, revealed that Yone was already not only "hubby" but also "pop."[27] If, in fact, Putnam had been the one to reveal Yone's duplicity to Ethel, he would hardly have been surprised when Ethel approached him for an advance. Yone had previously written to Putnam informing him of his plans to wed Ethel and asking Putnam for financial assistance if Ethel contacted him. Putnam had even pressed Yone to come clean and confess all to Ethel. Even as Yone ignored Putnam's requests, he appeared confident that Putnam would facilitate the reunion. He wrote, "Under any circumstance, I am sure you will help us. Yes, you will Frank."[28]

By March 1905 Ethel knew explicitly of Léonie's relationship with Yone. One of Ethel's friends consoled her by relaying that Léonie was "sloppy" in personal appearance, "not pretty," wears glasses, and "neither old nor young." When Léonie discovered Ethel's engagement to Yone, she responded with grace, stating to Ethel that she did not want to stand in the way of Yone's happiness. Léonie advised Ethel to wait until she could get a legal separation in order to be sure the baby would be "legitimized."[29] Rather than wait, Ethel severed her ties to Yone in March 1905 and embarked on a more permanent breakup. In June 1905 she informed Alice of her separation from Yone, as she placed her "man" Alice at the center of her affections. Declaring herself again as Alice's "Indian Bride," Ethel asked that she keep her always as the star of her heart.[30]

A month after her planned arrival date in Japan, Yone still appeared to be in the dark about the circumstances around Ethel's disaffection. On April 25, 1905, Yone rather mysteriously asked Charlie if Ethel had discovered his past with Léonie. He wrote in a postscript, "Did Ethel ask you about the Los Angeles' woman?" Yone assured "Dad" it was not as depressing as it seemed since "it was all settled—a long time ago."[31] Indeed two weeks before writing Charlie, Yone had already invited Léonie to come to live with him in Japan.[32] Léonie apparently did not respond to Yone's proposition and not until nine months later would he more earnestly begin again to suggest a move to Japan.[33]

By July Yone and Ethel's relationship had completely unraveled. In a series of "confession" letters, Yone told "all." Ethel reported to Alice, "It is quite over now and strange to say I am not at all unhappy any longer. I do not feel anything at all. After the first wrenching out and everything I breathe—freer—I believe."[34] According to friend and literary colleague Anne Kendrick Walker, Ethel would never be able to mend her shattered heart. She reported: "I never saw Ethel happy again. That was a blow that she could not ever recover from."[35] For Walker, Ethel's unmarried status until her death confirmed her assessment that Ethel's heart was frozen shut and had never recovered from Yone's betrayal.

Yet, contrary to Walker's assessment, Ethel picked herself up from the disaster with remarkable resilience. In fall of 1906, Ethel "made love too much" to a man who then began "to care too much" when she "didn't care enough."[36] In June 1911 overwhelming "love business" in addition to commitments to work and family kept Ethel from writing even to her Alice.[37] And then there was Alice. After Ethel's final breakup with Yone, she continued to insert passages of tenderness and affection into her letters for Alice, though more muted than her expressions six years previously.[38]

On October 3, 1905, Ethel wrote, "I'm quite crazy to see you," as she prepared for her trip to New York City, and concluded her letter "love to love you my man."[39] Two letters in 1907 in particular appeared more passionate. In November Ethel elaborated on how pictures of Alice brought her great pleasure. She requested more photographs, but only of Alice alone so that she could frame them. She declared Alice as "the beloved one,—my immortal and beautiful one," "a pleasure forever."[40] In a brief one-page letter in December, Ethel closed her letter to Alice, "Love and love go to you every day of the year. Love me—too—more and more—yours devoted."[41] While Ethel's affections toward Alice may have cooled, Ethel the "Indian bride," still found significant love and comfort in Alice, her "man."[42]

In October 1905 Yone craved intimacy. Ethel had abandoned him once and for all, and Léonie had made no suggestion of moving to Japan. Yone desperately hoped Charlie would finally join him. As leaves turned gloriously yellow, even the mesmerizing beauty of fall that normally cheered Yone could not ease the pain of his deep loneliness for Charlie as well as for America. Yone wished the "sweet old soul" Charlie could come for a few weeks at the least. He wove a tale of paradise to seduce Charlie to his quiet home in Tokyo. A thousand trees and flowers grew in the yard. Two servants made life comfortable. "I will treat you like a Lord," Yone declared. He made enough salary for both himself and another, and Yone had chosen Dad to join him. Charlie only needed to worry about the steamship fare, and Yone would take care of everything else. Though he had a few regular commitments during the week, he had plenty of time to spend with Charlie if he came to Japan.[43]

Yone recounted how he enjoyed reading Charlie's books again and again, particularly the one about "Paul."[44] In his reference to "Paul," Yone alluded to *For the Pleasure of His Company*, considered to be San Francisco's first gay novel. Paul Clitheroe, the protagonist of this novel, was reported to be Charlie himself in his furtive searches for male intimacy in the city.[45]

When evening approached, Yone wondered how Charlie was "sailing over the tide." He wrote tenderly: "Again I am hungry to read your work, and touch on your feeling and fancy. Dear Dad, I love you,—you know that." While the passion of the 1890s was now long gone, Yone again started to use the word love to express his sentiments for "Dad." Reminiscent of his letters ten years earlier, he signed his letter, "I am yours."[46] The notable tenderness likely arose from the depths of Yone's solitude as he yearned for companionship. For fulfillment he turned to Charlie.

In stark contrast, Yone's publications from Japan held no clue that Yone's truest heart might lie with a man. While earlier writings held great homoerotic potential, the written works published through Japanese publishing companies that followed his homecoming explicitly articulated heterosexual love and desire unlike ever before. Yone deliberately depicted himself as involved in heterosexual interactions. Moreover, not only would Yone avoid mentioning the particular intimacy between him and Charles in his Japanese writings, he also explicitly condemned male same-sex sexuality. Juxtaposed to his previously effusive public as well as private writing on love between men, Yone in Japan promoted a significantly different sexual persona.

In the newspaper *Yomiuri Shimbun* Yone stated his involvement in heterosexual romance in the years immediately following his return. On October 30, 1904, outlining his return to Japan, he compared himself to Rip Van Winkle as he met with all of his childhood friends who had now become adults. He recalled one neighborhood girl named Are with whom he previously played house. He noted, "She would be my wife and I would be her husband."[47]

In *Kichō no ki*, an account of his voyage to return to Japan published in 1904, Yone meticulously detailed his love for two women, Annabel Lee and Ethel Armes.[48] Yone credited his creativity to the mysterious Annabel Lee—mysterious since no record of an "Annabel Lee" appears in any of his recovered personal documents.[49] When he first met her in Boston, he knew he had come across a treasure. She appeared like a cherry blossom spreading light and reminded Yone of Edgar Allen Poe's Annabel Lee.[50] Her petite appearance, her white fingers, the abundant hair at times styled in a pompadour never ceased to move Yone. His soul expanded with passionate love with each thought of her. With time he hoped to take her away from the United States and transform her into a Japanese *yangu reidī*, or young lady. He wrote passionately, "I loved her—in the purest sense—and continue to love her today." He admired her brilliant wit, her serene demeanor.[51]

Yone's second heterosexual affair in *Kichō no ki* traced his affection for Ethel Armes, his *koibito*, or lover. "In Birmingham, Alabama I have a girlfriend," he declared.[52] He fell in love the very moment he met her at the Bungalow and immediately became her boyfriend. They chatted late into the night, and at the end of the evening as he accompanied her to her lodging, he felt an inexplicable euphoria. He would never forget the moment.[53] Yone would detail the affectionate intimacies they shared when he visited her in Birmingham and looked forward to the time when he could devote his entire life to her.[54] Through Annabel Lee and Ethel Armes, Yone constructed himself unambiguously as a man who falls in love with women rather than men.[55] Yone's passages on his affairs with women appear to have had the right effect. The brief review of *Kichō no ki* in the Japanese daily *Yomiuri Shimbun* singularly focused on his romantic content of the book. "In writer Yonejirō Noguchi's *Kichō no ki*, there is one passage where he meets his lover," began the article.[56]

In *Japan of Sword and Love*, a collection of English-language poems published by Kanao Bunyendo in 1905, Yone's poems consistently articulated heterosexual affection. In "Violet" Yone wrote of standing on the street and watching the people pass by. "Suddenly a girl's shape caught my eyes. 'Thou art my love lost,' I cried." She appeared like a flower. Her small ankles, flapping dress, and tassels of hair that looked like "whispering grasses on the sky-road" summoned him. As he rushed forward, he cried, "O Yen my beloved! O Yen San was my old lover lost." As she vanished, Yone ran after her, only to be left behind with a bunch of discarded violets[57]

Charlie was noticeably absent in Yone's various essays dedicated to countless American and British writers. In *Kichō no ki*, as Yone wrote extensive passages to literary figures such as Alfred Tennyson, Edith Thomas, Bret Harte, Robert Louis Stevenson, Gelett Burgess, and others, "dearest Charles" never appeared with any extensive comment. Indeed, as Yone documented sailing toward Japan, his entrance to the port of Hawaiʻi might have been an ideal moment to reference Stoddard's work and life since Stoddard had established himself through his writings on the archipelago.[58] In the *Yomiuri Shimbun* too, Yone highlighted authors such as Walt Whitman and Joaquin Miller but not Stoddard.[59] Finally, in *Eibei on jūsannen*, literary figures such as Edwin Markham, William Butler Yeats, and Frank Putnam enjoyed lengthy passages in Japanese. However, only a handful of sentences in Japanese appeared on Stoddard in the 220-page book.[60]

Previously published English-language material on Charlie did appear in *Eibei no jūsannen* with little editing. Stoddard's effusive introduction to Yone's *Voice of the Valley* appeared in full text as did Yone's passionate dedication to Charlie from *National Magazine*. While Stoddard's foreword revealed little explicitly, Yone's essay, as detailed earlier, articulated a unique intimacy between the two. In *Eibei on jūsannen*, where Yone included both English and Japanese texts, only the reprinted English essay would reveal the level of intimacy between Stoddard and Yone.[61] In late Meiji Japan, when few Japanese had foreign language training, the English language itself may have served as code that shielded Yone's same-sex affections on the page from the criticism of more homophobic readers. Yet in nearly all of Yone's written work after he returned to Japan, Yone appeared unable or unwilling to express same-sex affection even in the English language.

The collected essays in *Story of Yone Noguchi Told by Himself*, with varying original publication dates, most clearly illuminate the change in Yone's articulation of his sexual orientation. Totaling 255 pages, the work compiled seven previously published essays and five new ones that trace Yone's travels through the United States and England before he returned to Japan. While his later essays explicitly paint him as heterosexual, his earlier essays leave his sexual desire more ambiguous if not completely unaddressed. By the time he published the book, he may have felt that he had established his heterosexuality enough to reprint earlier articles that would have rendered his sexual orientation more ambiguous if printed by themselves. He had fulfilled his obligation to marry and have children. He remained unquestionably in a position of normalcy if not indisputable prestige.

Yone's English-language narrative about himself was first published in 1914 by a London publishing company named Chatto and Windus. In his first essay, "How I Learned English," Yone asserted his sexual orientation toward women within the first ten pages. He wrote of his "great sensitivity to female beauty," which was "in a speedy way of development." As he learned English from one particularly stunning beauty, he felt "restless," unable to focus on the lesson. As the "beautiful woman" sat by him, her luxuriant hair nearly touched Yone's blushing face.[62] There was no mention of Charlie or his Bungalow in Yone's account of his trek across the United States. Though meeting Charlie had been one of his main motivations to cross the continent in 1914, he wrote only, "I left for California for New York as the stepping-stone to old smoky London."[63]

In the second essay, a reprint from *Fortnightly Review* that Yone wrote around 1911, he again deliberately articulated his desire for women. According to this account, written over a decade after his travels, Yone noted that upon setting foot in the United States, the women "attracted" his "immediate attention which soon became admiration." He commented on their "lovely complexions" and "delightfully quick steps." He described the women as a "perfect revelation of freedom and new beauty" for his "Japanese eye." So equally beautiful and "even divine" did all the women appear that he could hardly distinguish their ages or their actual beauty. Every single woman appeared as if a "perfectly-raised California popp[y]."[64] For the next eleven years, his first impression never betrayed him. American women remained always his "admiration and delight."[65]

His declaration that all American women were beautiful to the point of being "divine" clearly contradicts an earlier essay he wrote in 1900 that was also reprinted in this autobiography. Yone wrote bitterly of Chicago women as not having "perfect balance," "talking loud all day," and making "mad noise" like "morning sparrows hunting for breakfast."[66] And though women in San Francisco had "beautiful faces," golden hair "dyed in everlasting sunshine and the freshest of air," and eyes that appeared like shooting stars on a "dreamy summer night," they stung often like a "wasp." He became "tired with them all." According to Yone, he needed "change" and left the Pacific coast.[67] In the chapter titled "Chicago" he wrote explicitly of his dislike of women and adoration of men. Moreover, Yone declared his awe of only distinctly male-gendered qualities. He declared, "Chicago is the wonder, the City of Men; not a city of women."[68] In 1900 the company of women did little to comfort Yone.

In the final chapter of his autobiography, Yone inserted the previously published *National Magazine* article declaring his intimacy with Charlie when he visited the Bungalow for the first time. He prefaced the reprint with a passage in which the first paragraph highlighted his two marriages and the existence of his four children. Yone wrote, "The readers will find somewhere in this book the name of Isamu, a boy from my first marriage; but I said nothing about Hifumi, Haruwo, and Masawo, these three children whom the present wife of mine, a Japanese, has brought to me. I am sure that the stories about them will furnish me another book." As an epilogue perhaps the paragraph would not have appeared oddly placed. However, as an introduction to a chapter dedicated to Charlie, the first paragraph seems not quite relevant to what immediately follows. Yet it does clearly highlight Yone's heterosexual commitments and his ability to engage in sexual intercourse with women as evidenced by his four children. In the second and third paragraphs, he gave a brief life history of the significance of Stoddard and discussed his own last moments with Charlie before beginning in his fourth paragraph, "So our love (love between Stoddard and me, by Buddha's name) was sealed one spring day, '97."[69]

While the introduction to Yone's final chapter could easily be attributed to Yone's disorganized writing, none of the other essays in this collection had a similarly mismatched first paragraph. Moreover, the insertion of Yone's older article on Charlie at the end of nearly 250 pages of heterosexual declarations would likely have made little impact on a readership that had no obvious reason to question Yone's love of women.

If a few Noguchi fans continued to hold out for a "gayer" Yone, his explicit comments in Japanese condemning same-sex sexuality among men would quickly dash their hopes. In 1908 Yone referred to the immorality of male same-sex sexuality in a Japanese-language commentary on poet and playwright Oscar Wilde, who was persecuted under suspicion of committing sodomy in 1895 and endured two years of hard labor.[70] As Yone referred to Wilde's "disgrace," his "sin of all sins," he ultimately focused on Wilde's genius. So rare was such a brilliant writer as Wilde that in fact society was foolish for punishing him for his crime and causing his premature death. Yone noted, "It's not that he has committed no sin," but rather that society's reaction toward Wilde was brutal and vicious. As Yone spoke out against homosexuality, he simultaneously called for mercy—not to squash sexual intolerance but rather to preserve literary brilliance.[71] The essay hinted at Yone's personal ambivalence regarding the gravity of same-sex sexuality as a heinous crime and unmistakably pointed to his clear understanding that homosexuality could ruin the most exceptional writer's career.

While Yone's denigration of male homosexuality in 1908 may have accurately reflected existing views in Japan, his writings likely contributed to further solidifying a more homophobic Japan. In fact, before the twentieth century Japan had a long history of acceptable intimate affections between men. Among Buddhist monks and samurai, in theater and in the military, male same-sex sexuality existed as common practice throughout various periods. Written works and images of men's love and affection for other men also flourished during times when sexual anxiety seemed to be the last thing on Japanese minds. Some Buddhist texts valued romantic relationships with men more than women since women were clearly the inferiors of men.[72]

In 1905 Inazo Nitobe wrote publicly on the integrity and nobility of same-sex sexuality among men. In Nitobe's treatise on Japan's ethical foundations, titled *Bushido*, he acknowledged the beauty and particular strength of relationships between man and man. "Founded on natural affections, common to all mankind," the same-sex "romantic attachment" often added to the bond of brotherhood. Nitobe explained that this attachment was doubtless intensified by the separation of sexes in youth—"a separation which did not occur in western chivalry or in Anglo-Saxon lands and thus this free intercourse of affection would not occur."[73] Nitobe's proclamation on cultural attitudes of Japan sold famously across the United States, as Americans flipped through its pages to comprehend Japanese gender roles and ethics. Translated into more than ten languages, *Bushido* reached international readers, who in turn responded with sweeping interest.[74]

Sexuality scholar Mark McLelland described homosexuality in late Meiji Japan as a "masculine and even masculinizing practice." Associated with male homosocial environments such as schools and universities, male same-sex sexuality was not understood as a minority activity but rather something that young men would naturally practice. As much as any virile man would be bound to sodomize a younger male, society increasingly began to stigmatize this activity—not because of its uniquely immoral or degrading nature as homosexuality, but rather as youthful sexual misbehavior similar to squandering tutorial money on geishas.[75]

Thus, in the beginning of the 1900s, Japan, a country that had long wrestled with and accepted many forms of unbridled male sexuality, began increasingly to differentiate between acceptable and unacceptable sexual behaviors. Drawing upon proliferating sexual theories such as those by Sigmund Freud, explicit articulations of "perverse" sexualities began to appear in popular literature in the nation's push for "civilized" morality.[76] Historian Gregory Pflugfleder notes that by the beginning of the Meiji era in the mid-nineteenth century, Japanese legal discourse actively discouraged male-male homoerotic behavior in part so as not to offend Western sensibilities.[77] In the early twentieth century, observers began to ask if same-sex love both for men and women might be on the rise.[78] In *Yomiuri Shimbun*, discussions of male love and same-sex sexuality that seemed more or less neutral in the 1890s grew increasingly pejorative in the decades that followed. Earlier tales of brave samurai devoting their lives to one another evolved into warnings that close bodily contact in judo breeds the "poison malady" of male-male love.[79] By the 1910s stories of same-sex couples committing double suicides owing to despair of their "perverse love," family members killing themselves or suing for defamation over shameful claims of their relatives' "beastly desire," and homicidal men killing their same-sex lovers sprinkled the pages of the *Yomiuri Shimbun*.[80] As Parisians protested the burial of famed essayist and "sodomite" Oscar Wilde in their city, one Japanese columnist declared that the grave should be met with approval so long as Wilde's tombstone did not further "immorality" with words such as "homosexuality" and "sodomy."[81] While support of Wilde's grave might seem to signal an acceptance of those who engage in same-sex affairs, the rejection of "homosexuality" as "immoral" underscored Japan's increasing discomfort around male-male love. In 1915 Yasusaburo Sakaki responded to the apparently increased reports of same-sex love by attributing the cause of this "pathological love" to a variety of family dysfunctions.[82] Yone, who contributed regularly to the newspaper and likely perused its pages, would have noticed the changing cultural climate around love and sex between men. In the same year as Sakaki's article, Yone more definitively referred to same-sex sexuality as "obscene" in an essay in *Yomiuri Shimbun* on illustrator Aubrey Beardsley.[83]

Yone gained status as a Japanese male in a country that put men and ethnic Japanese first. He became perhaps more reluctant to risk losing the privilege he could never have accessed as an "alien" in the United States. Tired of constantly dodging racism or playing the exotic, Yone enjoyed more lucrative opportunities as an English-language poetry "expert" in Japan.[84] He recounted his desire to return home in a notably defensive tone. Yone wrote, "I had gone to the U.S. and England, and neither had anything to boast about. There was not a single moment when I felt shame. I walked the correct path and grasped a life of relative ease."[85]

His personal records in fact reveal how much social position would come to mean after his homecoming. Within the cutthroat ranks of the Japanese intellectual elite, he chafed at comments from other scholars who doubted his literary merit.[86] Additionally, in his scrapbook he carefully framed a letter from his father declaring Yone's lineage as related by marriage to one of the samurais of the famous warlord Oda Nobunaga.[87] Finally, Yone objected to his son Isamu's use of the "famous" Noguchi name as Isamu, now a young artist, prepared to embark on his trip to Asia in 1930s. Yone suggested to his biracial son born out of wedlock that he not come to Japan carrying the last name "Noguchi." Ironically, Isamu would ultimately become the much more accomplished and well-reputed Noguchi between the two.[88] In a society growing increasingly intolerant of same-sex love between men, Yone, who already struggled to maintain prestige as an intellectual, could likely not afford to appear sexually different from the prevailing cultural mores.

Yet, just a few years earlier Yone and his Japanese cohorts willingly articulated if not practiced same-sex sexuality in an American or English-language context. While the power of historical legacies and cultural traditions of accepted male-male affection remains undeniable, Yone as well as Kosen Takahashi and Inazo Nitobe were most likely aware of Japan's shifting sentiments toward the pathologization of same-sex sexuality. However, as aliens in foreign land, they may have found a space in which they could express less conventional intimacies with undue passion. As Yone strove to be part of the American bohemian scene, he publicly embraced American same-sex friendships with an unusual zeal, even uncommon among Americans themselves. In the comfort of holding an "other" status, some Japanese interacting with the West may have felt more comfortable to pursue unconventional behavior, or even "Japanese traditions," that grew increasingly unacceptable in contemporary Japan.

When Yone faced difficulties making money in Japan, he additionally resolved to sell more "ethnic" articles to the American press.[89] "Oriental" evocations more deliberately appeared in English-language works published from Japan. Out of eleven English-language prose publications that he wrote from Japan from 1910 to 1934, nearly two-thirds explicitly articulated Orientalist imagery in referring to Japan.[90] In 1914, when Yone wrote of his first few days in the United States, he noted that he had to overcome his "Oriental shyness" in order to practice speaking English.[91] In the 1920 reprinted edition of *Seen and Unseen*, references to Japan more actively appeared even though in its 1897 edition the book of poems held no tones of Japonisme. In the four-page introduction written in 1920 for the updated edition, Yone included a passage on how he adopted solitude to write as a "Buddha priest in meditation" and "enjoyed . . . grand leisure in my walk on the road of mystery." He closed his introduction to the second edition with a call to Western writers. "And the writers of free verses and the so-called imagists in the present West, let me dare say, will be interested perhaps to know that a Japanese had written such verses like these some twenty four years ago." Yone's explicit separation of himself, the "Japanese," and the writers of the "West" rendered him distinct and exotic from the literary community he had originally hoped to join as a poet of equal status nearly a quarter of a century earlier.[92] As Yone presented himself as an exclusively heterosexual "native" expert on the mysteries of Japan, Yone double-crossed both Japanese and American readerships eager to embrace this bicultural intellectual.

In the early months of 1906, as Yone's engagement with Ethel smoldered and Charlie proved hesitant to come, Yone began more aggressively to call Léonie to Japan. In January, he reminded her of his earlier invitation and asked her to seriously consider his proposal. He underlined that it would be best for the baby so that he might grow "brightly and happily" and "escape from being fatherless." He confessed, "I was wrong in the past, and I repent greatly, and I wish to do [something] for him." He would abandon publishing bits and pieces of his written work as his sole income and take up a position in a school or company for more stability as Frank Putnam had long suggested.[93]

Yone hoped to help in bringing up the baby, and he elaborated on how earning money might prove easier in Japan for Léonie. "Foreign teachers" received more money than Japanese teachers for the same work, and with Yone's connections he could easily find Léonie a position. Though he had enough money to support himself and a small house, he did not have enough money to send back to Léonie and the baby in Los Angeles. If Léonie decided to join Yone in Japan, Yone expected her to work. In February he wrote more explicitly, "You must work a few hours every day if you come . . . because I can only make enough money to keep me decently." Yone's invitation to Léonie diverged significantly from his call to Charlie three months earlier, when he outlined a veritable utopia. An oasis of infinite trees and attentive service awaited Dad's arrival, and Yone would unquestionably support him. For Léonie, however, he had only cautionary words of encouragement. "If you come to Japan and don't mind to work four to five hours a day, we can solve our problem quite easily I think. We will work our salvation together." He assured her, "We will not starve if our hands are joined and work together, I think."[94]

Moreover, Yone painted a bleak future for Léonie if she chose not to join him. "Suppose you [stay] in America? I think no good fortune will smile on you, and perhaps you are to live from hand to mouth, and—having the child as extra." Ultimately, however, he would leave the decision to Léonie. "If you think you can bring up the baby safely in America, and educate duly, and want to keep him for yourself, I have nothing to say. You do what you please."[95] Still, he hoped that she would join him. Yone promised that he would be "true" to Léonie and "a good father" to the baby.[96] Little did Léonie know that in January of 1906, Yone had already married and set up house with Matsuko Takeda, a woman he had been employing to do domestic work.[97]

On February 24 Léonie responded firmly to Yone's letters. Of course, she wanted the "very best" for the baby. She resented Yone suggesting that she wanted to keep the baby all for herself, calling it "nonsense." She would be happy to share him with Yone yet remained unconvinced whether Japan indeed would be the better place to raise a child. Though they were "poor" and lived in ways perhaps "not quite civilized," Baby appeared happy, with roses glowing on his cheeks as he grew like a "flower under the sky." The two lived in a tent where rain and wind entered at will, and Baby ran shoeless and free as a "squirrel" on the hillside. He disliked both houses and shoes. The move to an ill-smelling city such as Tokyo with incessant rains and harsh winters would only turn Baby into a pale Japanese boy. If they were to move to Japan, she would more likely choose a location further south such as Kyoto. Léonie recognized the aesthetic education that Japan could provide but still remained unsure of what the move might mean for Baby's moral training and character. After all, she had read *Bushido* and observed both positive and negative characteristics. Furthermore, Léonie could always find work in the United States. She was just learning how to become an editor and hoped to start a magazine of her own, an endeavor that she found more interesting than teaching English in Japan.[98]

Léonie refused to join Yone in a union solely of obligation and not love. She traced how his life professionally as well as personally would have little reward. "Of course it is more important to be good than happy," Léonie wrote, yet where would Yone find the time and inspiration to write poetry? "In business? In the crowding cares and responsibilities? In the companionship of a wife you do not love?" As Yone grasped for company to ease his pangs of loneliness, Léonie appeared much more self-reliant in matters of the heart. Léonie elaborated on how Yone should not obligate himself to her. "You shut love out of your life—human love, which is also divine. Why? . . . Because Frank Putnam thinks you should? Because of awakened thought of responsibility toward your boy? Maybe you think you will make amends for the past. Past is past, you cannot amend it. Maybe you think me, Baby and I, need you, we do not. Therefore I think it better we live apart." Léonie noted that some day she might consider moving to southern Japan if she found work, and then Yone could see Baby all he wanted. They would have a proper separation and Yone could remarry according to his own judgment. Léonie concluded: "Baby and I have each other to love. Yes, that's better."[99] On April 2 Yone appeared to accept Léonie's decision to stay in California and noted her wisdom. He also had recently secured a part-time position at Keio University.[100]

Then in May Yone wrote a lengthier letter to Léonie in which he appeared more honest than ever before. He reassured Léonie that Ethel no longer had ties to his heart. "She has been rather careless or mean to me for some time. She is clever, doubtless. She has no interest in me, and also I have not. Everything is done and over," he explained. "One thing is sure—I do not love Miss Armes today."[101] Still, he conceded that there would be no sense moving to Japan if Léonie lived contentedly in California. He could not be certain that he could offer Léonie any new opportunities or even happiness. Furthermore, even though he was "much honored" in Japan, financial problems plagued him. With very little income and the summer fast approaching when the university would no longer pay, he entreated Léonie to send him more money from the publishers. "Be happy, Léonie. I respect you," concluded Yone in his letter.[102] Through the month of June he would continue to ask her to send more money from articles he sold.[103] Five months later, Léonie began preparations to join Yone in Japan after all.

In December of 1906, a few months before her departure, Léonie informed Stoddard of her imminent move to Japan and remarked, "I quite agree with you that poets—at least some of them—were not made for domestic uses. So I shall open the door of the cage as soon as I get over there." As she boarded the steamship, she made the voyage more for her son's education, to make a "Japanese boy" out of the now officially named Isamu, rather than to renew any relationship with Yone.[104] To the ever more reclusive Charlie, Léonie's move to Japan with Isamu pointed to the fact that Yone would likely never return to the United States.[105]

Yomiuri Shimbun reported Léonie's arrival in Yokohama on March 4, 1907: During the long voyage across the Pacific, she had apparently tried to be inconspicuous, a single woman traveling alone with a child just turned three, though Baby was in fact still two. Léonie seemed drawn to the Japanese passengers and would ask each one if they knew the Japanese poet who writes in English, Yone Noguchi. In the nonsmoking section Léonie became the subject of endless conversation among the Japanese. "She was likely the wife of the Japanese poet who writes his name as if he was a foreigner," they noted.[106] Passengers had heard rumors that Yone had left a wife in America. While some maliciously gossiped, others commented on the destiny of love and how Léonie had no choice but to cross the sea and embrace Japan as her new home.[107]

The voyage proved exhausting for the two. Isamu remained seasick for the length of the trip and ate almost nothing. When Yone met Léonie and Isamu, he wondered where the fat baby that Léonie had written about had gone. Instead, a thin, pale infant peered listlessly from his carriage. When the boy finally spoke, inquiring about the whereabouts of his home, Yone described his utterance as "no more than the dying voice of an autumn insect." Yone took them to his Hisakata home, where they settled in temporarily.[108]

As soon as Léonie could, she set up house independent of Yone and created a life for herself in Japan. By July 1907 she had mastered the sponge cake recipe Catherine had sent her, and Japanese businessmen and other notables, though "no longer young," studied English under her like "schoolboys." One student, Lieutenant Iwamura, in particular delighted her with his attentiveness to Léonie's personal needs if not her lesson plan. "I confess he is my favorite pupil. And why not? If I mention morning glory seeds, they are forthcoming. Singing insects? Here is a cage. Goldfishes? He will bring his sleeves full of them tomorrow. With such acts he wins my indulgence toward his frequent remissives in the matter of getting his lesson."[109] She had just returned from visiting the Iwamura home, a four-acre plot of land in Tokyo, one part farm and the other forest, where the lieutenant's father planted a thousand varieties of morning glories every year. In September she would begin teaching at a girls' school two mornings a week, though for "very small pay." Her ability to learn Japanese proved less forthcoming than her skill at making friends and finding work. While Isamu learned the language quickly, Léonie found it easier to teach English to all of Tokyo instead.[110]

As cheerful and humorous as Léonie's accounts of Japanese living appeared, life did not prove easy. She wrote to Catherine of doing "men's work" with little vacation. Despite Léonie's efforts she could only pull together 85 yen a month. After sending 20 yen to her mother, the remainder quickly disappeared with the cost of clothing, shoes, childcare, and the expensive imported American staples that she bought, such as bread, butter, sugar, chocolate, and oatmeal. Léonie reported: "Yone in his temple in Kamakura is happily oblivious of the cares and worries of this sordid world. There he spends his time sleeping, smoking, and writing divine poetry, emerging twice a week to lecture at Keio College." While Yone contributed a part of his salary to Léonie in March 1909, she for the most was "footing it alone."[111]

It was just as well to have Yone and his cigarettes out of her way. She had no interest in invading Yone's temple and continued to "run the ranch"

Photograph of Léonie Gilmour with her son Isamu and her students in Japan, c. 1910–1911. Courtesy of Isamu Noguchi Foundation and Garden Museum, Long Island City, New York.

with just herself and Isamu.[112] Isamu, though only a small child, recognized the remarkable amount of responsibility that Léonie shouldered in raising him. Young Isamu informed Yone one day that he hoped to become "a great man" some day, though he could not become "so great as mama." As much as Léonie toiled to raise Isamu, she refused to take credit for her heroic actions that even her now four-year-old son clearly recognized. She noted, "Poor little Isamu. His hero worship is strangely placed."[113]

Yone meanwhile continued to write to "Dad," as loneliness pushed him to appeal to those to whom he perhaps felt closest. On May 19, 1907, he wrote of finding "harmony of thought" during his retreat to the Buddhist temple Enkakuji in Kamakura. "Oh, Dad, if you were with me now! I will tell you a wisdom which is ten thousand years old, and sing you a poetry which comes from ten billion miles away. I am sure I am a better man to begin with, and a better writer to be sure." Léonie and Isamu had been up for a visit yet had returned to Tokyo to leave Yone in his "beloved silence." The quiet atmosphere away from city had cleared his mind to think from morning to evening and inspired Yone to write "all the time." Though initially he was "cursing" the whole of Japan, he had once again found happiness.[114]

When Yone grew impatient with Stoddard's long silence, he demanded, "Why don't you write me, Dad? I wrote you some time ago." "You must not neglect me. Well, well, I had been neglecting you for such a long time. I must be a wicked fellow to think I was perfectly honest and loyal to you. However, I was right in my heart and never forgot you."[115] Despite the ebbs and tides of passion between the two, Yone had always held Stoddard close in spirit. As he longed for him, Yone once again began to read *For the Pleasure of His Company* and an article in the *Monitor* on Stoddard. The book made Yone feel at one with Stoddard, and reading about the older western writer made him "somehow happy." Yone pleaded: "I wish you will write me a long letter every week; I can promise you that I will not fail to write you everything which happened here with me. Write me and tell about everything, Dad! I am lonesome."[116]

No doubt Charlie's increasing health problems shaped his inability to write as frequently or at length to Yone as he did previously. However, additional correspondence partners may also have distracted Charlie's already limited energy away from Yone. By 1905, Charlie wrote letters to another Japanese immigrant, Issio Kuge, who lived on the Hights

Photograph of Issio Kuge inserted into letter to Charles Warren Stoddard, 1905. Courtesy of Bancroft Library, Berkeley, California.

with Joaquin Miller. Kuge, who signed his letters to Stoddard "your little one," appreciated Stoddard's "affectionate" letters. The two would stay in consistent contact with one another even as Kuge returned to Japan and then came back to the United States once more. While Kuge would send pressed leaves and photographs of himself in his letters to Stoddard, the content of his recovered notes never reached the feverish passion of Yone's letters to Charlie.[117]

Stoddard wrote to his "beloved Issio" perhaps more passionately than did Issio to Stoddard. Charles often thought of him and longed to hear from him, fretting for his safety particularly after the 1906 earthquake and fire in San Francisco. He hoped and prayed that Issio had escaped injury: "Will you not write or tell me so Little One, my Little One?" In text similar to that he wrote to Yone, Charles also invited Issio to come live with him, this time in his California home in Monterey. "Will the Little One make my Bungalow his home for a while, that we may read together, write together, eat together—and together dream beautiful dreams? I wonder if he will? I pray for you, for the love I have bourn you through all this long silence, write to me here as soon as this reaches you."[118] Yone would not be the only "Japanese boy" with whom Stoddard would exchange endearments.

Though Yone's notes to Stoddard cooled compared to his previous writings to "Charlie," they continued to disclose a vulnerability absent from notes he wrote to his other literary colleagues. From Ina Coolbrith, Yone requested a book with which to teach his lecture on California poets. He closed, "I hope to hear a favorable reply from you."[119] To "Mr. Young" he apologized for not responding promptly and sent along bundles of his books for promotion. "Hereafter I can promise you that I will reply to you as soon as I receive your word."[120] Perhaps naturally, these notes diverged considerably in tone from the letters to Dad. After all, Yone had known Charlie for longer and much more intimately. In July 1907 Charlie awaited a letter from Yone. The western writer had moved to California and lived serenely, albeit without affection, in Monterey. He missed his belongings in Cambridge.[121]

As Yone resettled in Japan, his romantic life would not turn out as he had hoped. Spurned by Ethel, he would eventually reunite with an independent Léonie, who made almost no demands on his time. Though he had already married Matsuko Takeda, Yone felt increasingly heavy with loneliness. To comfort himself, he turned to his dearest "Dad," writing letters of tenderness and referring to how Charlie's gayest works comforted him. Yet even as his same-sex love for Charlie resurfaced with renewed affection, his public writings from Japan grew hesitant to reveal that the most significant love of his life would be a man, rather than a woman.

For Yone, his sexuality remained consciously determined by his social context. As a disciple of Zen, he would "not allow his individuality to control his actions."[122] Yone noted: "Drink tea when you are thirsty, eat food in your hunger. Rise with dawn, and sleep when the sun sets. But your trouble will begin when you let desire act freely; you have to soar above all personal desire."[123] And perhaps Yone likewise successfully soared above his most tempting desires. As much as he appeared to act freely according to his selfish ways in the trail of broken hearts he left behind, the choices he made were inextricably bound within the social constraints in which he lived. No decision in life would ever be of complete free will. Still, to some degree Yone successfully maneuvered through moral mandates that might otherwise have restricted his intimate life.

In 1901 Yone had discussed a potential book project with Léonie titled *My American Wife*. In it a Japanese man and his American wife traveled back to Japan to live with his parents. The American woman grew miserable from loneliness because of language and cultural differences. She dreamed of an old love story with an American man and realized that a "crow should be in comradeship with a crow!" When she could no longer stand her state, she ran off with a missionary. The Japanese husband without hesitation simply chose another woman to remarry. Yone noted the moral of the story as "Love is not the greatest factor in Japanese life." Indeed, if love had been the greatest factor in Japanese life, who might have Yone chosen for his crow in comradeship?[124] In the end, Yone would live and die in Japan only to make choices that he perceived as bounded by cultural expectations. By 1908 the love stories that proved the most memorable to Yone were those that asserted that love would never conquer all.[125] He had come a long way from believing in love as a life-giving salve just ten years earlier.

By January 1909 Charlie spent most of the day in bed. Tired and in pain from his rheumatism, he wrote little except to revise his will and prepare final notes to friends as he sensed his own impending death. On April 23 he suffered from a heart attack and died.[126] Though Charlie occupied Yone's thoughts less prominently than previously, their relationship in all of its impassioned and dispassioned phases remained remarkable for its longevity and intimate exchanges. While Yone's public presentation from Japan demonstrated unambiguous heterosexuality, Yone's private words revealed how Charlie held his heart more tightly than even the women with whom he considered marriage. For Yone and Charlie their "love" remained significant and unique for the most personal reasons. Despite Yone's physical and ideological move and the dilemmas that it may have brought, the connection proved to be a deeply emotional commitment that endured until Charlie's death.

Epilogue

I think it was a great mistake, Noguchi's returning to Japan to settle. He was making a name here and in England and now he will soon be forgotten by English readers.

Charles Warren Stoddard

Noguchi is far less important for his poetry than in his role as a fascinating transitional figure at a time when the modern West was just beginning to discover the Orient.

Susan Napier

The memory of Yone Noguchi faded significantly in the decades that followed his return to Japan. Almost a century after Noguchi left the United States, literary critic Edward Marx pressed for his recognition, a neglected pioneer of Asian American literature.[1] In his own homeland as well, Noguchi's name seemed to hold little lasting power. Though in 1989 Hosea Hirata wrote from Japan that Noguchi was "a legendary figure in the history of modern Japanese poetry," seven years later, in 1996, Keiko Wada wrote that the name Yone Noguchi did not "ring a bell" for most Japanese.[2] So unfamiliar had Noguchi become that on one Japanese online magazine titled Tansei.net the name of the father of the more famous Isamu Noguchi was written as "Yone Yamaguchi." Moreover, Noguchi's name never even came up in a recent Japanese article on San Francisco's bohemian community.[3] While Noguchi scholars decry the unjust oversight of an influential writer, other literary critics note that his work proved mediocre at best. In the swirling debates around Noguchi's literary importance, discussion of his intimate life remains nearly absent. Ironically, Noguchi's private life may hold more definitive historical significance than his literary works. As he negotiated multiple interracial same-sex and heterosexual affairs during times not known for racial and sexual tolerance, Noguchi's relationships bring voice to silenced same-sex romantic realities of Japanese immigrants in America and illuminate how race critically charged the seemingly all-white affairs of American bohemians. As rebellious as Yone's affairs might appear, they conformed to contemporary norms around race and sexuality at the turn of the century.

In the immediate years after his return to Japan, Noguchi's fame and prestige as an internationally acclaimed poet exploded. With his appointment at Keio University as professor of English, Noguchi quickly became Japan's leading expert on American and English literature.[4] Reviewers in the West continued to note skill in Noguchi's poetry, though the comments were often racialized. *The Globe and Commercial Advertiser* described Noguchi's poetry as "orientalis[t]" in its "daring metaphor and sensuous pantheistic quality" while "strongly occidental" in its depth of heart and self-analysis, characteristics that "cannot" occur in Japanese poetry. With "western" intensity and "exotic" form, Noguchi's poetry marked a transition that "must long prove interesting to the philosopher of literature." Ridgely Torrance of the *Critic* also noted that Noguchi's work proved innovative since it disproved the "favorite western axiom that the subtlety of the Japanese is all for line and color and nothing for emotion." In July of 1905, some circles even called Noguchi "Shakespeare in Japan."[5] Through the 1910s Noguchi appears to have had regular success publishing articles on Japan in *The Nation*, at that time a weekly literary supplement to the *New York Evening Post* with nationwide circulation.[6]

Within two decades following his homecoming, however, Western contemporaries began to ruthlessly shred Noguchi's writing. Reviews of Noguchi's five publications from 1921 to 1940 derided his ability as a writer and scholar as he published more extensively on the Japanese traditional arts. Critics hurled a variety of insults at the works, calling them "disappointing," "unintelligible," and "filled with irrelevant anecdotes." Reviewers personally attacked Noguchi, calling him "ignorant" and a poet who took too much "licentia poetica" to even attempt to write a book on art. For a number of his books, only their "handsome" binding and illustration seemed to be of redeeming value.[7]

That Western critics found more flaws in Noguchi's publications may have reflected in part the end of America's romance with Japan. As Japan's imperial ambition spread across Asia and the Pacific, the Far East nation no longer appeared as genteel as it did during the heyday of Japonisme. Reviewers would not be as willingly seduced by the "mystery" of Japan even in the form of Noguchi's oftentimes convoluted writing. Moreover, by the end of the 1920s, Japanese Americans faced full-blown anti-Japanese sentiment at home in the United States. Blatant racism likely stoked the fires of scathing criticisms directed at Noguchi. In contrast, among Japanese Americans in California, Noguchi continued to enjoy approval through the 1930s.[8]

Still, Noguchi's own literary shortcomings played some part in inciting the criticism, which came from a variety of scholars and essayists from Japan as well as in the United States. Japan-born educator and skilled writer of English Inazo Nitobe in 1903 described Noguchi's writing as charming, but inarticulate and incoherent.[9] Editor Shigetaka Shiga skewered Noguchi's writing abilities when he declared that his success in the West was based entirely on the novelty of his being a Japanese person writing in English. According to Shiga, Noguchi's work was no more than a rehashing of material already articulated by samurai Tatsuo Kumoi. Buddhist scholars would likely see Noguchi's work as merely English renditions of routine Buddhist phrases.[10]

As late as 1995, poet and translator Hiroaki Sato expressed amazement when discussing those who flattered Noguchi's writing. He could not understand why Charles Warren Stoddard, "an accomplished poet and writer," went as far as to call Noguchi "a word builder of startling originality and power." He found it "highly doubtful" that Noguchi was a forerunner of American free-verse poets as literary scholar Mitsuharu Kaneko claimed.[11] Calling Noguchi a "genial literary con," Sato attributed Noguchi's initial literary success to his being "a beautiful Japanese boy who wrote quaint English." Literary critic Susan Napier summarized Noguchi's work as "using Japan as an exotic Other, a 'fairy land,' as he himself would put it, peopled by characters closer to those of the 'Mikado' than to human beings."[12] The American and European popularity of Noguchi's writing seemed to more powerfully underline his exclusion as an unfamiliar "other" rather than inclusion into the American literary world. Westerners appeared first and foremost drawn to his exotic "Oriental" persona. Japanese supporters of Noguchi's work would then perceive the Occidental approval as an impressive stamp of credibility regardless of its motivation. By the 1920s, however, Noguchi's earlier appeal as an exotic writer had run its course and could no longer shoulder the load of his literary reputation.

Forty years after his death, a handful of scholars insist on Noguchi's significance in the literary world. Noguchi scholar Yoshinobu Hakutani notes his influence on Japanese poets such as Toson Shimazaki, Sakutaro Hagiwara, and Kotaro Takamura as well as American imagists such as Ezra Pound and Irish poet and Nobel laureate William Butler Yeats. According to Hakutani, "No other Japanese writer has written so much and so well in English as Yone Noguchi." As a "cross-cultural writer," Noguchi's role proved "unique" in literary history as a poet and interpreter of the . . . East and West." For Hakutani, Noguchi remained "perhaps the most gifted Japanese American poet." Edward Marx also noted the "pioneering" poet's "immense contribution to Japanese American literature,"[13]—so much so that Marx reprinted Noguchi's *American Diary of a Japanese Girl* with literary scholar Laura Franey in 2007. The publisher, Temple University Press, described *Diary* as "a groundbreaking work of Asian American fiction" that illuminated the "creative inventiveness" of an "important modernist writer."[14]

Asian American studies has been reluctant to embrace Noguchi.[15] Even if Noguchi's status as Asian in America might have qualified him to join the ranks of writers such as Sui Sin Far and Carlos Bulosan, his fulfillment of this minimal definition proves precarious. Spending a little over ten years in the United States, Noguchi appears as a traveling Japanese national rather than a Japanese American who found a home along the western rim of the continental United States. More important, his writing often perpetuated Orientalist notions of Japan in its use of Japonisme and therefore went against the fundamental purpose of uplift within Asian American literature at the turn of the century.

In the first half of the twentieth century, Asian American writers protested unfair stereotypes and discrimination to an often unsympathetic

American audience. Sui Sin Far, the pen name of the biracial Chinese Canadian Edith Eaton, fervently aligned herself with the maligned Chinese American community even though she herself could pass as white. Far purposefully published essays to promote the humanity of the Chinese American community.[16] Filipino American Carlos Bulosan also took risks in his work, asserting a racist and unjust America in an immigrant experience in which he endured hardship and overcame impossible hurdles. According to Bulosan, Filipino masculine charm and charisma would attract the attention of white women bored with uncompelling white American men.[17]

Unlike Far and Bulosan, Noguchi proved less courageous in the spinning of his own identity. A savvy opportunist, he rode the tide of exotic Japan while living in the United States and then marketed himself as a Westerner in the Japanese press to promote his English-language expertise. He underwent another strategic move to identify simply as Japanese when relations with the West became tense.[18] Social pressures and barriers compelled him to make the most of his situation. Still, Noguchi's Orientalist writings that fed white American fantasies of mystical Japan and his own opportunistic renderings of his identity additionally paint him as a questionable character in Asian American studies, a discipline dedicated to illuminating ways in which Asian Americans struggled against or resisted social injustice.

Sadly, even as he hoped to fit in seamlessly upon his homecoming as a Japanese man returning to Japan, Noguchi ultimately became *nihonjin denai nihonjn*, the Japanese who was not Japanese.[19] In the United States as well, he would not escape the marker of his race even in death. In 1947 the last paragraph of a three-paragraph *New York Times* obituary on Noguchi spotlighted his race. "The poet was small in stature, with dark brown eyes and very thick, long hair. He wore a small, thin mustache." After publishing nearly one hundred books by the time of his death, Yone would be credited only for his earliest work published in *The Lark* in just one sentence on his professional achievements. The obituary concluded, "His general appearance resembled that of an East Indian." Noguchi would be remembered ultimately as resembling an "East Indian" despite his prolific career.[20] In the twenty-first century, Noguchi with his complicated inclusions by exclusions—his belonging in both Japan and the United States as an outsider rather than an insider—might have served as a poster child for the term "transnational" in his asymmetrical incorporation of "East meets West."[21]

Despite these debates within and across Japan studies, literary history, and Asian American studies about the significance and impact of Noguchi's publications, his literary life has largely faded from historical memory. As obscure as Noguchi's literary contribution might have become, his personal affairs, closeted for over a century, bring remarkable insights to the histories of sexuality, bohemian America, and Asian America. Part of the first wave of Japanese immigrants to the continental United States, Noguchi impregnated his white editorial assistant, became engaged to a journalist from a prominent Southern family, and wrote torrid letters of love to a male western writer more than thirty years his senior. Ideas of race, specifically regarding Asians among turn-of-the-century writers and artists, would come to life in the intimate interactions of Charles Warren Stoddard, Léonie Gilmour, Ethel Armes, and all other whites who came in contact with the "boy poet" from the "Orient."

While U.S. legal restrictions and mores as well as Japanese sociocultural pressures played a significant part in the twists and turns of Noguchi's intimacies, Noguchi also determined the fate of his own relationships in accordance with his own personal desires. A handful of scholars suggest that Noguchi may have returned to Japan to marry Matsuko Takeda because of the unbearable stigma associated with having a white wife. Though Noguchi's inability to commit to Léonie remains undetermined, in the case of Ethel it was she who ultimately abandoned Noguchi because of his dishonesty regarding Léonie. As Noguchi insistently proclaimed his love for Ethel and then waited for her arrival in Japan, he made it abundantly clear that regimes of appropriate and inappropriate interracial desire, at least in a heterosexual context, had little impact in his choice of a partner. While Noguchi's affairs might appear exceptional, they point to how unremarkable people can live in between the cracks of propriety with little consequence.

If Noguchi's story were an Asian American gay story, it would not be about the brave soul who defied social convention risking life and liberty for personal fulfillment, but about the less conspicuous individual who, like much of the population, simply lived life each day quietly rather than in open defiance. While Noguchi's and Stoddard's dedication to their interracial, same-sex connection proved atypical even in bohemian America, the couple existed in ways complicit with white privilege and homophobia still rampant even within this unique community.

Welcomed into the inner sanctum of bohemia as Joaquin Miller's assistant prankster and Stoddard's new pen pal, Noguchi gained entry into what undoubtedly was one of America's few tolerant communities at the turn of the century and a distinctly separate world from mainstream America. Bohemians awash with Japonisme sought new experiences in the spirit of internationalism and eagerly embraced Noguchi's Japanese ethnicity. Stoddard in particular lavished love on the young poet. They lived somewhat cushioned from the nation's growing anti-Japanese sentiment and compulsory heterosexuality.[22] While this group of artists, writers, and other social misfits and revolutionaries perhaps promulgated an early model of a community of white liberals, it also passed down a tradition of cultural commodification.

Some bohemians lived abroad to more seriously explore cultures other than their own. Remote islands populated by "natives" provided an escape from "civilization" where white writers and artists of the time could rejuvenate themselves. Stoddard consistently exoticized Pacific Islanders as he wrote about his travels through the Hawaiian Islands as well as Tahiti. He described "South Sea Islanders" as "happier, healthier and more wholesome in everyway." For Joseph Strong "a cruise in the beautiful South Pacific" proved to be the ideal "nerve tourni." Stoddard additionally hoped to profit financially from the spectacle of the Pacific Islanders when he proposed a lecture circuit in which "native boys" would dance in the background. Though Stoddard and others of his ilk could discern differences among diverse cultures in the Pacific, they also perceived them as collectively the same, an exotic group of darker, more primitive people. For Stoddard, Noguchi, who was Japanese, would thus appear as an additional "sea porpoise" of the Pacific, holding much of the same mystique and allure as his Native Hawaiian male lovers.[23]

Yet even in the Pacific bohemian immersion only extended so far, as whites reenacted American imperialism in their interaction with Asians and Pacific Islanders. Personal interest and gain rather than any real sympathy would ultimately motivate these Americans to interact with the "brown natives." American writer Isobel Osbourne Field, called Belle by her friends, lived in Vailima, Samoa, and corresponded to Stoddard re-

The Strong family sent this picture of their family and home in Samoa to Charles Warren Stoddard in the late nineteenth century. Featured in the photograph among others are Joseph Strong (standing far left with the parrot), Isobel Osbourne Strong while she was still married to Joseph and their son Austin (seated together center), and Isobel's stepfather, Robert Louis Stevenson (seated center on the porch). Courtesy of Bancroft Library, Berkeley, California.

garding her adventures. Divorced but with a son, she wrote of becoming more and more "Samoanized."[24] Belle along with another white American woman friend, Annie, had "gone over" to the Samoans. One young chief Tupua was Belle's "special property." Her apparent fondness for Samoa and its people did not necessarily translate into mutual respect. Even as she and Annie pursued sexual relationships with alleged Samoan royalty, she held little regard for the "natives" as equals. When she wrote of Annie's stunning beauty, she described it as remarkable "enough to turn wiser heads than those belonging to Samoans."[25]

Belle's Christmas party may have most aptly demonstrated how Samoans fit into her own life. On December 25 she had a "jolly" party with roast turkey and punch—"a house party of white folk." Things and people Samoan only appeared as accessories to the event. "Native dancers" arrived to entertain guests in a house adorned with "native ornaments" and the "strong scent of cocoanut oil." Interestingly, in the early 1890s Belle once wrote to Stoddard, complaining of one friend as a "bigot."[26] Belle, a woman who adorned her house in Samoan decoration and perhaps even slept with a Samoan chief, believed she had the moral high ground to condemn the bigotry of others, even if she imagined herself to be superior to the very Samoans she appreciated. Belle boasted to Stoddard that through her and Annie's connection with two chiefs, they commanded nearly a hundred men who danced and wrote songs for the two.

Bohemians themselves experienced similar types of commodification of their own culture at the hands of bourgeois, more conservative whites in the city. By 1906 writers and artists no longer frequented Coppa's, considered to be the hub of bohemia just six years earlier. Nob Hill socialites, *haute volée*, and other culture vultures flocked to the small bistro on Montgomery Street, arriving in carriages and new automobiles to view the city's so-called wilder set. Men in bird coats and women in the latest in haute couture laughed at the murals and stared at the bohemians. Formerly inexpensive prices on the menu crept up, and bohemians found it increasingly difficult to find a table when they arrived to dine. After complaints from bohemians, Coppa formally designated a table for his old friends, not just out of respect but also to more distinctively mark the live exhibit. He doubled prices for "slummers" who came to gawk and began to sell the tablecloths and menus on which local writers and artists scribbled and doodled. The remarkable success of Coppa's came to mark the downfall of privacy for bohemians, who began to avoid the restaurant.[27] Yet, their own disgust with how mainstream Americans consumed their bohemian cultural mores appeared lost on writers and artists when it came to using people of color and native peoples for their own entertainment or profit. As they complained of bourgeois commodification of a once idyllic lifestyle, San Francisco bohemians refused to see their own replication of similar exploitation across racial lines.[28]

Even as bohemians welcomed individuals such as Noguchi to bring interest into their lives, the inclusion of nonwhites never meant full membership into the Bohemian Club. In a complete catalog of publications by Bohemian Club members printed in 1937, Noguchi's name and thus his many publications did not appear in the list of 210 writers. Nor did his name appear even once in the eight-volume official history of the San Francisco Bohemian Club.[29] Despite the stream of young Japanese men who stayed at Miller's home before Noguchi, not one single Japanese name appeared on the comprehensive membership rosters updated in 1895. In fact, no apparent people of color appeared in photographs or membership lists.[30] While historians have recorded the extensive club participation of Mexican American painter of "Aztec" descent Xavier Martinez, he too did not appear in the official documents of the Bohemian Club.[31] Additionally, when editor Frank Putnam wrote about Noguchi in the *Boston Transcript*, he described Noguchi as part of a cadre of "bohemian-like Japs," marking him as simultaneously a part of and separate from more "real" bohemians.[32] Stoddard perhaps most explicitly articulated Noguchi's position when he offered to write for Noguchi a letter of introduction to Iza Duffus Hardy as he set out for London. Stoddard reassured Noguchi that she would be like a "big sister" and welcome him without reservation. Stoddard elaborated, "You will be received by her as you were one of the Brotherhood." As Stoddard articulated Iza's generosity in treating Noguchi as if he was a member of the fraternity, he underscored how Noguchi in fact remained outside of the fraternal networks of the Bohemian Club.[33]

Previous works describe turn-of-the-century bohemian culture, made up of mostly white Anglo-Saxon Protestants in both California and New York, as accepting of Jews, Southern Europeans, and Eastern Europeans, and to a lesser degree Latinos, while completely excluding African Americans and Asians.[34] As much as bohemians enjoyed going to various dives in the Barbary Coast and restaurants in the Latin Quarter, Asian restaurants never appealed to bohemianism.[35] If consumption of a certain culture's food signaled at least some acceptance into the U.S. mainstream, as historian Donna Gabaccia asserts, then an aversion to Asian food more definitively pointed to its outright exclusion from the fabric of America.[36]

When Elsie Whitaker Martinez at sixteen years old developed her first romance with a Japanese poet on the Hights in 1905, her father, writer Herman Whitaker, vigorously opposed the union owing to his own racism against Asians. He went as far as to approach Miller to put an end to the relationship that never progressed beyond "chanting and incense."[37] In less than two years, Whitaker would allow his daughter to marry Xavier Martinez, also known as Marty, who was a friend and contemporary of the father Whitaker. Yet, when Marty married Elsie in 1907, he did not receive the customary chest of silver that the Bohemian Club gave as a gift to all of its members who married. When Elsie protested, bohemian Porter Garnett attributed the club's refusal to give Marty the chest of silver to the club members' conviction that the marriage would not last because of Marty's temperament. Though Marty laughed it off, underlying issues of racism likely informed the Bohemian Club's unequal recognition of his marriage.[38]

In the early 1900s Albert Sherwood Bierce declined Blanche Partington's invitation to visit the Chutes, an amusement park in San Francisco, to attend instead the "highly moral and educational" Buffalo Bill's Wild West Show, a production that exploited Native Americans as actors and glorified white America's violent disrespect of native people and culture.[39] Though Bierce's comments about the show's "highly moral and educational" value could be read as sarcasm, his choice to attend the event demonstrated at the very least his acceptance of the white supremacist premise of the Wild West Show. In Los Angeles, as Mexican and American Indian art and design drew in Charles Fletcher Lummis, he still promoted a racial myth of Southern California as a new homeland for the Aryan race.[40] In New York, while the inclusion of Jews into Bohemia gave "color" to the city's intellectual life, bohemians found African Americans and Asians to be completely void of any provocative thought.[41] Thus, even as bohemians immersed themselves in exotic cultures, they simultaneously remained wedded to the exclusion of nonwhites as equals in their daily lived realities. Charmian London viewed her string of indispensable Japanese house boys with condescension. In 1909 she advised Blanche Partington to give "the little Japs" the "white man's ethics" since it would be to their "education" and could bear "good ripe fruit."[42]

Even for the women closest to Yone who associated with but lay at the margins of the Bohemian Club community, sensitivities around race did not always appear to be their strongest suit. When Blanche Partington went on excursions with her friends and family, she found dressing up as a "Black Mammy" so entertaining that she would carefully post and preserve this image in her family album as a memento of her meaningful moments in life.[43] Even Léonie continued to use the word "Jap" in her correspondence though she knew that Japanese Americans found the term bitterly offensive. Léonie at times would also playfully mimic Japanese culture in her letters to her friend Catherine Burnell. In 1906 she signed her letter, "Your faithful friend and admirer, Léonichi Gilmourmiki Noguchi" in a move to comically reshape her name into what she believed were common Japanese name endings.[44]

Asians and Pacific Islanders hardly behaved in the romanticized ways that white bohemians imagined or hoped they would. In 1906 Manyougi, the Korean "boy" hired as a valet or "body servant" for author and honorary Bohemian Club member Jack London, grew unhappy with his position. According to Charmian Kittredge London, the wife of Jack London, Manyoungi had been "misbehav[ing]" in "every department of service" for two weeks before the fateful culmination at their nightly game of cards. Throughout the day Manyoungi had already been unwilling to address London with the specified title "master," using variations such as "Mr. London" and "boss." Charmian recalled: "His bold black eyes and studiedly nonchalant tongue advertised bid upon bid for discharge. And still new titles fell from his foolish lips." As the Londons settled into their evening cribbage game, Manyoungi met his end. He approached Jack and inquired, "Will God have some beer?" As "foolish" as Manyoungi may have appeared to Charmian, he had planned his actions deliberately to aggravate Jack. Manyoungi could easily have resigned from his post with the Londons as did so many other Asian "house boys" during this period. Yet he chose instead to torment the couple and risk not just his job but a "thrashing" as well.[45]

When Native Hawaiian Kahele, who befriended Stoddard in Hawai'i, came to San Francisco to visit, he almost immediately deserted Stoddard and began "sowing his heterosexual oats." Within a few days of his arrival, he left Stoddard to move to Los Angeles with his new Mexican wife.[46] Belle's adopted Samoan son Pola used to shake her fiercely and cry "stupid, stupid" when his patience, otherwise unflappable, ran low while trying to teach her the Samoan language. When Belle told Pola that she would have him taught carpentry so that he could build "the white man's house" and "make money," Pola, the second son of the chief of the village Tanugamanono, responded with scorn that the land belonged to him and that he had no need for work. Indeed, when Pola played "white men and Samoans" with his tin soldiers, the "brown men" always won with a wave of his arm that knocked down an entire battalion with a single sweep. "The Samoans win!" he declared.[47]

Additionally, in 1893 when Joseph Strong coordinated the South Sea exhibit for the World's Columbia Exposition in Chicago, the very props of his exhibit did not always cooperate to his liking. Strong wrote of living "pretty damn well" while the "Samoan boys" whom he used also as servants chafed under Strong's command. As they adjusted to life in the United States, they began to assert themselves in ways beyond Strong's sphere of influence. Strong complained bitterly to Stoddard: "Our boys are getting to know too much and its high time they went home. It is getting harder to control them each day." The Samoan men bought pistols "of every . . . size and shape" in Chicago to prepare for the next war when they returned to Samoa.[48] For Strong, irritated with the independence of *his* Samoans, embracing diversity would work only under his terms and when it served his purpose. According to historian Christine Stansell, these artistic "intellectuals" carried "racism so deep it went unmentioned."[49]

Furthermore, while bohemians nationwide recognized homoeroticism and bisexuality as central to bohemian life, they refused to be characterized as sexual deviants or homosexuals. Many took up with gender-appropriate spouses to project an acceptable heterosexual persona. Men "happily married" could then share their bed with other men without stigma. Noguchi observed that Miller, while married, at one point shared his bed with a man of color.[50] For those who knew that Stoddard grew unusually attached to men, the trait remained an "eccentric" affectation of bohemianism rather than sexual depravity.[51] In 1876, when Stoddard advised Joseph Strong that "girls were well enough in their way but not to go to bed with," Strong vigorously disagreed, writing that in bed was the very place in which he found women "charming." He noted, "I don't know what to take you for except somewhat as an artist."[52]

Notably, those who embraced affectionate male camaraderie could be staunchly against same-sex sexuality. Poet George Sterling, who referred to Jack London as his "darling Wolf," was "repelled" by Stoddard's attention. Stoddard began writing effusive letters of ardor to Sterling after he met him at the artist's colony in Carmel, California. Sterling confided to his mentor Ambrose Bierce that Stoddard was a "case of inversion of sex." Stoddard gave Sterling the "jims." If Sterling was not careful, "the old devil" might wind up "compromising him." After Stoddard's death in 1909, Bierce reassured Sterling that "my objection to him was the same as yours—he was not content with the way God had sexed him."[53] Thus, while Noguchi and Stoddard could acceptably share moments of closeness, it remained nonetheless an intimacy with limits. Explicit homosexuality remained forbidden.[54]

Additionally, when Noguchi confessed to Helen Bridyman his plans for marriage to Ethel Armes in 1904, Bridyman underlined the wisdom of his decision. "I am so glad you are taking the sane and healthful and normal point of view, after all. Long continued bachelordom is always a mistake: it marks a man, and makes him more or less selfish, even shallow."[55] Bridyman's comment to take the "healthful" and "normal" route and avoid the unwanted "mark" prevailed even within these homosocial circles.

Thus, even in more liberal bohemian America, full acceptance of both racial and sexual diversity remained unrealized. Blanche Partington seemed to embrace Noguchi only because she perceived him to be of the "noble Japanese type," very different from all the other Japanese in America who came from the "coolie class" and did not justly represent the "beautiful Japanese."[56] Ambrose Bierce once twitted Stoddard for going to the Pacific Islands to have love affairs with darker young men. Regarding Stoddard's most recent trip, Ambrose inquired: "Tell me all about everybody . . . and about your last voyage. Did you fall in love with another nigger boy?"[57] Still, bohemians in the early twentieth century, as in the nineteenth century, proved more tolerant than the rest of society. If bohemians valued ethnic or sexual exploration because of its exotic or adventurous appeal, it was at least better than total exclusion for members of ethnic minorities and men inclined toward same-sex love. Bohemia offered a space, however marginal, in which those excluded from mainstream society could "breathe a different air."[58]

Noguchi and Stoddard's intimacy grew within the confines of these bohemian mores of race and sexuality. Noguchi, a relative newcomer to American morality, more publicly announced his intimate affair with Stoddard in his 1904 article in *National Magazine*, believing to be within the bounds of acceptability. Alternatively, Stoddard, who had witnessed the consequences of a homophobic moral culture and legal system in the United States and Europe, sought to keep his private same-sex acts hidden from public view. His public proclamation regarding Noguchi diverged significantly from his more passionate affections in his countless letters to Noguchi. Literary scholar Roger Austen described Stoddard as living a "double life"—a gay life in the Pacific Islands and a heterosexual persona in the continental United States.[59] Noguchi, in contrast, believed that his *National Magazine* article participated in a larger bohemian discourse of collegial glad-hand and fraternal intimacy. What Noguchi perhaps did not realize was that he, perhaps more so than any other American of his time, publicly outlined what went on in the privacy of cozy sitting rooms in these well-accepted "friendships" between late Victorian men that remained behind closed doors.

Across race lines, Stoddard participated in a culture of Japanese desire where whites more usually pursued objects rather than relationships with Japanese men. To Stoddard, Noguchi would thus appear as a curio to covet rather than a comrade in the queer revolution. Though Stoddard believed his same-sex desire was "natural," he would not have been a likely crusader for gay rights during more homophobic times. When friends accused Stoddard of "having no blood to risk," he confessed, "I am a born coward."[60] Noguchi also deliberately articulated a heterosexual identity for himself after his return to Japan. As uncontroversial as they painted their interracial relationship to be, the reality of their intimacy in fact defied distinctions of appropriate desire promoted by contemporary xenophobes and moral conservatives alike. Intimacy between the two highlighted how individuals could live outside legal and social norms even while they consciously accommodated contemporary mores. Noguchi, Stoddard, and Noguchi's numerous lovers did not see themselves as sexual or interracial revolutionaries. In many ways they were everyday people merely in search of happiness and belonging without falling into the perils of social alienation.

What significance would the "outing" of Noguchi's same-sex affections ultimately hold? Many Noguchi scholars unquestioningly assume him to be a heterosexual experimenting during his younger years. Ikuko Atsumi noted: "I am sure he had various experiences when he was young. But it's not right for us to mention his sexuality unless we have firm proof."[61] No one has ever dared to presume the reverse—that Noguchi's true desires lay in men as he sexually dappled in women. A climate of increasing heternormativity may have pressured Yone to lead a lonely and conflicted life in which he remained unable to consummate his love for men. His frustration in turn may have fueled his disrespectful attitudes toward women.

Yone, similar to most men of his era, valued women largely as embodiments of beauty. For these men who glorified women as aesthetic objects, imagining the female gender as having any significant intellect or skill, as active participants in society, or as individuals deserving of respect and compassion became difficult if not impossible.[62] In March 1900 Yone wrote to Charlie about meeting writer Onoto Watanna in Chicago and included his thoughts on her deficiencies as a woman. "She is artfully clever, but she has no sound mind and sweet philosophy. She is woman afterall!" In 1901 Yone feared that Léonie would not forgive him after he criticized her editorial comments because he believed "wom[e]n [are] very revengeful." In 1900, when Yone described New York as a city of contradictions that baffled him, he wrote, "New York is like a woman: woman is the most difficult creature in existence." Finally, at the height of Yone's affection for Ethel Armes when she visited New York, he would carry a lantern to "search for [her] little mind."[63] Indeed these comments would not be indicative of a man who respected women's character or intellect, even those he kept closest to his heart.

Ironically, Yone's unwillingness to see his women partners as equals came at just the time when discourse from the West proposing equality between male and female lovers began infiltrating Japan through literature from Europe. While the concept often seemed difficult to grasp for Meiji intellectuals, for those attracted to Western styles of love, the principle of friendship and comradeship between lovers immediately became popular.[64] Yone, who also subscribed to many Western tenets of love as evidenced by his whole-hearted engagement in his American intimacies, likely valued his relationship with Charlie—the idealized combination of friendship and love—more significantly than his connections with women.

While scholars have deliberately chosen to ignore evidence that suggests the significance of Noguchi's same-sex intimacies, his intimate life stands as queer in the broadest sense of the word. As Noguchi shared warm kisses with Kosen and wrote passionate letters to Stoddard, he left Léonie with a child and promised marriage to Ethel. Noguchi could easily have been "bisexual," as anthropologist Karen Kelsky asserted as early as 1999.[65] Indeed, if measured against historian George Chauncey's yardstick of sexual identity for turn-of-the-century New York, Noguchi resolutely fits the profile of "bisexual" since he appeared capable of "responding sexually" to both men and women. Yet publications on arousal incisively underscore how "sexual response" more accurately points to physiological phenomena rather than being a determiner of personal desire. Thus men coerced into unwanted sex can become erect as well as orgasm.[66] This is not to suggest that Léonie and Matsuko repeatedly forced Noguchi into sexual intercourse, as evidenced by the birth of his children, but rather to illuminate how sexual response is hardly a conclusive indicator of an individual's sexual identity or even preference. Proliferating studies on sexual response continue to investigate the extent to which social factors, such as shame and moral values, also shape arousal. Noguchi could just as convincingly have been a closeted gay man, pressured by the prerogatives of heterosexual society.

No doubt, numerous paths might point to differing sexual orientations depending on how one defines a truly meaningful relationship. If only evidence of explicit sexual intercourse could determine Noguchi's most significant love, Léonie and his Japanese wife Matsu would be the only ones holding proof of Noguchi's affection through the birth of his children. If passion more accurately measured love, Ethel or even Kosen might be viable candidates based on the brief yet ardent declarations. Yet, if repeated articulations of affection and long-term commitment defined significant love, then Noguchi's relationship with Stoddard would stand out. Affixing a discrete sexual identity on someone else more often becomes a subjective exercise laden with values of the voyeur rather than the subject.

Demonstrating the conundrum of parsing out his sexuality is not at all meant to deny Noguchi a specific sexual identity, particularly bisexuality, which has suffered a long legacy of erasure as its own legitimate identity, but rather to highlight the at times absurd and maddening impulse to slot people into neat lesbian, gay, bisexual, or transgender identities.[67] If we were to follow postmodern and more specifically transgender rules of respecting people's self-declared identities, Noguchi would remain unquestioningly heterosexual owing to his sustained insistence on his desire for women after he returned to Japan.[68] *Queer Compulsions* thus is less about pinpointing Yone Noguchi's sexual identity and more about unearthing how dominant norms of race, gender, sexuality, and citizenship significantly shape people's intimate lives even as they might appear transgressive.

In the end, Noguchi's intimate life points to the complex relationship between moral mandates and lived realities. In turn-of-the-century America and late-Meiji Japan, where heterosexuality existed as an unquestioned given, Noguchi's intimacies reveal how lives did not always neatly mirror social expectations. These disjunctures, however, would not always point to revolution that resulted in better lives for those more marginalized. Noguchi's strategically rhetorical negotiation to find fulfillment in his personal life while maintaining some semblance of respectability not only brought trouble to himself but also wrought havoc upon the equally complicated lives of his unsuspecting intimates.[69] Much of it, though, remains hidden from public view.

The cloaking or "closeting" of Noguchi's intimate life both by himself and by later scholars of his work points to how sexuality had already become a signifier for the public versus private, the moral versus the depraved.[70] Noguchi's same-sex affections as part of his private life were deliberately hidden because of what critics would name as its indecent nature.[71] Yet revealing or "outing" Noguchi's sordid intimacies underscores not only the most obvious—that repressive regimes cause interpersonal trauma—but also the less obvious—that the most seemingly straightforward of historical narratives are rife with contestations of race, privilege, and personal fulfillment.[72] Imagining Noguchi's monuments and memorials as testaments to his personal as well as professional past unveils richer histories, stories of complicated negotiations of gender and sexuality in maneuvering through American and Japanese societal expectations.

In summary, Noguchi's little-known same-sex intimacies suggest how immigrants, particularly Japanese in America, played a critical role in the shaping of a homoerotic if not homosexual culture among men at the turn of the century. Their intimacies revealed alternative narratives not only in the early history of Japanese American sexuality, but also among histories of America's "romantic friendships," which have been dominated almost completely by American-born whites. Racial and cultural difference charged Noguchi's intimate interactions. Notably, while Noguchi expressed discontent with the Orientalism that manifested in his relationships, he simultaneously propagated exotic notions of Japan. Race and desire became a site of difference fueled at times by the very disgusted "Oriental" himself.

Finally, Noguchi's affair with Stoddard hinted at how immigrants in their new sense of freedom and alienation could potently contribute to public discourses on sexuality with little anxiety over their moral position. Though ideological mores in both the United States and Japan shaped Noguchi's embrace and later disdain of male-male erotic intimacy, he simultaneously acted out in remarkably unacceptable ways. Still, as whites raced to grow close to Noguchi in both friendship and love, none of them including Noguchi could ever completely escape the social context within which they lived. For American whites, Japonisme colored Noguchi as artistic, genteel, and desirably feminine. He became a commodity to enhance American arts, culture, and leisure. Within this web of cultural commodification, white women also became casualties burned by the very characteristics that they had naively assumed safe to covet. A refusal to see the real dilemmas bred by inequalities based on race or sexuality, as well as imperialism or gender, resulted in a wide array of victims. Racism and homophobia set the stage for Ethel's and Léonie's tragic affairs with Noguchi just as much as unequal power differentials between the United States and Japan. Disillusionment with Americans' openly anti-Asian practices and policies pushed Noguchi to return to Japan to the dismay of Gilmour as well as Stoddard. In his homeland, Noguchi would no longer be a "dime museum spectacle." But increasing social condemnation of same-sex sexuality led Noguchi to downplay his intimacy with Stoddard in countless ways even as Stoddard remained the only one to whom Noguchi consistently declared his love.[73] My intent is not to conclude that Noguchi's relationship with Armes and Gilmour served merely as beards to his more meaningful same-sex intimacies, but rather to urge that we consider how societal norms deeply inform decisions around intimacy. If she could have, Armes would likely have married Alice Wiggins or even Annie Briggs months before meeting Noguchi at Stoddard's home. Indeed, no act of sexuality is purely about realizing an essential desire deep within one's core.

As Noguchi moved from Japan to the United States, he took advantage of America's most educated women even as he remained disempowered in white America. Additionally, he grew intensely intimate with an older white man considered an accomplished figure in his field. In some ways he made his personal "best" in regards to his social positioning in America even as he felt trampled by racism. Noguchi's affairs aptly illuminate the ways in which privileges due to gender, race, and heterosexuality play out in a specific social context. As a male-born ethnic Japanese raised in Japan, Noguchi had no previous experience of the discrimination he would feel as a young adult living as an Asian immigrant in the United States. Though he landed in America anxious about his future, he also arrived feeling entitled to opportunities that would open up before him through hard work.[74] He believed to some extent that he could freely exercise his romantic and sexual impulses with little consequence. While Noguchi may have enjoyed male privilege in his relationship with white women, he remained exasperatingly marginalized in larger sociocultural ways in his interactions with the West. Thus, even as Noguchi misled and disrespected his white women lovers, he simultaneously felt ill treated and disenfranchised by Westerners around him.

By the 1910s his most intimate American relationships had lost all hope of salvation. After her breakup with Noguchi, Ethel Armes would go on to publish her own works and become Alabama's earliest state historian.[75] Though she would never marry, she adopted a child and created a family that included her closest friends. In 1949 C. M. Stanley, the editor of the *Alabama Journal*, remembered Armes as radiantly happy. Bedecked immaculately in a flowered summer dress, a large picture hat, and a matching parasol, Armes walked about with "laughing eyes." Stanley recalled her as "always in pleasant humor."[76]

For Léonie Gilmour, however, all would not end as well. She would never share a household with Noguchi and struggled financially to support herself and young Isamu. Only after Léonie had arrived in Japan would she discover that Noguchi had already married Matsuko Takeda. Though angry and disgusted, Léonie continued to sympathize with if not defend Noguchi as being trapped in cultural obligations that would never allow him to freely choose a spouse or even choose not to have a spouse. Léonie explained to her friend Catherine: "He followed the line of least resistance and married his maidservant, a homely and ignorant little wench who cooked his meals. He might have gone further and fared better. In Japan marriage is chiefly a matter of convenience—and she was right there. But somehow, I feel sorry—awfully sorry. He's a very good fellow."[77] She would later have a daughter with a man whom scholars suspect was not Noguchi and send a teenaged Isamu back to the United States for initially medical and later artistic training. By the 1940s Isamu would become an internationally acclaimed artist and sculptor, more powerfully bringing recognition to his father's last name than Yone was able to himself.[78]

Yone Noguchi's romance with the West appeared to have come to an end. In the decades after his homecoming, as Japan stretched its imperial tentacles, Noguchi became a vocal supporter of the nationalist cause. His promotion of Japanese nationalism may have begun as early as the 1890s, when the pain of discrimination in America pushed him to find solace in seeds of ethnic pride embedded in him when he left Japan.[79] Later, a second trip to England confirmed to him that European civilization was doomed to devolve into constant fighting. In 1914 Noguchi wrote in *The Nation* that "Western civilization" was founded upon "individualism," "egoism," and "self-satisfaction." Through his travels he had seen "enough proof" that "Western life was not a kind to lead one to soul's content and peacefulness, but always to disturbance and pain." After much dissatisfaction with the United States and England, Noguchi insisted that Japan resist Western "invasion."[80]

Thus Noguchi's experience with American racism mingled with his perception of European selfish individualism to form a fanatical pro-Japanese stance. From the safety of his country of birth, Japan, Noguchi would wildly thrust his once carefully guarded frustration at the West.[81] Rather than cower as the "white man's burden" to be saved and then possessed by the West, Noguchi, racially inferior but culturally commodified, reacted with anger. He strategized to "compete" and "fight" with the West by extolling Japanese "spiritual life." Noguchi called this promotion of Japan the American birth of his Orientalism, or *Nihonshugi* in Japanese. In stark contrast to theorist Edward Said's condemnation of Orientalism as racist and demeaning more than half a century later, for Noguchi Orientalism at this time held only positive implications to promote the wonders of Japan and assert its superiority in the face of Western condescension.[82]

As individualized as Noguchi's queer intimacies and attempts at racial play might appear, they suggest broader implications not only about the nature of gender, race, and sexuality, but also about the impact of culture on people's actions and identities.[83] Noguchi's personal decisions on how to promote himself personally and professionally would always be informed by an inextricable mash of existing gender, racial, and sexual ideologies. Though Noguchi at the turn of the century expressed annoyance with America's romance with Japan, he simultaneously believed that promotion of a romantic Japan would uplift the Orient in the Western mind. Noguchi in his gender and sexual expression often pandered to these romantic conceptions in his personal relationships with whites. Not until 1915 did Noguchi express realization that Orientalism might signal something wholly artificial as well as mystical rather than authentic.[84]

On Noguchi expert Edward Marx' web page a black and white image of Noguchi deliberately winks back at visitors. Though Marx outlines only Noguchi's literary accomplishments on his site, the winking Noguchi appears to hint at something more.[85] For Noguchi, who imagined himself a "constant lover," perhaps the most notable historical lessons he left would take the shape of his many loves—interracial and extramarital, directed at those of the same and different sex.[86] In 1926, however, Noguchi declared that not only did he not know the true meaning of love at twenty years old; he had never actually experienced love. He had deliberately divorced himself from love in the hope of forging a tragic life to feed his poetic genius.[87] Noguchi's 1926 disavowal of love underscores the futility of determining the "truth" behind the affairs of his heart. In the end, Noguchi's affairs as the story of an individual's intimate life would hold little meaning. Framing his personal affairs in the context of Western imperialism, racism, and homophobia becomes a more productive conversation than debating whether Noguchi was in love with Léonie, Ethel, or "Dad"; whether he was gay, bisexual, or heterosexual; or whether he experienced "true love" in his lifetime.

Noguchi's affairs vividly illustrate America's romance with Japan. This larger affair, much bigger than Noguchi's specific intimacies, narrates how negotiations of power, privilege, and alienation intimately infused people's private lives. For bohemians, race would play a critical role in inciting excitement and expressing affection even as they maintained white supremacy in their social networks and intimacies. Furthermore, as much as Noguchi remained an agent in the dramas that unfolded around him, unyielding standards of heterosexuality, monogamy, and family simultaneously fueled his motivation toward deception. For less courageous individuals such as Noguchi and Stoddard, openly rebelling against a prevailing norm would remain unimaginable. Noguchi, perhaps not unlike much of the population in 1900 let alone a century later, would be loath to declare, "I'm queer and I'm here"; to negotiate a polyamorous relationship with two women; or even to evoke imagery that grotesquely countered popular Japonisme as he sought to build better personal and professional networks. Creating pockets of viable existence under seemingly immovable social constraints was a means of negotiating the tangle of race, culture, and sexuality that Noguchi and many others faced while forging their own fulfillment during times not so conducive to self-actualization for immigrants and queers. In revealing long-silenced same-sex realities of Japanese immigrants in America, *Queer Compulsions* seeks to have meaning not just for the prurient among us, but for all of us who are compelled and troubled by the ways in which webs of imperialism, racism, homophobia, and misogyny shape the most intimate aspects of our lives.

Notes

Abbreviations

BSC	Bancroft Library, University of California at Berkeley, Berkeley, CA
CEL	Ikuko Atsumi, *Yone Noguchi Collected English Letters*
Dobbs Collection	Private collection of Gary Dobbs
Huntington MSS	Huntington Manuscripts, Huntington Library, San Marino, CA
Isamu Noguchi Museum	Isamu Noguchi Museum, Long Island City, NY
KSC	Scrapbook of Yone Noguchi, Keio Special Collections, Keio University, Tokyo

Preface

1. Adair Lara, "The Chosen Few: S.F.'s Exclusive Clubs Carry On Traditions of Fellowship, Culture—and Discrimination," SFGate.com, 18 July 2004, http://articles.sfgate.com/2004–07–18/news/17435505_1_bohemian-club-private-clubs-pacific-union-club (accessed 11 March 2010). Former President Richard Nixon, a Bohemian Club member since 1953, declined an invitation to speak at the club in 1971, noting privately that "Bohemian Grove which I attended from time to time . . . is the most faggy goddamned thing you could ever imagine with that San Francisco crowd. I can't shake hands with anybody from San Francisco."

INTRODUCTION

1. Yone Noguchi, "In the Bungalow with Charles Warren Stoddard: A Protest against Modernism," *National Magazine* (December 1904): 304–307.
2. The majority of Japanese in America resided in San Francisco until the late 1890s. Yuji Ichioka, *The Issei: The World of the First Generation Japanese Immigrants, 1885–1924* (New York: The Free Press, 1988), 7–9.
3. Sucheng Chan, *Asian Americans: An Interpretive History* (New York: Twayne Publishers, 1991), 51–52. See also Ronald Takaki, *Strangers from a Different Shore: A History of Asian Americans* (New York: Penguin Books, 1989); and Roger Daniels, *Politics of Prejudice: The Anti-Japanese Movement in California and the Struggle for Japanese Exclusion* (Berkeley: University of California Press, 1962).
4. Yen Le Espiritu, *Asian American Women and Men: Labor, Laws and Love* (Thousand Oaks, CA: Sage Publications, 1997).
5. John D'Emilio and Estelle Freedman, *Intimate Matters: A History of Sexuality in America* (Chicago: University of Chicago Press, 1997); Elizabeth Wilson, *Bohemians: Glamorous Outcasts* (New Brunswick, NJ: Rutgers University Press, 2000); Albert Parry, *Garrets and Pretenders* (New York: Covici Friede Publishers, 1933); Christine Stansell, *American Moderns: Bohemian New York and the Creation of a New Century* (New York: Henry Holt and Company, 2000); Martha Hodes, ed., *Sex, Love, Race: Crossing Boundaries in North American History* (New York: New York University Press, 1999).
6. During their twelve-year acquaintance they lived in the same country for less than five years.
7. Innumerable works exist on Yone Noguchi, largely in Japanese. The smaller number in English are more likely to discuss his intimate life. Those who address his domestic life such as Usaburo Toyama and Yoshinobu Hakutani typically focus on his lasting marriage to his Japanese wife Matsuko Takeda and the many children she bore. Other more detailed works such as that of Ikuko Atsumi also mention his brief engagement to Ethel Armes, while a pregnant Léonie Gilmour carried his illegitimate son. Toyama Usaburō, *Yone Noguchi kenkyū: ronbunshū*, 2 vols. (Tokyo: Zōkei Bijutsu Kyōkai Shuppankyoku, 1963–1965); Yoshinobu Hakutani, *Selected English Writings of Yone Noguchi*, 2 vols. (Rutherford: Fairleigh Dickinson University Press, 1990); Ikuko Atsumi, *Yone Noguchi Collected English Letters* (Tokyo: The Yone Noguchi Society, 1975).
8. Robert J. Maeda, "From Shape and Shadow: The Mother and Father of Isamu Noguchi," *Amerasia Journal* 22, no.3 (1996): 104–120; Wada Keiko,

"Noguchi Yonejirō no Rondon (2)—hajimete no shishū," *Ōsaka Gakuin Daigaku gaikokugo ronshū* 34 (September 1996): 112–114.

9. Yone Noguchi, *American Diary of a Japanese Girl, an Annotated Edition*, ed. Edward Marx and Laura E. Franey (Philadelphia: Temple University Press, 2007), xvii, 149.
10. Herbert Asbury, *Barbary Coast: An Informal History of the San Francisco Underworld* (New York: A. A. Knopf, 1933); Nan Alamilla Boyd, *Wide-Open Town: A History of Queer San Francisco to 1965* (Berkeley: University of California Press, 2003); George Chauncey, *Gay New York: Gender, Urban Culture, and the Making of a Gay Male World, 1890–1940* (New York: Basic Books, 1994). See also Wilson, *Bohemians*; Stansell, *American Moderns*.
11. Gregory M. Pflugfelder, *Cartographies of Desire: Male-Male Sexuality in Japanese Discourse, 1600–1950* (Berkeley and Los Angeles: University of California Press, 1999); Mihashi Osamu, *Meiji no sekushuariti: sabetsu no shinseishi* (Tokyo: Nihon Edita Sukūru, 1999).
12. Not until the Gentlemen's Agreement in 1908, four years after Noguchi's return to Japan, would picture brides arrive to "save" Japanese American sexuality by forming families throughout Hawai'i and the West. Yuji Ichioka, *The Issei*; Yuji Ichioka, "Ameyuki-san: Japanese Prostitutes in Nineteenth Century America," *Amerasia* 4, no. 1 (1977): 1–21; Lucie Cheng Hirata, "Free, Indentured, Enslaved: Chinese Prostitutes in Nineteenth-Century America," *Signs: Journal of Women in Culture and Society* 5, no. 1 (1979): 3–29; Jennifer Ting, "Bachelor Society: Deviant Heterosexuality and Asian American Historiography," in *Privileging Positions: The Sites of Asian American Studies*, ed. Gary Y. Okihiro et al. (Pullman: Washington State University Press, 1995), 271–280; Madeline Y. Hsu, "Unwrapping Orientalism, Unwrapping Orientalist Constraints: Restoring Homosocial Normativity to Chinese American History," *Amerasia Journal* 29, no. 2 (2003): 230–253. For a more detailed account of the history of Asian American sexuality, see Amy Sueyoshi, "Sexuality and Asian Pacific Islander History," Asian Pacific American Collective History Project, 2004 (online); available from http://apachp.net/.
13. Carroll Smith-Rosenberg "Female World of Love and Ritual," *Signs* 1, no. 1 (1975): 1–29; Alan Bray, *Homosexuality in Renaissance England* (London: Gay Men's, 1982). See also Martha Vicinus, *Intimate Friends: Women Who Loved Women, 1778–1928* (Chicago: University of Chicago Press, 2004); Jeffrey Richards, " 'Passing the Love of Women': Manly Love and Victorian Society," in *Manliness and Morality: Middle Class Masculinity in Britain and America, 1800–1940*, ed. J. A. Mangan and James Walvin (Manchester, UK: Palgrave Macmillan, 1987): 92–122. For a more detailed historiography

on romantic friendship, see Amy Sueyoshi, "Finding Fellatio: Friendship, History and Yone Noguchi," in *Embodying Asian American Sexualities*, ed. Gina Masequesmay and Sean Metzger (Lanham, MD: Lexington Books, 2009): 157–172. Lillian Faderman underscores the dearth of people of color in the revised introduction to her 2001 reprint of *Surpassing the Love of Men*. Lillian Faderman, *Surpassing the Love of Men: Romantic Friendship and Love between Women from the Renaissance to the Present* (New York: Perennial, 2001). Literary critic Eve Sedgwick called for more analysis on the relationship between female and male homosocial structures. Eve Kosofsky Sedgwick, *Between Men: English Literature and Male Homosocial Desire* (New York: Columbia University Press, 1984), 18.

14. Martin Bauml Duberman, Martha Vicinus, and George Chauncey, Jr., eds., *Hidden from History: Reclaiming the Gay and Lesbian Past* (New York: New American Library, 1989); David M. Halperin, "How to Do the History of Homosexuality," *GLQ: Gay and Lesbian Quarterly* 6, no. 1 (2000): 87–124. See also John Howard, *Men Like That: A Southern Queer History* (Chicago: University of Chicago Press, 1999), xiv.
15. For essays summarizing the state of U.S. queer histories, see Marc Stein, "Theoretical Politics, Local Communities: The Making of a U.S. LGBT Historiography," *GLQ: Gay and Lesbian Quarterly* 11, no. 4 (2005):605–625; Nan Alamilla Boyd, "Who Is the Subject? Queer Theory Meets Oral History," *Journal of the History of Sexuality* 17, no. 2 (May 2008): 177–189; Karen E. Lovaas, John P. Elia, and Gust A. Yep, "Shifting Ground(s): Surveying the Contested Terrain of LGBT Studies," *Journal of Homosexuality* 52, nos. 1/2 (2006): 1–18.
16. Henry Yu, "Mixing Bodies and Cultures: The Meaning of America's Fascination with Sex between 'Orientals' and 'Whites,' " in *Sex, Love, Race: Crossing Boundaries in North American History*, ed. Martha Hodes (New York: New York University Press, 1999), 444–463; Nayan Shah, "Between 'Oriental Depravity' and 'Natural Degenerates': Spatial Borderlands and the Making of Ordinary Americans," *America Quarterly* 57, no. 3 (September 2005): 703–725.
17. Inderpal Grewal and Caren Kaplan, "Global Identities: Theorizing Transnational Studies of Sexuality," *GLQ* 7, no. 4 (2001): 663–679.
18. For an excellent example see Eng-Beng Lim, "Glocalqueering in New Asia: The Politics of Performing Gay in Singapore," *Theatre Journal* 57 (2005): 383–405. See also Joseph Massad, "Re-Orienting Desire: The Gay International and the Arab World," *Public Culture* 14, no. 2 (Spring 2002): 361–385.
19. Howard spotlights Earl Finch in both his introduction and his epilogue and documents only a handful of same-sex intimacies. No doubt, he faced the

usual challenges in primary sources that all historians of queer sexuality face. John Howard, *Concentration Camps on the Home Front: Japanese Americans in the House of Jim Crow* (Chicago: University of Chicago Press, 2008).

20. Judy Tzu-chun Wu, *Doctor Mom Chung of the Fair-Haired Bastards: The Life of a Wartime Celebrity* (Berkeley and Los Angeles: University of California Press, 2005).
21. Historian Susan Johnson discusses how sexuality has been marginalized as a serious intellectual endeavor in the field of history. Susan Johnson, " 'My Own Private Life': Toward a History of Desire in Gold Rush California," in *Rooted in Barbarous Soil: People, Culture, and Community in Gold Rush California*, ed. Kevin Starr and Richard Orsi (Berkeley: University of California Press for the California Historical Society, 2000), 316–346.
22. For more on fetishizing language patterns of U.S. people of color within scholarly works, see bell hooks, *Black Looks: Race and Representation* (Boston: South End Press, 1992).
23. In Japanese American immigration or Issei history specifically, scholars have more often used both Japanese- and English-language sources in their analysis. See Ichioka, *Issei*, as well as Eiichiro Azuma, *Between Two Empires: Race, History, and Transnationalism in Japanese America* (New York: Oxford University Press, 2005).
24. Historian Mark McLelland notes how "backward" and "less liberated" Japan has been seen as borrowing extensively from the "advanced" West. Mark McLelland, *Queer Japan: From the Pacific War to the Internet Age* (New York: Rowman and Littlefield Publishers, 2005), 3, 6–7.

One: An Ocean Apart

1. Ian Neary, "Burakumin at the End of History—History of Social Class in Japan," *Social Research: An International Quarterly of the Social Sciences* 70, no. 1 (Spring 2003): 269–296.
2. Shunsuke Kamei, *Nashonarizumu no bungaku* (Tokyo: Kodansha, 1988), 210–211; Hiroaki Sato, "Yone Noguchi: Accomplishments and Roles," *Journal of American and Canadian Studies* 13 (1995), http://www.info.sophia.ac.jp/amecana/Journal/13–5.htm. Yone in his memoir cited the name of his priest-uncle as Daishun Ukai. Yone Noguchi, *The Story of Yone Noguchi Told by Himself* (Philadelphia: George W. Jacobs and Company, 1915), 202.
3. Roger Austen, *Genteel Pagan: The Double Life of Charles Warren Stoddard*, ed. John W. Crowley (Amherst, MA: University of Massachusetts Press, 1991), 77–78. For another useful work on Stoddard's life and career, see Robert L. Gale, *Charles Warren Stoddard* (Boise, ID: Boise State University, 1977).

4. Austen, *Genteel Pagan*, 65, 78. For the letter from Ambrose Bierce advising Stoddard to be wary of his actions, see Ambrose Gwinnett Bierce, Hampstead, England to Charles Warren Stoddard, 28 September 1873, HM10105, Huntington Manuscripts, Huntington Library, San Marino, CA (hereafter cited as Huntington MSS).
5. Seventeenth-century Stoddards had attended Harvard to become physicians and ministers. Even in 1843 Charles Warren Stoddard's paternal grandfather was a wealthy physician practicing in nearby Pembroke, New York. Stoddard's father, Samuel Burr Stoddard, in comparison was an "uneducated ne'er-do-well." Austen, *Genteel Pagan*, 3.
6. In 1867 Stoddard converted to Catholicism. Numerous scholars have speculated on the motivation behind this conversion. Ibid., 4, 35.
7. "Diversity" here points to the large number of ethnic whites as well as Americans from different states. Ibid., 9.
8. Ibid., 4, 10.
9. Ibid., 15, 17, 19, 26, 39.
10. A year later, in 1870, he prepared for another South Sea adventure, this time to Tahiti. And in 1872, as he boarded a ship bound for Samoa, he ended up disembarking in Hawai'i. Ibid., 48, 55–56.
11. Stoddard's biographer Roger Austen explained Stoddard's sentiments frankly when he wrote "to love other males freely, he felt he had to go to 'barbaric' countries." Ibid., 46.
12. Ibid., xxviii.
13. Edward Said, *Orientalism* (New York: Vintage Books, 2003); Robert Aldrich, *Colonialism and Homosexuality* (New York: Routledge, 2003). I thank Keith Camacho for pointing me to Aldrich's work.
14. Charles Warren Stoddard, *Hawaiian Life, or Lazy Letters from Low Latitudes* (Chicago and New York: F. T. Neely Publisher, 1894).
15. Austen, *Genteel Pagan*, 75.
16. Charles Warren Stoddard, *A Troubled Heart and How It Was Comforted at Last* (Notre Dame, IN: Joseph A. Lyons, 1885), 11–12.
17. Austen, *Genteel Pagan*, 53, 57–58.
18. Ibid., 82–84, 93, 94, 106, 121, 122, 129, 130, 131, 134.
19. Ibid., 135.
20. While Stoddard continued teaching one course on the history of English literature that he had requested when he took the position, his newly arrived rival Egan taught Anglo-Saxon, Chaucer, Shakespeare, philology of Tudor English, history of English journalism, and the art of versification among other courses. As the university faced a financial crisis, economic reality dictated that one of the two would likely be forced to resign. At the

time of Stoddard's expulsion from the university, only two or three students were enrolling in his lecture course. Ibid., 136, 144.

21. Noguchi, *The Story of Yone Noguchi Told by Himself*, 1.
22. Ibid., 6. For a Japanese-language source see Shiga Nobuo, "Noguchi Yonejirō to Isamu Noguchi: Futari no nijūkokusekisha," *Kaigai ijō* 592 (March 2000), 22.
23. Edward Marx, " 'A Different Mode of Speech': Yone Noguchi in Meiji America," in *Recollecting Early Asian America: Essays in Cultural History*, ed. Josephine Lee, Imogene L. Lim, and Yuko Matsukawa (Philadelphia: Temple University Press, 2002), 290–292; Noguchi, *The Story of Yone Noguchi Told by Himself*, 6.
24. Marx, " 'A Different Mode of Speech,' " 290–292; Shiga, "Noguchi Yonejirō to Isamu Noguchi," 22; Noguchi, *The Story of Yone Noguchi Told by Himself*, 7.
25. Marx, " 'A Different Mode of Speech,' " 292; Shiga, "Noguchi Yonejirō to Isamu Noguchi," 22.
26. The sea voyage itself proved difficult for Yone. He could not eat or drink for days on end yet continued to vomit through the journey as the ship rolled over the Pacific. The voyage made him a "thorough sea-hater." Noguchi, *The Story of Yone Noguchi Told by Himself*, 1, 25–26. See also Shunsuke Kamei, "Yone Noguchi an English Poet of Japan: An Essay," in Yone Noguchi, *Collected Poems*, ed. Usaburo Toyama (Tokyo: Yone Noguchi Society, 1965).
27. Miss Morning Glory, *American Diary of a Japanese Girl* (New York: Fredrick A. Stokes Publishing House, 1901), 16, 35, 36. In this chapter and the following ones, I use Yone's *American Diary of a Japanese Girl* in part as a document of his actual experiences in America. In 1925 Yone stated that *Diary* was an account of his American life. Yonejirō Noguchi, *Yonejirō Noguchi senshū: 3 kaigai bungaku shiron* (Tokyo: Kuresu Shuppan, 1998), 64.
28. *Crocker-Langley San Francisco Directory* (San Francisco: H. S. Crocker Company, 1897), 476; Noguchi, *The Story of Yone Noguchi Told by Himself*, 27.
29. Noguchi, *The Story of Yone Noguchi Told by Himself*, 28.
30. Ibid., 29.
31. Sato, "Yone Noguchi: Accomplishments and Roles."
32. Noguchi, *The Story of Yone Noguchi Told by Himself*, 8. While Yone passionately blamed his English language instructors, his own poor attendance in his conversation class may have contributed to his communication difficulties.
33. Ibid., 28–30.

34. For more on the experience of Japanese immigrant schoolboys, see Ichioka, *Issei*.
35. During one of his retreats, he noted that at one point when he was not yet twenty years old, it was he who ran the *Soko Shimbun*. Still, working for the paper proved no less stressful and in fact more unstable than domestic work. *Soko Shimbun* had a readership of no more than two hundred, and the five to six newspaper employees who slept in the office could hardly scrape up money for dinner every evening. When the landlord decided to put up new houses, he "begged" them to simply move away without demanding unpaid rent. Yone wrote of volunteering his services. Noguchi, *The Story of Yone Noguchi Told by Himself*, 16, 31. *Soko Shimbun* was more than likely titled *Soko Shimpo* or even *Soko Jiji* by the time Yone settled in San Francisco. According to historian Yuji Ichioka, the first daily Japanese American newspaper *Soko Shimbun* changed its name to *Soko Shimpo* in 1893 and *Soko Jiji* in 1895. If Yone in fact disembarked in San Francisco in December 1893 as he reported in his biography, it would not have been until 1894 at the earliest that he began volunteering for the Japanese-language paper. For a brief history of *Soko Shimbun*, see Brian Niiya, ed., *Japanese American History: An A-to-Z Reference from 1868 to the Present* (New York: Facts on File, 1993), 30.
36. While Yone ate only rice for dinner, Yone and nine of his friends feasted on a two-course "Chinese banquet" that cost thirty-five cents total for lunch. Frank Putnam, "Yone Noguchi," *Boston Transcript*, 8 April 1902; Noguchi, *The Story of Yone Noguchi Told by Himself*, 10–12, 32.
37. Shiga, "Noguchi Yonejirō to Isamu Noguchi," 22. For details on the shoplifting incident, see Noguchi, *The Story of Yone Noguchi Told by Himself*, 12–14.
38. Noguchi, *The Story of Yone Noguchi Told by Himself*, 21, 29.
39. Noguchi, *Yonejirō Noguchi senshū*, 38; Noguchi, *The Story of Yone Noguchi Told by Himself*, 38, 55–56.
40. Marx, " 'A Different Mode of Speech,' " 298–299. Noguchi, *The Story of Yone Noguchi Told by Himself*, 15. In other accounts Yone notes that he is unable to remember why he left the Menlo Park lodging house after four to five months of washing dishes. Noguchi, *Yonejirō Noguchi senshū*, 38.
41. The name of Joaquin Miller's home has alternatively been spelled "the Heights" by various journalists. I have chosen to use the less conventional spelling of the Oakland Hills retreat because Miller himself referred to his home in this fashion. For examples see Joaquin Miller, *Complete Poetical Works* (San Francisco: The Whitaker and Ray Company, 1902).
42. Noguchi, *Yonejirō Noguchi senshū*, 39.

43. In her interview in the 1960s, Elsie Whitaker Martinez distinctly recalled meeting "Yone Noguchi, the famous poet," on the Hights. Elsie Whitaker Martinez, interviewed by Willa K. Baum and Franklin Dickerson Walker, San Francisco Bay Area Writers and Artists: Oral History Transcript/ Elsie Martinez, Bancroft Library, University of California at Berkeley, 1962–1969.
44. "Mirā no sansō o tazuneru Yone Noguchishi," *Yomiuri Shimbun*, 1 February 1920, 7.
45. Noguchi, *Yonejirō Noguchi senshū*, 39.
46. Elsie Whitaker Martinez, interviewed by Willa K. Baum and Franklin Dickerson Walker, San Francisco Bay Area Writers and Artists: Oral History Transcript/Elsie Martinez, Bancroft Library, University of California at Berkeley, 1962–1969.
47. Noguchi, *Yonejirō Noguchi senshū*, 40–43; Noguchi, *The Story of Yone Noguchi Told by Himself*, 57; Frank Putnam, "Yone Noguchi." At least two additional conflicting accounts of the first meeting between Yone and Joaquin Miller exist. Both erase the role of Alice Oliver and spotlight Miller's warm embrace of Yone. I have chosen Yone's account to maintain a narrative in which his perspective—though at times convoluted or conflicting—remains central in the retelling of his intimate life. For the other two accounts see "Noguchi the Dreamer," *Washington Post*, 5 January 1902; and "How Two Famous Poets Met," *National Magazine*, October 1901. According to Joaquin Miller scholar M. M. Marberry, Alice Oliver was Joaquin Miller's lover and mother of three of his sons, one of whom died in infancy. M. M. Marberry, *Splendid Poseur: Joaquin Miller—American Poet* (New York: Crowell, 1953), 208, 234.
48. Miss Morning Glory, *American Diary of a Japanese Girl*, 210.
49. Noguchi, *Yonejirō Noguchi senshū*, 40–43; Noguchi, *The Story of Yone Noguchi Told by Himself*, 57; Atsumi, *Yone Noguchi Collected English Letters*; Sato, "Yone Noguchi"; Marx, " 'A Different Mode of Speech,' " 288–306; Parry, *Garrets and Pretenders*; "Noguchi the Dreamer," *Washington Post*, January 5, 1902.
50. Cincinnatus Hiner Miller (Joaquin Miller), "Yone Noguchi: An Article," c. 1898?, HM15706, Huntington MSS.
51. "Noguchi the Dreamer," *Washington Post*, 5 January 1902; Joaquin Miller and Yone Noguchi, *Japan of Sword and Love* (Tokyo: Kanao Bunyendo Publishers, 1905), 53; Noguchi, *The Story of Yone Noguchi Told by Himself*, 56.
52. Cincinnatus Hiner Miller (Joaquin Miller), "Yone Noguchi: An Article," c. 1898?, HM15706, Huntington MSS.

53. Yonejirō Noguchi, *Eibei no jūsannen* (Tokyo: Shunyōdō, 1905), 113, 114. For Miller's ambition to promote Asian-white marriages, see Elsie Whitaker Martinez, interviewed by Willa K. Baum and Franklin Dickerson Walker.
54. Noguchi, *The Story of Yone Noguchi Told by Himself*, 58; *San Francisco Chronicle*, 22 November 1896, Scrapbook of Yone Noguchi, Keio Special Collections, Keio University, Tokyo (hereafter cited as KSC).
55. Noguchi, *The Story of Yone Noguchi Told by Himself*, 58.
56. Noguchi, *Yonejirō Noguchi senshū*, 42.
57. Ibid., 41–42.
58. Noguchi, *Yonejirō Noguchi senshū*, 42. In 1909 Miller explained about the Japanese, "They all eat sparingly and drink not at all, in the sense that the white man drinks." Miller and Noguchi, *Japan of Sword and Love*, 51.
59. Noguchi, *Yonejirō Noguchi senshū*, 42.
60. Ibid., 46, 55. See also Noguchi, *The Story of Yone Noguchi Told by Himself*, 69.
61. While the *Washington Post* reported that Miller did most of the cooking with Yone assisting from time to time, Yone remembered Miller's mother preparing meals for everyone three to four days out of the week. At one particular breakfast when Miller cooked frogs as a special dish, Yone could not bring himself to eat the "delicacy" as he thought of the frogs who sang him a lullaby as he drifted off to sleep the night before. Staring at the frog leg in his dish, Yone nearly cried in grief. Noguchi, *Yonejirō Noguchi senshū*, 60–61; Miss Morning Glory, *American Diary of a Japanese Girl*, 184, 214; "Noguchi the Dreamer," *Washington Post*, 5 January 1902.
62. When there was no beef available, Yone would substitute squirrel that Miller had gunned down. Yone could barely imagine Miller successfully hunting for squirrels. After all, Yone argued, how could an animal with four legs be outrun by Miller's slower two? Noguchi, *Yonejirō Noguchi senshū*, 60–61; Miss Morning Glory, *American Diary of a Japanese Girl*, 190.
63. Miller never complained about Yone's cooking but would add excessive amounts of salt and pepper behind his back to the dismay of Yone and Miller's mother. Noguchi, *Yonejirō Noguchi senshū*, 60–61; "Noguchi the Dreamer," *Washington Post*, 5 January 1902; Noguchi, *The Story of Yone Noguchi Told by Himself*, 58, 74–75.
64. From Joseph Dwight Strong, Oakland, to Charles Warren Stoddard, before April 1896, HM38113, Huntington MSS; From Joseph Dwight Strong, Oakland, to Charles Warren Stoddard, before April 1896, HM38115, Huntington MSS.
65. Miss Morning Glory, *American Diary of a Japanese Girl*, 203.

66. For Noguchi growing his hair like Miller and playing pranks on guests see Parry, *Garrets and Pretenders*, 234.
67. During this poorest time of his life, he wore the same hat and velvet outfit on the Hights for three years. When Miller noticed Yone's torn socks, he bought him several new pairs. Generous friends also frequently gave him fare to cross the San Francisco Bay. Noguchi, *Yonejirō Noguchi senshū*, 62; Noguchi, *The Story of Yone Noguchi Told by Himself*, 76.
68. Noguchi, *The Story of Yone Noguchi Told by Himself*, 58–59.
69. So popular did the Oakland home prove that a play about the Hights also took the stage in New York. Noguchi, *Eibei no jūsannen*, 113, 114.
70. Indeed, the panorama proved so spectacular that California governor John C. Frémont was rumored to have tented at the very location and designated the entrance to the San Francisco Bay as the "Golden Gate" during the 1840s. Miller, *Complete Poetical Works*, 321–322; Noguchi, *Eibei no jūsannen*, 4, 7; Noguchi, *The Story of Yone Noguchi Told by Himself*, 21.
71. Noguchi, *Yonejirō Noguchi senshū*, 42, 44; Noguchi, *The Story of Yone Noguchi Told by Himself*, 45, 60–62.
72. Noguchi, *Yonejirō Noguchi senshū*, 63.
73. Maeda, "From Shape and Shadow," 106; Marx, " 'A Different Mode of Speech,' " 300; Warren Unna, *The Coppa Murals: A Pageant of Bohemian Life in San Francisco at the Turn of the Century* (San Francisco: The Book Club of California, 1952), 3.
74. Gelett Burgess, "The Night Reveries of an Exile," *Lark*, no. 15 (1896): n.p.
75. Noguchi, *Eibei no jūsannen*, 4, 7.
76. Scrapbook of Yone Noguchi, KSC.
77. Noguchi, *Eibei no jūsannen*, 4, 7, 13–15.
78. *San Francisco Chronicle*, 22 November 1896, Scrapbook of Yone Noguchi, KSC.
79. Dated 10 December 1896, Scrapbook of Yone Noguchi, KSC.
80. Gelett Burgess, n.t., *San Francisco Examiner*, 25 November 1896, Scrapbook of Yone Noguchi, KSC; Jay William Hudson, n.t., *San Francisco Chronicle*, [1896?], Scrapbook of Yone Noguchi, KSC.
81. Jay William Hudson, n.t., *San Francisco Chronicle*, [1896?], Scrapbook of Yone Noguchi, KSC.
82. Noguchi, *The Story of Yone Noguchi Told by Himself*, 44.
83. Gelett Burgess, n.t., *San Francisco Examiner*, 25 November 1896, Scrapbook of Yone Noguchi, KSC.
84. Jay William Hudson, n.t., *San Francisco Chronicle*, [1896?], Scrapbook of Yone Noguchi, KSC. Joaquin Miller in fact wrote a more personal letter

supporting Yone during his plagiarism scandal. Though Yone could not read the letter because of Miller's "perfectly terrible" handwriting, he saved the note carefully to his death. Joaquin Miller, Hights, to Yone Noguchi, Sausalito, CA, 5 December 1896, Yone Noguchi Papers, BANC MSS 71/39c, Bancroft Special Collections, Bancroft Library, Berkeley, CA (hereafter cited as BSC).

85. When the *San Francisco Chronicle* refused to print Burgess' defense of Yone and his alleged act of plagiarism, Burgess sent his editorial to the *Chronicle*'s rival, the *San Francisco Examiner*, for publication. Gelett Burgess, n.t., *San Francisco Examiner*, 25 November 1896, Scrapbook of Yone Noguchi, KSC.
86. Porter Garnett, [n.t.], *San Francisco Call*, [n.d.], Scrapbook of Yone Noguchi, KSC.
87. The lines Yone wrote, "I dwell alone / In world of moan, / My soul is stagnant dawn," came from Poe's poem "Eulalie," where Poe wrote, "I dwelt alone / In a world of moan, / And my soul was a stagnant tide." Yonejirō Noguchi, *Eibei no jūsannen*, 9.
88. Noguchi, *The Story of Yone Noguchi Told by Himself*, 18, 19.
89. Noguchi, *Eibei no jūsannen*, 10.
90. In an ironic twist of perhaps karmic fate, poet and playwright Laurence Housman would inadvertently publish an edited version of Yone's poem "Cradle Song" as his own in 1919. When Yone's "Cradle Song" appeared later in the *Sunday Times*, he grew indignant, believing that Yone had plagiarized it from him. His memory though, quickly returned, and he realized that in fact the reverse was true. He apologized profusely for his blunder in his 1937 autobiography. Laurence Housman, *The Unexpected Years* (London: Jonathan Cape, 1937), 201–202. I thank Deborah Cohler for pointing me to Housman.
91. Noguchi, *The Story of Yone Noguchi Told by Himself*, 19.
92. In twenty-one poems Yone used the word "alone," "lonely," "loneliness," or "lonesome." Yone Noguchi, *Seen and Unseen: Monologues of a Homeless Snail* (San Francisco: Gelett Burgess and Porter Garnett, 1897).
93. Noguchi, *Seen and Unseen*, n.p.
94. Ibid.
95. Noguchi, *Seen and Unseen*, nos. 1, 3, 19, 24, 43, 50.
96. Yone Noguchi, *Voice of the Valley* (San Francisco: William Doxey, 1897), 16, 42.
97. Yone Noguchi, *Twilight* (May 1898), Huntington MSS; Yone Noguchi, *Twilight* (June 1898), Huntington MSS.
98. W. S. Gilbert, *The Mikado* (New York: Boni and Liveright Inc., 1917).

99. "Through the Opera Glass," *Wasp*, 30 October 1897, 14–15; "A Musical Comedy," *San Francisco Chronicle*, 17 October 1897, p. 5; "Dramatic and Musical Review," *San Francisco Chronicle*, 7 November 1897, p. 5. Owen Hall, *The Geisha* (London: Ascherberg, Hopwood and Crew, 1896).
100. For an excellent article on the implications of *Madame Butterfly*, see Mari Yoshihara, "The Flight of Japanese Butterfly: Orientalism, Nationalism, and Performances of Japanese Womanhood," *American Quarterly* 56, no. 4 (2004): 975–1001. For a creative more recent Asian American critique of *Madame Butterfly* see David Henry Hwang, *M. Butterfly* (New York: Penguin, 1989).
101. Lynn Gordon, "The Gibson Girl Goes to College: Popular Culture and Women's Higher Education in the Progressive Era, 1890–1920," *American Quarterly* 39, no. 2 (Summer 1987): 211–230; Carroll Smith-Rosenberg, *Disorderly Conduct*, 246–296.
102. Noguchi, *The Story of Yone Noguchi Told by Himself.*
103. Miss Morning Glory, *American Diary of a Japanese Girl*, 60, 75, 80.
104. Scholarly publications on *Mikado* in fact show that many English at the time knew of W. S. Gilbert's intent to write a satire of England rather than represent an authentic Japan in his musical. W. A. Darlington, *The World of Gilbert and Sullivan* (New York: Thomas Y. Crowell Company, 1950). For critical reviews of *Mikado* and *Geisha* occurring outside of San Francisco, see Amy Sueyoshi, "Race-ing Sex: The Competition for Gender and Sexual Identity in Multi-Ethnic San Francisco, 1897–1924" (Ph.D. diss., University of California at Los Angeles, 2002).
105. Miss Morning Glory, *American Diary of a Japanese Girl*, 238–240.
106. Yone Noguchi, New York, to Charles Warren Stoddard, 1903?, HM37937, Huntington MSS. Watanna, whose mother was in fact Chinese and whose father was a white Canadian, deliberately presented herself as Japanese for her literary career based on writings on exotic Japan. For more on Watanna, see Diana Birchall, *Onoto Watanna: The Story of Winnifred Eaton* (Urbana: University of Illinois Press, 2001). In 1907, several years after Yone first became acquainted with Watanna's work, he went as far as to dedicate an essay pointing out all of the incorrect Japanese references line by line in *Japanese Nightingale*. Yone Noguchi, "Onoto Watanna and Her Japanese Work," *Taiyo* 13, no. 8 (June 1907): 18–21; Yone Noguchi, "Onoto Watanna and Her Japanese Work," *Taiyo* 13, no. 10 (July 1907): 19–21, http://www.h.ehime-u.ac.jp/~marx/YN/articles/Watanna-Taiyou.htm (accessed 23 November 2007).
107. Miss Morning Glory (Yone Noguchi), *American Letters of a Japanese Parlor-Maid* (Tokyo: Fuzanbō, 1905), 116.

108. Austen, *Genteel Pagan*, xxv, 132–133.
109. William Hosley additionally argued that the particular yearning between the United States and Japan intensified with their similar status as developing nations in a global field previously dominated by Europeans. William Hosley, *The Japan Idea: Art and Life in Victorian America* (Hartford, CT: Wadsworth Athenaeum, 1990), 29.

Two: Two Shy Stars

1. For Yone's dream, see Yone Noguchi, San Francisco, to Charles Warren Stoddard, ? September 1897, HM37891, Huntington MSS. For publication of the poem, see Noguchi, "In the Bungalow with Charles Warren Stoddard," 308.
2. Alexander Saxton, *Indispensable Enemy: Labor and Anti-Chinese Movement in California* (Berkeley: University of California Press, 1971); Roger Daniels, *The Politics of Prejudice: The Anti-Japanese Movement and the Struggle for Japanese Exclusion* (Berkeley: University of California Press, 1962); Sucheng Chan, *Asian Americans: An Interpretive History* (New York: Twayne, 1991); Bill Ong Hing, *Making and Remaking Asian America through Immigration Policy: 1850–1990* (Stanford, CA: Stanford University Press, 1993); Paul R. Spickard, *Mixed Blood: Intermarriage and Ethnic Identity in Twentieth Century America* (Madison, WI: University of Wisconsin Press, 1989). See also Tomás Almaguer, *Racial Faultlines: The Historical Origins of White Supremacy in California* (Berkeley: University of California Press, 1994).
3. Peggy Pascoe, "Race, Gender, and Intercultural Relations: The Case of Interracial Marriage," *Frontiers* 12, no. 1 (1991): 5–19; Rachel F. Moran, *Interracial Intimacy: The Regulation of Race and Romance* (Chicago: University of Chicago Press, 2001), 31; Candice Lewis Bredbenner, *A Nationality of Her Own: Women Marriage, and the Law of Citizenship* (Berkeley: University California Press, 1998); Hing, *Making and Remaking Asian America*; Megumi Dick Osumi, "Asians and California's Anti-Miscegenation Laws," in *Asian and Pacific American Experiences: Women's Perspectives*, ed. Nobuya Tsuchida (Minneapolis, MN: Asian/Pacific Learning Resource Center and General College University of Minnesota, Minneapolis, 1982): 1–37.
4. Henry Kiyama, *Four Immigrants Manga: A Japanese Experience in San Francisco*, trans. Frederick L. Schodt (Berkeley: Stone Bridge Press, 1999); Spickard, *Mixed Blood*.
5. The use of "secretary" here indicates a high-level executive position similar to "director." "Torao Kawasaki—Japanese Consulate, Battery and Sansome,

San Francisco," Survey on Race Relations, Special Collections, Hoover Library, Stanford University, Stanford, CA.

6. Literary historian James Levin argued that the turn of the century was sexually repressive for both same-sex sexuality and heterosexuality alike. James Levin, *The Gay Novel in America* (New York: Garland Publishing, Incorporated, 1991).
7. Peter Gay, *The Tender Passion* (New York: Oxford University Press, 1986), 202; Roger Austen, *Playing the Game: The Homosexual Novel in America* (New York: The Bobbs-Merrill Company, 1977), xxxvi.
8. Bohemian Club, *The Annals of the Bohemian Club* (San Francisco: Hicks-Judd Company, 1898–1909); Stansell, *American Moderns*, 251, Wilson, *Bohemians*, 183.
9. Poet and playwright Oscar Wilde was accused of committing sodomy in the 1890s. For more on Wilde, see Michael S. Foldy, *The Trials of Oscar Wilde: Deviance, Morality, and Late-Victorian Society* (New Haven, CT: Yale University Press, 1997). "Preacher Convicted of Revolting Acts," *San Francisco Chronicle*, 12 July 1898, p. 4.
10. Alan Dale, *A Marriage below Zero* (New York: G. W. Dillingham, 1889); Biennial Report of the Attorney General of the State of California 1900–1902 (Sacramento: A. J. Johnston, 1902); The People v. William Day, 135 Cal. 360 (1902).
11. Roger Austen, *Genteel Pagan*, xxviii.
12. According to historians of the San Francisco Bohemian Club, bachelor artists and writers began gathering for intellectual banter and artistic collaboration in the 1870s. Bohemian Club, *Annals of the Bohemian Club*, vol. 1 (1898), 15, 17; Warren Unna, *The Coppa Murals*, 42.
13. Bohemian Club, *Annals of the Bohemian Club*, vol. 1, 16. Kearny, Stockton, Pacific, and Union Streets composed the boundaries of the Latin Quarter. The area is better known today as the North Beach district's innermost enclave of restaurants and night clubs. Gerald Adams, *The Neighborhood of San Francisco* (San Francisco: *San Francisco Examiner*, 1977), 13.
14. City bohemians also regularly traveled to Marin County for picnic, blanket, and bonfire weekends in Tocaloma near Point Reyes. Bohemian Club, *Annals of the Bohemian Club*, vol. 1, 15, 17; Unna, *The Coppa Murals*, 42. So well liked was Stoddard within the Bohemian Club that even as late as 1911 members gathered to celebrate "Stoddard Day at the Club." Ina Coolbrith to Blanche Partington, 27 January 1911, Partington Family Papers, BANC MSS C-H 84, BSC.
15. Bohemian Club, *Annals of the Bohemian Club*, vol. 1, 32–33. The Bohemian Club instituted an annual "Ladies' High Jinks" for women associated with

club members. Bohemian Club, *Annals of the Bohemian Club*, vol. 2 (1900), 11.

16. Bohemian Club, *Annals of the Bohemian Club*, vol. 2, 64–73, 117–120, 146, 212–213; Bohemian Club, *Christmas Jinks: December 1891* (San Francisco: C. A. Murdock and Company, Printers, 1891), n.p.
17. William Dean Howells, New York City, to Charles Warren Stoddard, Washington, DC, 8 April 1896 HM41520, Huntington MSS; Joseph Dwight Strong, San Francisco, to Charles Warren Stoddard, 31 January 1898, HM38152, Huntington MSS. According to "Coppan chronicles," west coast bohemia began under the guidance of French-born American artist Jules Tavernier, painter Joseph Strong, and writer Robert Louis Stevenson. Unna, *The Coppa Murals*, 3.
18. Elbert Hubbard, *So Here Then Is a Little Journey to the Home of Joaquin Miller* (East Aurora, NY: The Roycrofters, 1903), 22–24.
19. Yone Noguchi, Oakland, to Charles Warren Stoddard, 19 March 1897, Charles Warren Stoddard Papers, BANC MSS C-H 53, BSC.
20. Richard Hovey, New York City, to Yone Noguchi, 12 May 1897, in Atsumi, *Yone Noguchi Collected English Letters* (hereafter cited as CEL), no. 9; Julian Hawthorne, New Rochelle, NY, to Yone Noguchi, 7 July 7, 1897, CEL, no. 10; Francis Sherman to Yone Noguchi, 19 April 1897, CEL, no. 11.
21. Henry van Dyke to Yone Noguchi, 12 April 1897, CEL, no. 5; Edith M. Thomas, Staten Island, NY, to Yone Noguchi, 15 April 1897, CEL, no. 7.
22. Charles Warren Stoddard, Washington, DC, to Yone Noguchi, April 1897, CEL no. 4.
23. Ibid.
24. Henry van Dyke to Yone Noguchi, 12 April 1897, CEL, no. 5; Edith M. Thomas, Staten Island, NY, to Yone Noguchi, 15 April 1897, CEL, no. 7. For additional examples, see Y. Mable, New York City, to Yone Noguchi, 14 April 1897, CEL, no. 6; J. O'Hara(?), Santa Rosa, to Yone Noguchi, 18 April 1897, CEL, no. 8.
25. Yone Noguchi, Oakland, to Charles Warren Stoddard, 16 April 1897, HM37874, Huntington MSS.
26. Yone Noguchi, Oakland, to Charles Warren Stoddard, 25 April 1897, HM37875, Huntington MSS. For additional reference to Yone's youth by Yone, see Yone Noguchi, Oakland, to Charles Warren Stoddard, 2 May 1897, HM37876, Huntington MSS.
27. David M. Halperin, "How to Do the History of Homosexuality," 101.
28. I thank Bobby Cheung for reminding me to more explicitly address the BDSM nature of Yone and Charles' affair. (BDSM is a compound acronym for Bondage and Discipline; Domination and Submission; and Sadism

and Masochism.) For the theoretical significance of contemporary queer "Daddy/boy" relationships, see C. Jacob Hale, "Leatherdyke Boys and Their Daddies: How to Have Sex without Women or Men," *Social Text* 52/53 (Autumn–Winter 1997): 223–236. Theorist Gayle Rubin cautions against stigmatizing all forms of marginalized relationships—queer, kinky, as well as intergenerational—in the struggle for sexual liberation. Gayle Rubin, "Thinking Sex," in *The Lesbian and Gay Studies Reader*, ed. Henry Abelove, Michèle Aina Barale, and David M. Halperin (New York: Routledge, 1993), 3–44.

29. Four years later, Yone's approach to his nationality would change drastically.
30. Chinese themes also played a strong role in this Christmas Jinks with an oration titled "Recollections of Chinatown" by W. H. L. Barnes and a Chinese play titled "Shy-shy, or The Emperor's Sister" concluding the event. Bohemian Club, *Christmas Jinks*, 2; Porter Garnett, *The Bohemian Jinks: A Treatise* (San Francisco: Hicks-Judd Co., 1906), 11. The 1892 Midsummer High Jinks themed "Buddha" is more formally known as the "Sermon of the Myriad Leaves." Bohemian Club, *Bohemian Club, 1872: A Chronicle of Our Years: Commemorating the Seventy-Fifth Anniversary of the Founding of the Bohemian Club of San Francisco* (San Francisco: Grabhorn Press, 1947), 16; Bohemian Club, *Annals of the Bohemian Club*, vol. 3 (1909), 168, 187–194, 262.
31. Austen, *Genteel Pagan*, 89; Yone Noguchi, Oakland, to Charles Warren Stoddard, 22 May 1897, HM37878, Huntington MSS.
32. Yone Noguchi, Oakland, to Charles Warren Stoddard, 25 May 1897, HM37879, Huntington MSS; Yone Noguchi, "the hights," Oakland, to Charles Warren Stoddard, 6 July 1897, HM37885, Huntington MSS. Yone Noguchi, San Francisco?, to Charles Warren Stoddard, 1 July 1897, HM37884, Huntington MSS; Yone Noguchi, Oakland, to Charles Warren Stoddard, 30 May 1897, HM37880, Huntington MSS.
33. Yone Noguchi, *The Voice of the Valley*, 10–11.
34. Yone Noguchi, "the hights," Oakland, to Charles Warren Stoddard, 6 July 1897, HM37885, Huntington MSS.
35. Yone Noguchi, San Francisco, to Charles Warren Stoddard, 27 July 1897, HM37887, Huntington MSS.
36. For the summer series of letters, see Yone Noguchi, Oakland, to Charles Warren Stoddard, 6 June 1897, HM37881, Huntington MSS; Yone Noguchi, Oakland, to Charles Warren Stoddard, 7 June 1897, HM37882, Huntington MSS; Yone Noguchi, Oakland, to Charles Warren Stoddard, 13 June 1897, HM37883, Huntington MSS; Yone Noguchi, San Francisco?, to Charles

Warren Stoddard, 1 July 1897, HM37884, Huntington MSS; Yone Noguchi, "the hights," Oakland, to Charles Warren Stoddard, 6 July 1897, HM37885, Huntington MSS; Yone Noguchi, Oakland, to Charles Warren Stoddard, 15 July 1897, HM37886, Huntington MSS; Yone Noguchi, San Francisco, to Charles Warren Stoddard, 27 July 1897, HM37887, Huntington MSS; Yone Noguchi, San Francisco, to Charles Warren Stoddard, 28 July 1897, HM37888, Huntington MSS; Yone Noguchi, San Francisco, to Charles Warren Stoddard, 9 August 1897, HM37889, Huntington MSS; Yone Noguchi, San Francisco, to Charles Warren Stoddard, 18 August 1897, HM37890, Huntington MSS. On July 28 he queried, "My Dearest Charlie: Don't you like to hear so often from me?" And without so much as waiting for a response, Yone parried in the following sentence, "I do not care. . . . I continue to write for you." Yone Noguchi, San Francisco, to Charles Warren Stoddard, 28 July 1897, HM37888, Huntington MSS.

37. Yone Noguchi, "the hights," Oakland to Charles Warren Stoddard, 6 July 1897, HM37885, Huntington MSS.
38. Yone Noguchi, Oakland, to Charles Warren Stoddard, 13 June 1897, HM37883, Huntington MSS; Yone Noguchi, San Francisco?, to Charles Warren Stoddard, 1 July 1897, HM37884, Huntington MSS.
39. Yone wrote: "There are measureless flowers in this world. But we love a few of them. Why you are a flower which I love; Nay, I am a flower which you came to love me!" Yone Noguchi, Oakland, to Charles Warren Stoddard, 7 June 1897, HM37882, Huntington MSS.
40. Yone Noguchi, San Francisco, to Charles Warren Stoddard, 18 August 1897, HM37890, Huntington MSS.
41. Ibid.
42. The "Golden Gate" here refers to the opening of the San Francisco Bay where it meets the Pacific Ocean.
43. Yone Noguchi to Charles Warren Stoddard, ? September 1897, HM37892, Huntington MSS; Yone Noguchi, San Francisco, to Charles Warren Stoddard, 30? October 1897, HM37896, Huntington MSS. Not until nearly a full year later would Yone come to appreciate the city's streetcars and overcast skies.
44. Yone Noguchi, San Francisco, to Charles Warren Stoddard, 30? October 1897, HM37896, Huntington MSS. In the early 1900s Yone would write similarly of Japan as a place that nurtured creativity. "I left all my poetry with Japan. Dear land of inspiration, no more with me!" Miss Morning Glory, *American Diary of a Japanese Girl*, 7–8.
45. Though he had not yet inquired about the schedule of steamers to Japan, Yone tentatively planned to depart in late September or early October.

Yone Noguchi to Charles Warren Stoddard, ? September 1897, HM37892, Huntington MSS; Yone Noguchi, San Francisco, to Charles Warren Stoddard, 30? October 1897, HM37896, Huntington MSS.

46. Yone Noguchi to Charles Warren Stoddard, 12 May 1898, HM37905, Huntington MSS.
47. From Yone Noguchi, San Francisco, to Charles Warren Stoddard, ? October 1897, HM37893, Huntington MSS.
48. Yone Noguchi, San Francisco, to Charles Warren Stoddard, ? September 1897, HM37891, Huntington MSS.
49. Yone Noguchi, San Francisco, to Charles Warren Stoddard, ? September 1897, HM37891, Huntington MSS; Yone Noguchi to Charles Warren Stoddard, ? October 1897, HM37894, Huntington MSS; Yone Noguchi to Charles Warren Stoddard, 8? October 1897, HM37895, Huntington MSS; Yone Noguchi, San Francisco, to Charles Warren Stoddard, 30? October 1897, HM37896, Huntington MSS.
50. Yone Noguchi, San Francisco, to Charles Warren Stoddard, 30? October 1897, HM37896, Huntington MSS.
51. Yone Noguchi, San Francisco, to Charles Warren Stoddard, ? November 1897, HM37898, Huntington MSS; Yone Noguchi, San Francisco, to Charles Warren Stoddard, 11 December 1897, HM37899, Huntington MSS; Yone Noguchi, San Francisco, to Charles Warren Stoddard, ? December 1897, HM37901, Huntington MSS; Yone Noguchi, San Francisco, to Charles Warren Stoddard, ? January 1898, HM37903, Huntington MSS; Yone Noguchi, San Francisco, to Charles Warren Stoddard, 27 April 1898, HM37904, Huntington MSS. The last time he sends "kisses" to Charlie is in a letter dated December 8, 1898. Yone Noguchi, San Francisco, to Charles Warren Stoddard, 8 December 1898, HM37914, Huntington MSS. Of the sixteen recovered letters from November of 1897 to December of 1898, eleven contain kisses in a variety of forms. In fact, every piece of correspondence from Yone to Charlie until August of 1898 contained kisses, and it would only be in the last four months of 1898 that the kisses begin to taper off.
52. Yone Noguchi, San Francisco, to Charles Warren Stoddard, ? December 1897, HM37901, Huntington MSS.
53. Ibid.
54. Yone Noguchi, San Francisco, to Charles Warren Stoddard, 27 April 1898, HM37904, Huntington MSS.
55. Yone Noguchi to Charles Warren Stoddard, 12 May 1898, HM37905, Huntington MSS; Yone Noguchi, the heights, Dimond, CA, to Charles Warren Stoddard, 6 August 1898, HM37909, Huntington MSS.

56. Yone Noguchi to Charles Warren Stoddard, 12 May 1898, HM37905, Huntington MSS.
57. Yone Noguchi, Dimond, CA, to Charles Warren Stoddard, HM37906, Huntington MSS, 4 July 1898; Yone Noguchi, San Francisco, to Charles Warren Stoddard, HM37907, ? July 1898, Huntington MSS; Yone Noguchi, the heights, Dimond, CA, to Charles Warren Stoddard, 6 August 1898, HM37909, Huntington MSS; Yone Noguchi, the heights, Dimond, CA, to Charles Warren Stoddard, 13 August 1898, HM 37910, Huntington MSS.
58. Yone's letters still expressed his "great love" for Charlie and the "pleasure" and "encouragement" Charlie's letters brought, but his letters had lost the passionate intensity in previous passages describing their "divine" relationship that made even the "angels jealous." For examples showing decreasing passion, see Yone Noguchi, The Heights, Dimond, CA, to Charles Warren Stoddard, September 1898, HM37912, Huntington MSS; Yone Noguchi, San Francisco, to Charles Warren Stoddard, 17 November 1898, HM37913, Huntington MSS.
59. Yone Noguchi to Blanche Partington, 20 December 1898, CEL, no. 30. Still, in a later publication, as Yone wrote of the beauty of the Pacific Ocean by the Cliff House, he described San Francisco as an "insane asylum" as well as a city where "people have made a science of robbery." "Professional lady killers" in the city who powdered their faces and carried large canes also disgraced the entire state. Yone apparently came to appreciate the gifts of nature that the city held more than the urban inhabitants themselves. Yonejirō Noguchi, *Eibei no jūsannen*, 56–57, 77.
60. Yone [Noguchi] to Blanche Partington, n.d., Partington Family Papers, BANC MSS C-H 84, BSC.
61. "Blanche Partington," *New York Times*, 16 March 1951, p. 31.
62. Richard Langtry Partington became a portraitist; Gertrude Partington Albright became a successful painter and etcher; and Phyllis Partington, known on the stage as Frances Peralta, became a Metropolitan Opera singer in New York City. Blanche regularly wrote for the *San Francisco Call*. "Guide to the Partington Family Papers, ca. 1892–1946," BSC, p. 6; http://www.oac.cdlib.org/findaid/ark:/13030/kt40000344. "Finding Aid to the Partington Family Papers: Additions, 1865–1979, bulk 1865–1949," BSC, p. 3; http://www.oac.cdlib.org/findaid/ark:/13030/kt6g5004zc.
63. Ambrose Bierce, St. Helena, CA, to Blanche Partington, 15 August 1892, Partington Family Papers, BANC MSS C-H 84, BSC; Ambrose Bierce, St. Helena, CA, to Blanche Partington, 28 September 1892, Partington Family Papers, BANC MSS C-H 84, BSC; Ambrose Bierce, Angwin, CA, to

Blanche Partington, 14 December 1892, Partington Family Papers, BANC MSS C-H 84, BSC; Ambrose Bierce, Angwin, to Blanche Partington, 5 February 1893, Partington Family Papers, BANC MSS C-H 84, BSC; Ambrose Bierce to Blanche Partington, 10 April 1893, Partington Family Papers, BANC MSS C-H 84, BSC. For more on Ambrose Bierce, see Carey McWilliams, *Ambrose Bierce: A Biography* (New York: A and C Boni, 1929).

64. Diary of Blanche Partington, August 1898, Partington Family Papers, BANC MSS C-H 84, BSC; Diary of Blanche Partington, 4 October 1898, Partington Family Papers, BANC MSS C-H 84, BSC.
65. This use of race is hardly unique to turn-of-the-century bohemians. Sociologist Mary Waters discusses this concept with regard to American whites in the late twentieth century. Mary C. Waters, *Ethnic Options: Choosing Identities in America* (Berkeley: University of California Press, 1990).
66. For the use of "Buddha" see T. F. D., Vaud, Switzerland to Charles Warren Stoddard, 10 April 1906, HM38498, Huntington MSS. For the use of "Carlos" see Carrie Wyatt, Montera, WA, to Charles Warren Stoddard, Monterey, CA, 16 March 1908, HM38513, Huntington MSS. For examples of the use of "Aloha," see Joseph Dwight Strong, San Francisco, to Charles Warren Stoddard, 7 January 1898, HM38151, Huntington MSS; Charles Warren Stoddard, Saratoga, CA, to Dewitt Miller, 3 November 1906, HM38403, Huntington MSS; Charles Warren Stoddard, Monterey, CA, to Dewitt Miller, 17 October 1908, HM38415, Huntington MSS.
67. Ina Coolbrith, San Francisco, to Blanche Partington, [c. 1897–1899], Partington Family Papers, BANC MSS C-H 84, BSC; Ambrose Bierce to Blanche Partington,14 February 1893, Partington Family Papers, BANC MSS C-H 84, BSC.
68. Ambrose Bierce, Berkeley, CA, to Blanche Partington, 23 December 1893, Partington Family Papers, BANC MSS C-H 84, BSC; Ambrose Bierce, Washington, DC, to Blanche Partington, 6 February 1913, Partington Family Papers, BANC MSS C-H 84, BSC; Charmian London, Glen Ellen, CA, to Blanche Partington, n.d. [before July 1910], Partington Family Papers, BANC MSS C-H 84, BSC.
69. Cincinnatus Hiner Miller (Joaquin Miller), "Yone Noguchi: an article," [c. 1898?], HM15706, Huntington MSS.
70. Diary, 1911, Partington Family Papers, BANC MSS C-H 84, BSC; Diary, 1898, Partington Family Papers, BANC MSS C-H 84, BSC.
71. Bohemian Club, *Bohemian Club, 1872*; Gary John Graves, "Bohemian Grove Theatrics: A History and Analysis from the Club's Beginnings in 1872 up

until the Encampment in 1992" (Ph.D. diss., University of California at Berkeley, 1994).

72. Charles Warren Stoddard, "The Daughter of Pharoah To Bohemia," 8 September 1890, Huntington MSS.
73. For more information on contemporary issues of returning human remains and other cultural and sacred objects to lineal descendants, culturally affiliated Indian tribes, and Native Hawaiian organizations, see http://www.nps.gov/history/nagpra/ (accessed 5 October 2007).
74. Helen Bridyman to Yone Noguchi, New York, 18 April 1904, in CEL, no. 314. Later letters reveal that the woman "wild to see" Noguchi's place was "Miss Williamson." Helen Bridyman, Brooklyn, to Yone Noguchi, New York, 25 April 1904, CEL, no. 318. For the added dinner guests, see Helen Bridyman, Brooklyn, to Yone Noguchi, New York, 26 April 1904, CEL, no. 319.
75. Helen Bridyman, Brooklyn, to Yone Noguchi, New York, 26 April 1904, CEL, no. 319. Helen, a devout lover of Japan, enjoyed reading Noguchi's poetry in her backyard beside two chestnut and cherry trees, where she felt as though she were in "miniature Japan." Helen Bridyman, Brooklyn, to Yone Noguchi, New York, 8 May 1904, CEL, no. 325.
76. "Intimate Study of Yone Noguchi," *Human Life*, October 1905, n.p.
77. Diary of Blanche Partington, 4 October 1898, Partington Family Papers, BANC MSS C-H 84, BSC.
78. Yone Noguchi, San Francisco, to Blanche Partington, Oakland, 11 October 1898, CEL, no. 20. Yone's musings about Blanche's age in his letter to her delighted Blanche, as she shared it with her ailing mother to cheer her up. Diary of Blanche Partington, 12 October 1898, Partington Family Papers, BANC MSS C-H 84, BSC.
79. Yone Noguchi, San Francisco, to Blanche Partington, Oakland, ? October 1898?, CEL, no. 21.
80. Ibid.; Yone Noguchi, San Francisco, to Blanche Partington, Oakland, ? October 1898?, CEL, no. 22; Yone Noguchi, San Francisco, to Blanche Partington, Oakland, 5 November 1898, CEL, no. 23; Yone Noguchi to Blanche Partington, 1 December 1898, CEL, no. 26; Yone Noguchi to Blanche Partington, ? December 1898?, CEL, no. 28; Yone Noguchi to Blanche Partington, 9 ? 1898, CEL, no. 25; Yone Noguchi, San Francisco, to Blanche Partington, 17 December? 1898, CEL, no. 29; Yone Noguchi to Blanche Partington, 20 December 1898, CEL, no. 30; Yone Noguchi, San Francisco, to Blanche Partington, 10 January 1899, CEL, no. 33.
81. Diary of Blanche Partington, 23 October 1898, Partington Family Papers, BANC MSS C-H 84, BSC.

82. "Intimate Study of Yone Noguchi," *Human Life*, October 1905, n.p.
83. Yone Noguchi, San Francisco, to Blanche Partington, 7 June ?, CEL, no. 38.
84. Yone Noguchi, San Francisco, to Charles Warren Stoddard, 8 December 1898, HM37914, Huntington MSS.
85. Noguchi, *The Story of Yone Noguchi Told by Himself*, 49–52.
86. Miss Morning Glory, *American Diary of a Japanese Girl*, 109, 116, 117, 164; Yone Noguchi, San Francisco, to Blanche Partington, San Francisco, 10 April 1899, CEL, no. 37.
87. Yone Noguchi, The Heights, Dimond, CA, to Charles Warren Stoddard, 26 August 1899, HM37916, Huntington MSS; Yone Noguchi, The Heights, Dimond, CA, to Charles Warren Stoddard. 11 September 1899, HM37917, Huntington MSS; Yone Noguchi, The Heights, Dimond, CA, to Charles Warren Stoddard, 15 January 1900, HM37918, Huntington MSS. For examples of less affectionate writing to Blanche as opposed to Charlie, see Yone Noguchi, Oakland, to Blanche Partington, 12 July 1899, CEL, no. 40; Yone Noguchi, The Heights, to Blanche Partington, 19 July 1899, CEL, no. 41; Yone Noguchi, The Heights, to Blanche Partington, 23 August 1899, CEL, no. 43; Yone Noguchi, The Heights to Blanche Partington, "First Tuesday" August 1899, CEL, no. 44; Yone Noguchi, San Francisco, to Blanche Partington, 25th [no month or year], CEL, no. 45; Yone Noguchi to Blanche Partington, 5 September 1899, CEL, no. 46. For additional similar letters from September through December 1899, see Yone Noguchi, The Heights, to Blanche Partington, 21 September 1899, CEL, no. 47; Yone Noguchi, Dimond, to Blanche Partington, 27 October 1899, CEL, no. 48; Yone Noguchi to Blanche Partington, 16th [1899?], CEL, no. 49; Yone Noguchi, The Heights, to Blanche Partington, [December 1899?], CEL, no. 50.
88. Bray, *Homosexuality in Renaissance England*; Sedgwick, *Between Men*, 1; Alan Sinfield, *The Wilde Century: Effeminacy, Oscar Wilde and the Queer Moment* (London: Cassell, 1994). Valerie Traub, "Friendship's Loss: Alan Bray's Making of History," *GLQ: Gay and Lesbian Quarterly* 10, no. 3 (2004): 339–365. The difference lies in part in the dissimilar source material used for female and male friendship studies. While scholarship on women tends to rely heavily on personal documents such as letters and diaries, publications on male homosociality extensively utilize court records—in addition to literature, poetry, and plays—that more explicitly reference sexual intercourse.
89. Charles Warren Stoddard, "Notes Wise, Unwise and Otherwise," 1900, Charles Warren Stoddard Papers, BANC MSS C-H 53, BSC.

Three: To the Bungalow and Beyond

1. Yone Noguchi, San Francisco, to Charles Warren Stoddard, 16 May 1900, HM37919, Huntington MSS.
2. Yone Noguchi, Chicago, to Charles Warren Stoddard, 11 June 1900, HM37922, Huntington MSS.
3. Yone Noguchi, *Story of Yone Noguchi Told by Himself*, 23.
4. Yone Noguchi, Avon, New York, to Blanche Partington, Oakland, CA, 17 August 1900, CEL, no. 58; Noguchi, *Story of Yone Noguchi Told by Himself*, 86.
5. Noguchi, *Story of Yone Noguchi Told by Himself*, 85, 89.
6. Yone Noguchi, Avon, New York, to Blanche Partington, Oakland, CA, 17 August 1900, CEL, no. 58.
7. Ibid. Recovered letters reveal that Yone asked Charlie for money at least twice during their relationship. Their affair, however, was likely not based on an exchange of money. Yone infrequently asked for financial support, and Charlie appeared to have little money to lavish on others. In the earlier request for money, Charlie remained unable to help Yone. In fact, Charlie frequently lived with friends since he often had no money even to pay the rent and he hated to work. Yone Noguchi, Brooklyn, NY, to Charles Warren Stoddard, Nahant, MA, 3 July 1900, CEL, no. 56.
8. Markham, A[nna] C[atherine], Brooklyn, NY, to [Blanche] Partington, 30 July 1900, Partington Family Papers, BANC MSS C-H 84, BSC; Noguchi Yonejirō, "Gojussai no shokan," *Yomiuri Shimbun*, 8 February 1926, p. 4; "Yone Noguchi, Avon, NY, to Blanche [Partington], 17 August 1900, Partington Family Papers, BANC MSS C-H 84, BSC; Yone Noguchi, Brooklyn, to Frank Putnam, 3? July 1900, Yone Noguchi Collection, BANC MSS 82/130, BSC.
9. Austen, *Genteel Pagan*, xxxviii, xxxix, 134, 135.
10. Yone Noguchi, Oakland, to Charles Warren Stoddard, 24 September 1900, Yone Noguchi Papers, BANC MSS 82/130, BSC.
11. Noguchi, "In the Bungalow with Charles Warren Stoddard," 306.
12. Ibid.
13. Noguchi Yonejirō, *Kichō no ki* (Tokyō: Shunyōdō, 1904), 62–63.
14. Masayo Duus, *The Life of Isamu Noguchi: Journey without Borders*, trans. Peter Duus (Princeton, NJ: Princeton University Press, 2004), 28.
15. Ethel's friend and colleague Anne Kendrick Walker conveyed Ethel's first impression of Yone in an article in the *Birmingham Age-Herald* in June 1905. C. M. Stanley, "An Alabama Romance and Its Painful End," *Montgomery Advertiser*, 2 July 1950.

16. CEL, 12. Atsumi likely made this conclusion from Yone's own writings. In a 1904 Japanese-language publication on his American stay, Yone described feeling certain he had been struck by love at that very moment. Noguchi, *Kichō no ki*, 62–63. I argue in Chapter 5 that Yone deliberately portrayed himself as heterosexual in his later Japanese writings to deflect attention from his earlier homoerotic publications.
17. Yone Noguchi, New York City, to Léonie Gilmour, 4 February 1901, CEL, no. 62.
18. CEL, 12; Elizabeth to Ethel Armes, n.d., Charles Warren Stoddard, BSC. Though always reported as Irish, Léonie Gilmour, was in fact Native American as well. Her great-grandmother was the daughter of a French fur trader and a Cherokee woman. Duus, *The Life of Isamu Noguchi*, 21–23.
19. Duus, *The Life of Isamu Noguchi*, 22–23.
20. Only two letters in July 1901 appeared more extensive. In one letter, Yone dedicated pages to asking for forgiveness over an editorial slight. He evidently had insulted Léonie by disagreeing with her criticisms. In an additional letter he extensively outlined his idea for a story he hoped to title "My American Wife." While both letters were notably longer and more substantive than any of his other letters, they nonetheless focused on Yone's writing rather than explicitly expressing any affection between the two. Yone Noguchi, New York City, to Léonie Gilmour, "Friday" July 1901, CEL, no. 84; Yone Noguchi, New York City, to Léonie Gilmour, [July 1901?], CEL, no. 85.
21. Yone Noguchi, New York City to Léonie Gilmour, 21 February 1901, CEL, no. 63; Yone Noguchi, New York City, to Léonie Gilmour, 4 March 1901, CEL, no. 67.
22. Yone Noguchi, New York City, to Léonie Gilmour, March or April 1901?, CEL, no. 68.
23. Yone Noguchi, Bayonne, NJ, to Léonie Gilmour, "Wednesday noon" 10 September 1901, CEL, no. 94.
24. Yone Noguchi, New York City, to Léonie Gilmour, 1901?, CEL, no. 70.
25. Yone Noguchi, New York City, to Léonie Gilmour, 31 May 1901, CEL, no. 82. For an additional example, see Yone Noguchi to Léonie Gilmour, 2 October 1901, CEL, no. 96.
26. For examples, see Yone Noguchi, New York City, to Léonie Gilmour, 4 March 1901, CEL, no. 67; Yone Noguchi, New York City, to Léonie Gilmour, March 1901?, CEL, no. 65; Yone Noguchi, New York City, to Léonie Gilmour, "Saturday" 1901?, CEL, no. 71; Yone Noguchi, New York City, to Léonie Gilmour, 2 April 1901, CEL, no. 73; Yone Noguchi, New York City to Léonie Gilmour, "Thursday" April or May 1901?, CEL, no.

75; Yone Noguchi, New York City, to Léonie Gilmour, 1901?, CEL, no. 80; Yone Noguchi, New York City, to Léonie Gilmour, July 1901?, CEL, no. 86; Yone Noguchi, Bayonne, NJ, to Léonie Gilmour, 22 October 1901, CEL, no. 99. Noguchi expert Ikuko Atsumi notes that correspondence between Yone and Léonie resembled an exchange between co-authors working on a publication rather than letters between lovers. Atsumi Ikuko, "Yone Noguchi kankei eibun shokan ni tsuite—eibei bungakusha tachi to no kōryū to josei," in *Shijin Yone Noguchi kenkyū*, vol. 3, ed. Toyama Usaburō (Tokyo: Zōkei Bijutsu Kyōkai Shuppanbō, 1975), 106.

27. Yone Noguchi, New York, to Charles Warren Stoddard, Island Heights, NJ, 23 July 1901, CEL, no. 88; Yone Noguchi, New York, to Charles Warren Stoddard, Island Heights, NJ, 26 July 1901, CEL, no. 90; Yone Noguchi, Bayonne, NJ, to Charles Warren Stoddard, Washington, DC, [postmark 7 October 1901], CEL, no. 97.
28. As he confided to Dewitt Miller, he expressed guilt about leaning on his friends during his time of emotional hardship. "Why do I say all this to you? Forgive me." Charles Warren Stoddard, Washington, DC, to Dewitt Miller, Philadelphia, 15 October 1901, HM38383, Huntington MSS.
29. "A Life's Labryinth, December 1901," Charles Warren Stoddard Papers, BANC MSS C-H 53, BSC.
30. Yone Noguchi, Washington, DC, to Frank Putnam, n.d., Yone Noguchi Papers, BANC MSS 82/130, BSC.
31. "A Life's Labryinth, December 1901," Charles Warren Stoddard Papers, BANC MSS C-H 53, BSC.
32. As noted in Chapter 1, Gelett Burgess wrote of Yone being "in love with sadness" in the introduction of Yone's book *Seen and Unseen*. Yone confessed to being married to the state of being sad. In 1900 Yone declared to Frank that he "could not live without" his "wife Melancholia." Yone Noguchi to Frank Putnam, June 1900, Yone Noguchi Papers, BANC MSS 82/130, BSC.
33. *Washington Post*, 5 January 1902, Keio Special Collections, Keio University, Tokyo, Japan (hereafter cited as KSC).
34. For Yone's complaints about his winter residency at the Bungalow, see Yone Noguchi, New York City, to Frank Putnam, n.d., Yone Noguchi Papers, BANC MSS 82/130, BSC; "A Life's Labryinth, December 1901," Charles Warren Stoddard Papers, BANC MSS C-H 53, BSC; Yone Noguchi, New York City, to Frank Putnam, n.d., Yone Noguchi Papers, BANC MSS 82/130, BSC.
35. Yone Noguchi, Bayonne, NJ, to Léonie Gilmour, 22 October 1901, CEL, no. 99.

36. Yone Noguchi to Charles Warren Stoddard, Washington, DC, (postmark 26 November 1901), CEL, no. 105.
37. CEL, 11. For the same conclusion in Japanese, see Atsumi, "Yone Noguchi kankei eibun shokan ni tsuite," 112.
38. Noguchi, *The Story of Yone Noguchi Told by Himself*, 32, 77.
39. In an intimate correspondence between two lovers, Charles Fecker wrote to Evaline Holt "dearest babe" and signed the letter "Papa." "Fecker in his True Light," *San Francisco Chronicle*, 7 September 1898, p. 5. This use of "Dad" and "kid" or "baby" as erotic signifiers resonates in twenty-first-century sexual cultures as well. See Peter L. Dancer, Peggy J. Kleinplatz, and Charles Moser, "24/7 SM Slavery," *Journal of Homosexuality* 50, 2/3 (2006): 83.
40. Judy Tzu-Chun Wu, *Doctor Mom Chung of the Fair-Haired Bastards: The Life of a Wartime Celebrity* (Berkeley and Los Angeles: University of California Press, 2005), 122.
41. Though Austen describes Stoddard's desires as "pedophilic," Stoddard in fact pursued young men in their late teens and early twenties. These men were more likely adults than children. Austen, *Genteel Pagan*, xxxv, xxxviii.
42. Charles Warren Stoddard, Monterey, CA, to Dewitt Miller, 14 January 1908, HM38410, Huntington MSS.
43. Charles Warren Stoddard, Monterey, CA, to Dewitt Miller, 21 April 1908, HM38412, Huntington MSS.
44. Yone Noguchi, Japan, to Charles Warren Stoddard, 27 January 1905, BSC; George Sterling, Oakland, to Charles Warren Stoddard, 14 March 1908, BSC; Austen, *Genteel Pagan*, xlvi, xlv, 142.
45. Charles Warren Stoddard, Washington, DC, to Yone Noguchi, London, England, 3 November 1902, CEL, no. 123.
46. Yone Noguchi, New York, to Charles Warren Stoddard, 1 November 1902, HM37940, Huntington MSS.
47. Ethel Armes, Birmingham, AL, to Alice Wiggins, Franklin, MA, 6 November 1902, Private collection of Gary Dobbs (hereafter cited as Dobbs Collection).
48. Ibid.
49. Charles Warren Stoddard, Washington, DC, to Yone Noguchi, New York City, 7 November 1902, CEL, no. 124. Notably, as Charlie discouraged Yone from marriage, he expressed no protest when Ethel informed him of her engagement to a man she elusively called "Bennie." Noting this discrepancy in Charlie's reaction toward Yone versus Ethel's engagement, Ethel wrote to Yone, "He loves you more." Ethel Armes to Yone Noguchi, Brixton, England, [postmark 22 December 1902], CEL, no. 127.

50. Ethel Armes, Birmingham, AL, to Alice Wiggins, Franklin, MA, 6 November 1902, Dobbs Collection.
51. Ethel Armes to Yone Noguchi, Brixton, England, [postmark 22 December 1902], CEL, no. 127; Ethel Armes, Birmingham, AL, to Alice Wiggins, Franklin, MA 6 November 1902, Dobbs Collection; Ethel Armes, Birmingham, AL, to Alice Wiggins, 6 June 1904, Dobbs Collection.
52. Regarding the move itself and how it relates to furthering his career, see Yone Noguchi, London, England, to Charles Warren Stoddard, 24 November 1902, HM37923, Huntington MSS; Yone Noguchi, London, England, to Léonie Gilmour, New York City, USA, 24 November 1902, CEL, no. 125; Yone Noguchi, London, England, to Léonie Gilmour, ? November 1902, CEL, no. 126.
53. Ethel Armes to Yone Noguchi, Brixton, England, [postmark 22 December 1902], CEL, no. 127.
54. Charles Warren Stoddard, Washington, DC, to Yone Noguchi, London, 28 January 1903, CEL, no. 152; Charles Warren Stoddard, Washington, DC, to Yone Noguchi, London, 31 January 1903, CEL, no. 154; Yone Noguchi, London, to Charles Warren Stoddard, Washington, DC, 3 February [1903?], CEL, no. 157.
55. Austen, *Genteel Pagan*, 144.
56. Ibid., 145.
57. Charles Warren Stoddard, Washington, DC, to Yone Noguchi, London, 28 January 1903, CEL, no. 152.
58. Billy Coombs was one individual whom Stoddard believed mistakenly married a woman. Charles Warren Stoddard, Monterey, CA, to Dewitt Miller, 11 December 1908, HM38417, Huntington MSS; Charles Warren Stoddard, Monterey, CA, to Dewitt Miller, 17 October 1908, HM38415, Huntington MSS.
59. Charles Warren Stoddard, Washington, DC, to Yone Noguchi, London, 31 January 1903, CEL, no. 154.
60. Charles Warren Stoddard, Washington, DC, to Yone Noguchi, London, 2 February 1903, CEL, no. 153.
61. Notably, Frank Putnam's letter of congratulations to Yone did not carry the same passion as Charlie's. On February 6, Putnam wrote in much more muted tones. "How pleased I am with your success in London—and how satisfying it is to reflect that success is deserved. You have a very fine and true poetic gift. Frank Putnam, Boston, to Yone Noguchi, 6 February 1903, CEL, no. 99.
62. Yone Noguchi to Léonie Gilmour, 2 February [1903], CEL, no. 156; Yone Noguchi, London, to Léonie Gilmour, 19 February 1903, CEL, no. 167;

Yone Noguchi, London, to Léonie Gilmour, 24 February 1903, CEL, no. 172; Yone Noguchi, London, to Léonie Gilmour, 5 March 1903, CEL, no. 174; Yone Noguchi, England, to Léonie Gilmour, 12 March 1903, CEL, no. 175; Yone Noguchi, London, to Léonie Gilmour, 19 February 1903, CEL, no. 167; Yone Noguchi, New York, to Léonie Gilmour, 19 April 1903, CEL, no. 185.

63. Yone Noguchi, London, to Charles Warren Stoddard, before April 1903, HM 37924, Huntington MSS.
64. Yone Noguchi, New York, to Charles Warren Stoddard, 16 July 1903. HM 37928, Huntington MSS. Charlie read Yone's letter with great distress to hear that friends, namely, William Denslow, depicted him as a lazy mooch. Stoddard defended himself, explaining that he had been called to his lonely friend's home in Cambridge to keep him company since he lived all alone with his mother and sister now passed away. Stoddard then proceeded to call Denslow a "plodder" who works "night and day." "All people can not do that," declared Stoddard. Charles Warren Stoddard, Cambridge, MA, to Yone Noguchi, New York City, 16 July 1903, CEL, no. 222.
65. Yone Noguchi, New York, to Charles Warren Stoddard, Boston, September 1903, HM 37934, Huntington MSS; Yone Noguchi to Charles Warren Stoddard, [1903?], HM 37925, Huntington MSS.
66. Yone Noguchi, East Milton, MA, to Charles Warren Stoddard, 4 April 1903, HM 37932, Huntington MSS; Yone Noguchi, Boston, to Charles Warren Stoddard, April 1903, HM 37933, Huntington MSS; Yone Noguchi, New York, to Charles Warren Stoddard, 11 July 1903, HM 37930, Huntington MSS; Yone Noguchi to Charles Warren Stoddard, 1903?, HM 37931, Huntington MSS; Yone Noguchi, East Milton, MA, to Charles Warren Stoddard, 1903?, HM37935, Huntington MSS; Yone Noguchi, New York, to Charles Warren Stoddard, 1903?, HM37936, Huntington MSS; Yone Noguchi, New York, to Charles Warren Stoddard, 1903?, HM37937, Huntington MSS; Yone Noguchi, East Milton, MA, to Charles Warren Stoddard, 1903?, HM37938, Huntington MSS; Yone Noguchi, London, to Charles Warren Stoddard, 20 March 1903, HM37939, Huntington MSS; Yone Noguchi, New York, to Charles Warren Stoddard, 18 October 1903, HM37941, Huntington MSS; Yone Noguchi, New York, to Charles Warren Stoddard, 26 September 1903, HM37942, Huntington MSS.
67. Charles Warren Stoddard, New York City, to Yone Noguchi, New York City, 18 April 1903, CEL, no. 184. While Charlie's letters more often expressed affection than Yone's notes, they too no longer carried intense longing as did his writing just two months earlier. For examples see Charles Warren Stoddard, New York City, to Yone Noguchi, New York City, 22 April 1903,

CEL, no. 188; Charles Warren Stoddard, New York City, to Yone Noguchi, New York City, 23 April 1903, CEL, no. 189; Charles Warren Stoddard, New York City, to Yone Noguchi, 25 April 1903, CEL, no. 191; Charles Warren Stoddard, Cambridge, MA, to Yone Noguchi, New York City, 13 June 1903, CEL, no. 207; Charles Warren Stoddard, New York City, to Yone Noguchi, New York City, 20 April 1903, CEL, no. 187; Charles Warren Stoddard, Nantucket, MA, to Yone Noguchi, New York City, 30 August 1903, CEL, no. 231.

68. Charles Warren Stoddard, Washington, DC, to Yone Noguchi, New York City, 2 April 1903, CEL, no. 180.
69. Charles Warren Stoddard, "The Resurrection and Life of Charles Warren Stoddard" [c. 1903], Charles Warren Stoddard Papers, BANC MSS C-H 53, BSC; Charles Warren Stoddard, New York City, to Yone Noguchi, New York City, 18 April 1903, CEL, no. 184.
70. Charles Warren Stoddard, New York City, to Yone Noguchi, New York City, 22 April 1903, CEL, no. 188; Charles Warren Stoddard, New York City, to Yone Noguchi, New York City, 23 April 1903, CEL, no. 189; Charles Warren Stoddard, New York City, to Yone Noguchi, 25 April 1903, CEL, no. 191; Richard le Galliene, New York City, to Yone Noguchi, New York City, [postmark 26 May 1903], CEL, no. 199; Edith Thomas, West New Brighton, Staten Island, to Yone Noguchi, New York City, 30 May [1903], CEL, no. 201; Edith Thomas, New York City, to Yone Noguchi, New York City, 2 June [1903], CEL, 202; Edith Thomas, New York City, to Yone Noguchi, New York City, [postmark 4 June 1903], CEL, no. 205.
71. Yone Noguchi, New York, to Léonie Gilmour, 24th [1903], CEL, no. 208.
72. Charles Warren Stoddard, Cambridge, MA, to Yone Noguchi, New York City, 8 July 1903, CEL, no. 219; Charles Warren Stoddard, Cambridge, MA, to Yone Noguchi, New York City, 14 July 1903, CEL, no. 221.
73. For Yone's dream of sleeping with Stoddard, see Yone Noguchi, New York, to Charles Warren Stoddard, Boston, September 1903, HM37934, Huntington MSS. For travel plans to visit Stoddard, see Charles Warren Stoddard, Cambridge, MA, to Yone Noguchi, New York City, 17 August 1903, CEL, no. 228; Charles Warren Stoddard, Cambridge, MA, to Yone Noguchi, New York City, 15 September 1903, CEL, no. 237; Yone Noguchi to Léonie Gilmour, 17 September [1903], CEL, no. 239.
74. Charles Warren Stoddard, Cambridge, MA, to Yone Noguchi, New York City, 20 August 1903, CEL, no. 229.
75. Yone Noguchi to [?], Tuesday morning [July 1903], CEL, no. 216.
76. Duus, *The Life of Isamu Noguchi*, 29, 30.

77. Yone Noguchi to Léonie Gilmour, 18 November 1903, CEL, no. 254; Yone Noguchi to Léonie Gilmour, 17 September [1903], CEL, no. 239.
78. Elizabeth to Ethel Armes, n.d., Charles Warren Stoddard Papers, BANC MSS C-H 53, BSC; Duus, *The Life of Isamu Noguchi*, 39.
79. For Léonie's statement on why she put weight on the note based on Yone's character, see Elizabeth to Ethel Armes, 23 March 1905, Charles Warren Stoddard Papers, BANC MSS C-H 53, BSC.
80. Noguchi, *The Story of Yone Noguchi Told by Himself*, 185.
81. Ethel Armes, Birmingham, AL, to Alice Wiggins, Franklin, MA, 22 December 1903, Dobbs Collection.
82. Ethel Armes, Birmingham, AL, to Alice Wiggins, Franklin, MA, 22 December 1903, Dobbs Collection; Ethel Armes to Yone Noguchi, Brixton, England, [postmark 22 December 1902], CEL, no. 127; Ethel Armes, Birmingham, AL, to Alice Wiggins, 6 June 1904, Dobbs Collection.
83. Yone Noguchi, New York, to Charles Warren Stoddard, Island Heights, NJ, (postmark 6 August 1901), CEL, no. 91; Yone Noguchi, Bayonne, NJ, to Charles Warren Stoddard, Washington, DC, [postmark 7 October 1901], CEL, no. 97; Yone Noguchi, New York City, to Léonie Gilmour, Friday afternoon [February or March 1901?], CEL, no. 64. For additional examples of Yone using "Jap," see Yone Noguchi, New York, to Charles Warren Stoddard, Island Heights, NJ, 23 July 1901, CEL, no. 88; Yone Noguchi, New York, to Charles Warren Stoddard, Island Heights, NJ, 26 July 1901, CEL, no. 90; Yone Noguchi to Léonie Gilmour, 23 May [1902?], CEL, no. 121.
84. Yone Noguchi to Charles Warren Stoddard, Washington, DC, [postmark 26 November 1901], CEL, no. 105; Yone Noguchi, New York City, to Léonie Gilmour, "Saturday" 1901?, CEL, no. 72; Yone Noguchi to Léonie Gilmour, 19th [February 1902?], CEL, no. 115.
85. Yone Noguchi to Léonie Gilmour, July 1901, CEL, no. 84. From Léonie's perspective, Yone's apology may have appeared absurdly condescending. To the Bryn Mawr graduate, Yone remained a high school graduate from the "Orient" who did not prove to be a particularly good student of the English language. Complimenting the college-educated, native-English speaker on her "little story" with "better" English and "delicious" writing may have proved less than convincing. What remained less transparent was his apparent insincerity in claiming that he "never" spoke well of others. In his letters to Charlie, Yone frequently gushed with compliments not just for Charlie, but also for Joaquin Miller, albeit to a lesser degree.
86. English author Richard le Gallienne noted Yone's Noguchi's use of "Japanese" in his pamphlets in a clipping pasted inside of the following book available at

the Bancroft Library Special Collections: Yone Noguchi, *From the Eastern Sea* (London: Unicorn Press, 1903).

87. Funk & Wagnalls Company, 44–60 e. 23rd st. nyc [publishing house], to Yone, [address unknown], 3 May 1901, CEL, no. 66; Helen Bridyman, Brooklyn, to Yone Noguchi, New York, 1 May 1904, CEL, no. 322.
88. Miss Morning Glory, *American Diary of a Japanese Girl*. For literary critics who interpreted Yone's *American Diary of a Japanese Girl* as a critique, see Yone Noguchi, *American Diary of a Japanese Girl, an Annotated Edition*, ed. Edward Marx and Laura E. Franey. For literary critics who interpreted Yone's *American Diary of a Japanese Girl* as complicit with existing Orientalist notions of Japan, see Cathryn Halverson, " 'Typical Tokio Smile': Bad American Books and Bewitching Japanese Girls," *Arizona Quarterly* 63, no. 1 (Spring 2007): 49–80.
89. Cathryn Halverson elaborates on how American writer Mary MacLane as well as Yone Noguchi capitalized on the "vogue for beautiful Japanese girls" at the turn of the century. Halverson, "'Typical Tokio Smile,'" 51.
90. Yone Noguchi, Bayonne, NJ, to Charles Warren Stoddard, Washington, DC, 5 November [1901], CEL, no. 100. For more on Noguchi's use of *American Diary of a Japanese Girl*, see Amy Sueyoshi, "Miss Morning Glory: Orientalism and Misogyny in the Queer Writings of Yone Noguchi," *Amerasia Journal—Special Issue: Further Desire* 37, no. 2 (2011): 2–27.
91. Theorist W. E. B. Dubois may have first articulated this phenomenon for people of color when he wrote of "double consciousness" among African Americans in the nineteenth century who lived in world that allowed them "no true self-consciousness" but rather an identity shaped by perceptions of others, namely, whites. Eric J. Sundquist, ed., *The Oxford W. E. B. Dubois Reader* (New York: Oxford University Press, 1996), 102.
92. Yone Noguchi, New York City, to Léonie Gilmour, 5 July [1903], CEL, no. 217. Anthropologist Aihwa Ong wrote of a similar phenomenon when she traced wealthy Chinese businessmen in the late-twentieth-century United States propagating "model minority" stereotypes such as hard-working and good-with-money to further their capitalist endeavors. She went as far as to call them "cocreators in Orientalism." Aihwa Ong, *Flexible Citizenship: The Cultural Logics of Transnationality* (Durham, NC: Duke University Press, 1999), 131.
93. For Miller writing diminutively about Japanese men, see Joaquin Miller and Yone Noguchi, *Japan of Sword and Love* (Tokyo: Kanao Bunyendo, 1905), 1, 3, 8–9, 23, 47. For Yone asserting Japan as an undeniable force of power, see pp. 4, 56–58.

94. Keiko Wada similarly wrote of how Yone deliberately used Japan to ride the tide of Japonisme. Wada Keiko, "Noguchi Yonejirō no Rondon: Japonizumu no arashi," *Ōsaka Gakuin Daigaku gaikokugo ronshū* 39 (March 1999): 56.

Four: Queer Intimacies

1. David Boyer suggests that it may have been common for closeted gay men and lesbian women unwittingly to accompany each other to their high school proms in the late twentieth century. Yone and Ethel might similarly be read as a pairing of two queers. David Boyer, *Kings and Queens: Queers at the Prom* (Brooklyn, NY: Soft Skull Press, 2004), 5.
2. Austen, *Genteel Pagan*, 153.
3. Yone Noguchi, New York, to Charles Warren Stoddard, 22 January 1904, HM37944, Huntington MSS; Yone Noguchi, New York, to Charles Warren Stoddard, 15 February 1904, HM37949, Huntington MSS.
4. Ethel Armes, Birmingham, AL, to Alice Wiggins, Franklin, MA, 22 December 1903, Dobbs Collection.
5. Ethel Armes, Birmingham, AL, to Alice Wiggins, 14 May 1904, Dobbs Collection; Yone Noguchi, New York, to Charles Warren Stoddard, 18 May 1904, HM37945, Huntington MSS; Ethel Armes, Birmingham, AL, to Alice Wiggins, 6 June 1904, Dobbs Collection.
6. Ethel Armes, Birmingham, AL, to Alice Wiggins, Franklin, MA, 8 June 1904, Dobbs Collection; Ethel Armes, Birmingham, AL, to Alice Wiggins, Franklin, MA, 28 June 1904, Dobbs Collection.
7. Ethel Armes, Birmingham, AL, to Alice Wiggins, Franklin, MA, 28 June 1904, Dobbs Collection.
8. For martial depictions of Japanese men in the early twentieth century, see Daniels, *Politics of Prejudice*. For late-twentieth-century imagery of the Asian male as emasculated, see David L. Eng, *Racial Castration: Managing Masculinity in Asian America* (Durham: Duke University Press, 2001).
9. Amy Sueyoshi, "Mindful Masquerades: Que(e)rying Japanese Immigrant Dress in Turn-of-the-Century San Francisco," *Frontiers: A Journal of Women Studies* 26, no. 3 (2005): 67–100. For a parallel commodification of Japanese femininity by white women on the east coast, see Mari Yoshihara, *Embracing the East: White Women and American Orientalism* (New York: Oxford University Press, 2003).
10. Hosley, *The Japan Idea*; Julia Meech and Gabriel P. Weisberg, *Japonisme Comes to America: The Japanese Impact on the Graphic Arts, 1876–1925* (New York: Harryn Abrams, 1990); Toshio Watanabe, *High Victorian Japonisme*

(New York: Peter Lang, 1991). For sources in Japanese, see Fukai Akiko, *Japonisumu in fasshion: umi o wattata kimono* (Tokyo: Heibonsha, 1994); Kodama Sanehide, *Amerika no Japonizumu* (Tokyo: Chūokōronsha, 1995); Wada, "Noguchi Yonejirō no Rondon: Japonizumu no arashi." See Louis Gonse, *L'Art Japonais* (London: Ganesha Publishing, 2003), for reportedly one of the earliest publications promoting Japonisme in the arts. Originally printed in 1883, Ganesha Publishing reprinted the work in 2003.

11. "Island Heights Notebook, 17 May 1904," BSC.
12. Yone Noguchi, Rochester, NY, to Léonie Gilmour, [February 1902?], CEL, no. 114
13. Yone Noguchi, Gilroy, CA, to Blanche Partington, 15 June 1899, CEL, no. 39.
14. A trip to the Cliff House may have been one of Markino's more traumatic experiences. As he settled down to paint, a group of ruffians descended upon him, tore his canvas, broke his paint-box, and hurled his brushes and paints into the ocean. Markino had saved for nearly four months for the materials. Feeling helpless, he could do nothing but weep in the spot for hours. He thought to himself that Japanese leaving their country would always be treated as an inferior race. As Markino traveled more broadly, he found that in London, Washington, DC, and New York, the "Japanese were not as much hated as in California." Yoshio Markino, *A Japanese Artist in London* (Philadelphia: George W. Jacobs and Company, 1910), 4–6, 72.
15. Miss Morning Glory, *The American Letters of a Japanese Parlor-Maid*, 185; Miss Morning Glory, *American Diary of a Japanese Girl*, 153.
16. Yone Noguchi, Rochester, to Léonie Gilmour, 25 March 1902, CEL, no. 118; [n.a.], [n.t.], [likely 1898?], Scrapbook of Yone Noguchi, KSC. Indeed, when Yone returned to Tokyo in 1904, his spirits took a significant turn for the better. Immediately after his homecoming he wrote: "I have been getting rid of the sad muses lately. I whistle into the air. I smile up to the sun." Noguchi, "In the Bungalow with Charles Warren Stoddard," 305.
17. Yone Noguchi to Charles Warren Stoddard, before August 1904, HM37950, Huntington MSS. Yone additionally reported to Blanche Partington on his "hard, honest experience" in America as a "young Oriental poet." Yone Noguchi to Blanche Partington, June 7th, CEL, no. 38.
18. Yone Noguchi, New York, to Charles Warren Stoddard, Island Heights, NJ, 23 July 1901, CEL, no. 88. Notably, his publisher disagreed. Yone eventually decided on a fellow Japanese, Genjiro Yeto, a "fine artist" who would do his book "justice." Yone Noguchi, New York City, to Léonie Gilmour, n.d., Isamu Noguchi Museum, Long Island City, NY (hereafter cited as Isamu Noguchi Museum). Critics who hated the text of Yone's *American Diary of a*

Japanese Girl had only compliments for the Genjiro Yeto illustrations. *News*, 8 December 1902; *Journal*, 26 October 1902, Scrapbook of Yone Noguchi, KSC.

19. "How foolishly Japanese look in brown skin and dreamy eyes! Brown itself is the color of melancholy and stupidity." Yone equated brownness with night and whiteness with day, elaborating that "white-skinned Americans" are "hard working, as the daytime is the time of work. The Orientals are the people of rest and dreams." Noguchi, *The Story of Yone Noguchi Told by Himself*, 90. Yone again articulated superiority of whiteness over brownness in a Japanese language publication five years later. Noguchi, *Eibei no jūsannen*, 60. For more on internalized racism among U.S. people of color, see bell hooks, *Killing Rage: Ending Racism* (New York: Henry Holt, 1995), 119–132.
20. Noguchi, *Eibei no jūsannen*, 87.
21. Yone Noguchi, Rochester, NY, to Léonie Gilmour, [February 1902?], CEL, no. 114; Yone Noguchi, Brooklyn, NY, to Charles Warren Stoddard, Nahant, MA, 3 July 1900, CEL, no. 56; Yone Noguchi, The Heights, Dimond, CA, to Charles Warren Stoddard, 15 January 1900, HM37918, Huntington MSS.
22. Yone Noguchi to Charles Warren Stoddard, Washington, DC, Spring 1900, CEL, no. 51.
23. Yone Noguchi, Rochester, NY, to Léonie Gilmour, [February 1902?], CEL, no. 14. Interestingly, Yone discovered that the man he assisted had in fact given Yone bread and meat a couple of years earlier when he tramped through California.
24. "It's me, it's me!"
25. Markino, *A Japanese Artist in London*, 71–74.
26. Kosen Takahashi, San Francisco, to Blanche Partington, 24 March 1899, CEL, no. 35; From Kosen Takahashi, San Francisco, to Blanche Partington, 29 March 1899, CEL, no. 36.
27. Daniel Quinn was renowned at the time as the greatest Greek scholar in America. Ethel Armes, Birmingham, AL, to Alice Wiggins, Franklin, MA, 22 December 1903.
28. Ethel Armes, Franklin, MA, to Alice Wiggins, Cambridge, MA, 25 January 1899, Dobbs Collection.
29. Ibid.
30. Ibid.
31. Ibid. Ethel would later solicit Alice to give her feedback on her writing. The two were literary colleagues as well. Ethel Armes, Birmingham, AL, to Alice Wiggins, 14 May 1904, Dobbs Collection; Ethel Armes, Birmingham, AL, to Alice Wiggins, 6 June 1904, Dobbs Collection.

32. Ethel Armes, Franklin, MA, to Alice Wiggins, Cambridge, MA, 25 January 1899, Dobbs Collection. In 1898 *Wasp*, a San Francisco satirical journal, reported on how kissing had become an epidemic. "Is an Osculatory Epidemic Probable?" *Wasp*, 13 August 1898, 5.
33. Ethel Armes, Franklin, MA, to Alice Wiggins, Cambridge, MA, 25 January 1899, Dobbs Collection.
34. Ethel Armes, Birmingham, AL, to Alice Wiggins, Franklin, MA, 22 December 1903, Dobbs Collection. Ethel and Alice appeared to have had an ongoing joke about their regional differences. In June 1910 Ethel suggested to Alice the "obliteration" of her "New England nasal sounds and pronunciation." Ethel Armes, Birmingham, AL, to Alice Wiggins, Franklin, MA, 14 June 1910, Dobbs Collection.
35. Ethel Armes, Birmingham, AL, to Alice Wiggins, Franklin, MA, 8 June 1904, Dobbs Collection.
36. Ethel Armes, Birmingham, AL, to Alice Wiggins, Franklin, MA, 6 November 1902, Dobbs Collection.
37. Ibid.
38. In this November letter, Ethel believed that all was now done with Yone. Ethel Armes, Birmingham, AL, to Alice Wiggins, Franklin, MA, 6 November 1902, Dobbs Collection.
39. Ibid.
40. Ann McGrath, "White Brides: Images of Marriage across Colonizing Boundaries," *Frontiers: A Journal of Women Studies* 23, no. 3 (2002): 76–108; Rayna Green, "The Pocahontas Perplex: The Image of Indian Women in American Culture," *Massachusetts Review* 16, no. 4 (1975): 698–714; Robert S. Tilton, *Pocahontas: The Evolution of an American Narrative* (New York: Cambridge University Press, 1994); Elias Boudinot, *An Address to Whites* (Philadelphia: Geddes, 1926). See also Ann McClintock, *Imperial Leather: Race, Gender, and Sexuality in the Colonial Contest* (New York: Routledge, 1995); Ann Laura Stoler, "Sexual Affronts and Racial Frontiers: European Identities and the Cultural Politics of Exclusion in Colonial Southeast Asia," in *Tensions of Empire: Colonial Cultures in a Bourgeois World*, ed. Frederick Cooper and Ann Laura Stoler (Berkeley: University of California Press, 1997), 198–237; Albert L. Hurtado, *Intimate Frontiers: Sex, Gender, and Culture in Old California* (Albuquerque: University of New Mexico Press, 1999); Martha Hodes, ed., *Sex, Love, Race: Crossing Boundaries in North American History* (New York: New York University Press, 1999).
41. Ethel Armes, Birmingham, AL, to Alice Wiggins, Franklin, MA, 6 November 1902, Dobbs Collection.

42. Ethel Armes, Birmingham, AL, to Alice Wiggins, Franklin, MA, 22 December 1903, Dobbs Collection.
43. Ethel Armes, Birmingham, AL, to Alice Wiggins, 6 June 1904, Dobbs Collection; Ethel Armes, Birmingham, AL, to Alice Wiggins, Franklin, MA, 8 June 1904, Dobbs Collection.
44. Ethel Armes, Franklin, MA, to Alice Wiggins, Cambridge, MA, 25 January 1899, Dobbs Collection.
45. For more than a few white women writers in late Victorian America, explicit same-sex desire appeared as a viable love different from heterosexuality and available for public discussion. Halverson, "'Typical Tokio Smile.'"
46. Ethel Armes, Birmingham, AL, to Alice Wiggins, Franklin, MA, 6 November 1902, Dobbs Collection. Though inclined more toward women, Ethel in the twenty-first century might have identified herself as a pansexual, an individual with potential for romantic or sexual attraction toward people regardless of their gender identity or biological sex. Jin Haritaworn, Chin-ju Lin, and Christian Klesse, "Poly/Logue: A Critical Introduction to Polyamory," *Sexualities* 9, 5 (2006): 515–529.
47. Ethel Armes, Birmingham, AL, to Alice Wiggins, Franklin, MA, 22 December 1903, Dobbs Collection.
48. Ethel Armes, Birmingham, AL, to Alice Wiggins, Franklin, MA, 6 November 1902, Dobbs Collection.
49. Ibid.
50. Charles Warren Stoddard to Yone Noguchi, 15 July 1904, CEL, no. 342.
51. Yone Noguchi, New York, to Charles Warren Stoddard, 4 June 1904, HM37947, Huntington MSS. Ironically, as Stoddard appeared to hold reservations about Ethel's character as an appropriate wife, Ethel had nothing but high praise for Stoddard and thought of him frequently. Yone Noguchi to Charles Warren Stoddard, 30 August 1904, HM 37954, Huntington MSS.
52. Yone Noguchi, New York, to Charles Warren Stoddard, 22 July 1904, HM37952, Huntington MSS; Yone Noguchi, New York, to Charles Warren Stoddard, 15 February 1904, HM 37949, Huntington MSS; Yone Noguchi, New York, to Charles Warren Stoddard, 11 May 1904, HM 37945, Huntington MSS; Yone Noguchi to Charles Warren Stoddard, before August 1904, HM 37950, Huntington MSS; Yone Noguchi, Dimond, CA, to Charles Warren Stoddard, August 1904, HM 37956, Huntington MSS.
53. Yone Noguchi, New York, to Charles Warren Stoddard, 4 June 1904, HM37947, Huntington MSS.
54. Yone Noguchi, New York, to Charles Warren Stoddard, 18 July 1904, HM37946, Huntington MSS.

55. Yone Noguchi, New York, to Charles Warren Stoddard, 18 July 1904, HM37946, Huntington MSS; Yone Noguchi, New York, to Charles Warren Stoddard, 22 July 1904, HM37952, Huntington MSS.
56. Charles Warren Stoddard, Cambridge, to Yone Noguchi, New York City, 28 July 1904, CEL, no. 350; Austen, *Genteel Pagan*, 157.
57. Yone Noguchi, Oakland, to Charles Warren Stoddard, August 1904, BSC; Yone Noguchi, New York, to Charles Warren Stoddard, 29th [1904?], CEL, no. 353.
58. Charles Warren Stoddard, Cambridge, MA, to Yone Noguchi, 1 August 1904, CEL, no. 356.
59. Coppa's first appears in the 1904 San Francisco city directory as "Coppa & Piantanida, restaurant," at 622 Montgomery. *Crocker Langley San Francisco Directory for the Year Commencing 1904* (San Francisco: H. S. Crocker Co., 1904).
60. Unna, *The Coppa Murals*, n.p. (photograph before page 1), 1–4, 8, 12–13.
61. Carmel writer Jimmy Hopper observed that "the pretty ones didn't have to write very much to get in." Unna, *The Coppa Murals*, 8–9. At the end of the evening, when Coppa's closed, bohemians walked down Merchant Street to the other end of Montgomery Street to a small French restaurant and bar. Ibid., 47.
62. Ina Coolbrith, San Francisco, to Blanche Partington, n.d. [prior to 1902], Partington Family Papers, BANC MSS C-H 84, BSC. Coolbrith faced many difficulties with the Bohemian Club men, including having her work plagiarized by Joaquin Miller. Ina Coolbrith to Blanche Partington, n.d., Partington Family Papers, BANC MSS C-H 84, BSC.
63. "Island Heights Notebook, 22 August 1904," Papers of Charles Warren Stoddard, BSC.
64. Yone Noguchi to Charles Warren Stoddard, Cambridge, MA, 1 August 1904, CEL, no. 356.
65. Charles Warren Stoddard, Cambridge, MA, to Yone Noguchi, 1 August 1904, CEL, no. 356.
66. Ethel Armes, Birmingham, AL, to Alice Wiggins, Franklin, MA, 28 June 1904, Dobbs Collection.
67. Ethel Armes, Birmingham, AL, to Alice Wiggins, Franklin, MA, 19 July 1904, Dobbs Collection.
68. Since they last saw each other, Ethel had quit her position with the *Washington Post* and returned to Birmingham to spend more time with her mother. Noguchi, *Kichō no ki*, 64–65.
69. As her father said grace, Anne's "mammy," the "perfect maid," served the delicacies. Anne recalled "my mammy" being "affrighted" with Yone and hold-

ing the waffles off almost beyond his reach. Ethel had described the Walkers as a "typical Southern family." C. M. Stanley, "An Alabama Romance and Its Painful End," *Montgomery Advertiser*, 2 July 1950. See also Noguchi, *Kichō no ki*, 64–65.

70. Historian Daniel Letwin describes Birmingham as the "Magic City," the industrial centerpiece of the New South by the turn of the century. Daniel Letwin, *The Challenge of Interracial Unionism: Alabama Coal Miners, 1878–1921* (Chapel Hill, NC: University of North Carolina Press, 1998), 3. For more on the New South, see Edward L. Ayers, *The Promise of the New South: Life after Reconstruction* (New York: Oxford University Press, 1992).
71. Jacquelyn Dowd Hall, "The Mind That Burns in Each Body: Women, Rape and Racial Violence," in *Powers of Desire: The Politics of Sexuality*, ed. Ann Snitow, Christine Stansell, and Sharon Thompson (New York: Monthly Review Press, 1983), 328–349; W. Fitzhugh Brundage, *Lynching in the New South: Georgia and Virginia, 1880–1930* (Urbana, IL: University of Illinois Press, 1993); Gail Bederman, *Manliness and Civilization: A Cultural History of Gender and Race in the United States, 1880–1917* (Chicago: University of Chicago, 1995).
72. For interracial unionism in Birmingham, see Letwin, *The Challenge of Interracial Unionism*, 3–4. See also Brian Kelly, *Race, Class and Power in the Alabama Coalfields, 1908–1921* (Urbana: University of Illinois Press, 2001). For the publication by Armes, see Ethel Armes, *The Story of Coal and Iron in Alabama* (New York: Arno Press, 1973). This work on the coalfields earned Armes the title Alabama's "first historian."
73. Letwin, *The Challenge of Interracial Unionism*, 149.
74. In the 1890s several hundred white miners received approval from the mine boss to take the day off to pursue and lynch an African American miner suspected of raping a white woman. Ibid., 31.
75. "Toleration" refers to historian Martha Hodes' distinction of "forebearance for that which is not approved" as opposed to "tolerance," which would indicate a "liberal spirit toward those of a different mind." Martha Hodes, *White Women, Black Men: Illicit Sex in the American South* (New Haven, CT: Yale University Press, 1997) 3.
76. Ida B. Wells Barnett may have been the first to point out that lynching was wholly political in "Lynching: Our National Crime," written in 1909. Mildred E. Thompson, *Ida B. Wells Barnett: An Exploratory Study of an American Black Woman, 1893–1930* (Brooklyn, NY: Carlson, 1990). See also Martha Hodes, "The Sexualization of Reconstruction Politics: White Women and Black Men in the South after the Civil War," *Journal of History of Sexuality* 3, no. 3 (January 1993): 402–417; Nell Irvin Painter, " 'Social

Equality,' Miscegenation, Labor, and Power, *The Evolution of Southern Culture,* ed. Numan Bartley (Athens, GA: University of Georgia Press, 1988), 47–67; Jacquelyn Dowd Hall, *Revolt against Chivalry: Jessie Daniel Ames and the Women's Campaign against Lynching* (New York: Columbia University Press, 1979).

77. Even when Asians in America clearly appeared not white, they were not necessarily considered Black either. Sociologist James Loewen notes that though Chinese in Mississippi in the nineteenth century were assigned a "near-Negro" position and had no more legal protection or political influence than Delta Blacks, neither African American nor whites quite thought of the Chinese as "Negroes." James Loewen, *The Mississippi Chinese: Between Black and White*, 2nd ed. (Prospect Heights, IL: Waveland Press, 1988), 60.
78. Alexander Saxton, *The Indispensable Enemy: Labor and the Anti-Chinese Movement in California* (Berkeley: University of California Press, 1971); Robert G. Lee, *Orientals: Asian Americans in Popular Culture* (Philadelphia: Temple University Press, 1999); Julie Novkov, "Racial Constructions: The Legal Regulation of Miscegenation in Alabama, 1890–1934," *Law and History Review* 20, no. 2 (Summer 2002): 225–277; Peggy Pascoe, "Miscegenation Law, Court Cases, and Ideologies of 'Race' in Twentieth Century America," *Journal of American History* 83 (1996): 44–69.
79. Historian Katherine Ellinghaus in her work on Native American men and white women in the United States in the early 1900s notes how male members of SAI, the Society of American Indians, who held occupations such as physicians, lawyers, and preachers, lived "within" rather than outside the margins of mainstream American society. Their solidly middle-class status allowed them to marry acceptably similarly educated white women on their road toward successful "assimilation." Katherine Ellinghaus, "Margins of Acceptability: Class, Education and Interracial Marriage in Australia and America," *Frontiers: A Journal of Women Studies* 3, no. 3 (2002): 55–75. See also Katherine Ellinghaus, *Taking Assimilation to Heart: Marriages of White Women and Indigenous Men in Australia and the United States, 1887–1937* (Lincoln: University of Nebraska Press, 2006).
80. Amy Sueyoshi, "Race-ing Sex," 240.
81. Noguchi, *Kichō no ki*, 68–69.
82. Ibid., 65. Though Ethel's mother, Lucy Hamilton Kerr, initially had "no real objection" to the marriage, some time after Yone's visit to the Armes home in Birmingham, she began to express reservations about the union. Yone hoped letters from Charlie to Ethel flattering him would eventually win over Lucy. Yone Noguchi to Charles Warren Stoddard, August 1904,

HM37957, Huntington MSS; Yone Noguchi, Tokyo, Japan, to Charles Warren Stoddard, 27 September 1904, HM37951, Huntington MSS; Yone Noguchi, Japan, to Charles Warren Stoddard, 10 October 1904, HM37953, Huntington MSS; Yone Noguchi, Tokyo, to Charles Warren Stoddard, 27 January 1905, CEL, no. 365.

83. Yone Noguchi, Birmingham, AL, to Charles Warren Stoddard, August 1904, HM37943, Huntington MSS.
84. Ethel added her own note to Stoddard. "Dearest Dad," she wrote, "this is just to send my love also.—We are happy! Ethel." Her addition no doubt burned rather than comforted Charlie as he continued to oppose their wedding. Yone Noguchi, Birmingham, AL, to Charles Warren Stoddard, August 1904, HM37943, Huntington MSS.
85. Yone wrote: "Ethel likes to have you say some lovely things about me so she can show your letters to her mother." "Can't you do that? Pray, make me happy, Dad! If we can persuade Ethel's mother, how happy we can be! I wish you will say in your letter to Ethel that I will make a very good husband and love her eternally and so forth." Yone Noguchi to Charles Warren Stoddard, August 1904, HM37957, Huntington MSS.
86. Ethel Armes, Birmingham, AL, to Alice Wiggins, Franklin, MA, 16 August 1904, Dobbs Collection.
87. Ethel Armes, Birmingham, AL, to Alice Wiggins, Franklin, MA, 10 November 1904, Dobbs Collection.
88. Ethel Armes, Birmingham, AL, to Alice Wiggins, Franklin, MA, 22 December 1903, Dobbs Collection.
89. Helen Ray Bierce, Redlands, CA, to Blanche Partington, 3 October 1894, Partington Family Papers, BANC MSS C-H 84, BSC. For additional affectionate letters from Helen to Blanche, though less ardently so, see Helen Ray Bierce, Redlands, CA, to Blanche Partington, 8 August 1894, Partington Family Papers, BANC MSS C-H 84, BSC; Helen Ray Bierce, Redlands, CA, to Blanche Partington, 3 January 1895, Partington Family Papers, BANC MSS C-H 84, BSC; Helen Ray Bierce, Redlands, CA, to Blanche Partington, 10 February 1895, Partington Family Papers, BANC MSS C-H 84, BSC. For the rumored affair between Ambrose Bierce and Blanche Partington, see James McWilliams, "Devil in the Details," *The Austin Chronicle*, 17 May 2002. Available online at http://www.austinchronicle.com/gyrobase/Issue/story?oid=oid%3A86557 (accessed 8 April 2010).
90. Charmian London, Oakland, to Blanche Partington, 8 March 1907, Partington Family Papers, BANC MSS C-H 84, BSC; Charmian London, Honolulu, to Blanche Partington, 10 July 1907, Partington Family Papers,

BANC MSS C-H 84, BSC; Charmian London, "about 700 miles from Marquesa," to Blanche Partington, 1 December 1907, Partington Family Papers, BANC MSS C-H 84, BSC; Charmian London, Glen Ellen, CA, to Blanche Partington, 3 September 1909, Partington Family Papers, BANC MSS C-H 84, BSC.

91. *Washington Post*, 5 January 1902, KSC; Austen, *Genteel Pagan*, 101.
92. Sociologist Mary C. Waters outlined a similar use of ethnic identity among middle-class white Americans in the 1980s as being largely symbolic and voluntary, mattering only when celebrating holidays with a "special twist," cooking a "special ethnic meal," or remembering a phrase or two in a foreign language. This flux and choice in using ethnic identity largely for purposes of leisure parallels how whites awash in privilege such as turn-of-the-century bohemians could appropriate other people's race or ethnicity to enliven their personal lives. Mary C. Waters, *Ethnic Options: Choosing Identities in America* (Berkeley: University of California Press, 1990), 147.
93. Yone Noguchi to Frank Putnam, n.d., Yone Noguchi Collection, BANC MSS 82/130, BSC.
94. For Yone's voyage out of San Francisco harbor, see Noguchi, *Kichō no ki*, 5–6. For Yone's sentiments about the future of his romantic and professional life, see Yone Noguchi to Charles Warren Stoddard, 27 September 1904, HM 37951, Huntington MSS.
95. Yone Noguchi to Charles Warren Stoddard, August 1904, HM37955, Huntington MSS. So insistently would Yone repeatedly declare his love for Ethel that at times he appeared as though he were trying to convince himself of his love for her. Yone Noguchi, Japan, to Charles Warren Stoddard, 10 October 1904, HM37953, Huntington MSS; Yone Noguchi, Tokyo, to Charles Warren Stoddard, 27 January 1905, CEL, no. 365.
96. Yone Noguchi to Charles Warren Stoddard, 30 August 1904, HM 37954, Huntington MSS. Yone would reiterate his "love" for Ethel subsequently in additional letters.

Five: Double Crossings

1. Yone Noguchi, Tokyo, Japan, to Charles Warren Stoddard, 27 September 1904, HM37951, Huntington MSS; Yone Noguchi, Japan, to Charles Warren Stoddard, 10 October 1904, HM37953, Huntington MSS.
2. Historian Frank Dikötter similarly notes how shifting ideas of sexuality in China came about through the emergence of a "plurality of intertwined modernities" from both the East and the West. Frank Dikötter, *Sex, Culture, and Modernity in China* (Honolulu: University of Hawai'i Press, 1995).

3. Noguchi, *Kichō no ki*, 81–82. For a description of his homecoming in English see Noguchi, *The Story of Yone Noguchi Told by Himself*, 166–169.
4. Noguchi, *Kichō no ki*, 82–84, 115–116. For details in English of his welcome, see Noguchi, *The Story of Yone Noguchi Told by Himself*, 182–183.
5. Léonie Gilmour, Los Angeles, to Catherine Burnell, 30 October 1904, Special Collections, Isamu Noguchi Museum.
6. Duus, *The Life of Isamu Noguchi*, 33–35.
7. Léonie Gilmour, Los Angeles, to Catherine Burnell, 30 October 1904, Isamu Noguchi Museum.
8. Ibid.
9. Léonie Gilmour to Catherine Burnell, n.d., Isamu Noguchi Museum; Léonie Gilmour, New York City, to Catherine Burnell, Stratford, CT, 20 November 1900, Isamu Noguchi Museum; Léonie Gilmour to Catherine Burnell, Stratford, CT, 4 May 1900, Isamu Noguchi Museum; Léonie Gilmour to Catherine Burnell, Stratford, CT, 25 April 1900, Isamu Noguchi Museum; Léonie Gilmour, Los Angeles, to Catherine Burnell, 30 October 1904, Isamu Noguchi Museum.
10. Léonie Gilmour to Catherine Burnell, Stratford, CT, 14 September 1902, Isamu Noguchi Museum; Léonie Gilmour, Los Angeles, to Catherine Burnell, 30 October 1904, Isamu Noguchi Museum.
11. Historian Carroll Smith-Rosenberg made a similar argument when she pointed to how middle-class white women found great comfort and support with other women in their lives such as relatives and friends. Carroll Smith-Rosenberg, "Female World of Love and Ritual: Relations between Women in Nineteenth-Century America," *Signs* 1, no.1 (1975): 1–29.
12. In October 1905 Léonie appeared to have named the baby Yosemite, yet Yone disapproved of the name and promised to send a "good name" soon after additional "pondering." Léonie Gilmour, Los Angeles, to Catherine Burnell, 4 October 1905, Isamu Noguchi Museum.
13. Duus, *The Life of Isamu Noguchi*, 36.
14. Elizabeth to Ethel Armes, n.d., Charles Warren Stoddard Papers, BANC MSS C-H 53, BSC.
15. D'Emilio and Freedman, *Intimate Matters*.
16. Elizabeth to Ethel Armes, n.d., Charles Warren Stoddard Papers, BANC MSS C-H 53, BSC. He confessed in his autobiography that he largely ignored the baby's existence until he met him for the first time when he was two years old. Noguchi, *The Story of Yone Noguchi Told by Himself*, 186.
17. Yone Noguchi, Tokyo, to Gustav Stickley, Syracuse, 25 December 1904, CEL, no. 363; Yone Noguchi, Tokyo, to Mr. Lemies, Philadelphia, 29

December 1905, CEL, no. 364; Yone Noguchi to Léonie Gilmour, 6 April 1905, CEL, no. 366.

18. Duus, *The Life of Isamu Noguchi*, 36; Léonie Gilmour to Catherine Burnell, 1 January 1905, Isamu Noguchi Museum.
19. Yone Noguchi, Tokyo, to Charles Warren Stoddard, 27 January 1905, CEL, no. 365. In 1905 Stoddard's life slowed considerably owing to bouts of grippe and inflammatory rheumatism. What doctors would later diagnose as heart disease no doubt had been affecting his health as well. Austen, *Genteel Pagan*, 163, 167.
20. Yone Noguchi, Tokyo, to Charles Warren Stoddard, 27 January 1905, CEL, no. 365.
21. Noguchi, "In the Bungalow with Charles Warren Stoddard," 305.
22. Yone additionally reprimanded readers for not appreciating the "genius" Stoddard's "lovely" writing, a remarkable "breeze" with an indescribable "scent." Ibid., 306–307.
23. Noguchi, *Seen and Unseen*; Noguchi, *The Voice of the Valley*.
24. Yone may have begun considering remaking his sexual persona as early as 1903, when he published *From the Eastern Sea*, in which several poems articulating desire for women appear. Out of forty-six poems total, five explicitly articulated desire for a woman. Fourteen expressed Yone's desire more ambiguously. For the five poems see Yone Noguchi, *From the Eastern Sea*, 4th ed. (Tokyo: Fuzanbō, 1905), 12–13, 21–26, 28–30, 38, 68. Justifiably some might interpret this collection of poetry as well as his relationships with men and women as evidence of Yone's bisexuality. However, as a historian influenced by queer theory, I am more interested in investigating why things change over time than in presuming that the sum of one's life makes evident an established static identity, sexual or otherwise.
25. Noguchi, "In the Bungalow with Charles Warren Stoddard," 307.
26. Elizabeth to Ethel Armes, 23 March 1905, Charles Warren Stoddard Papers, BANC MSS C-H 53, BSC; Léonie Gilmour, Los Angeles, to Catherine Burnell, 4 October 1905, Isamu Noguchi Museum.
27. Thomas Walsh recounted the demise of Yone's nuptial plans to Stoddard as heard from the wife of Edwin Markham. Thomas Walsh, Mount Arlington, VA, to Charles Warren Stoddard, 23 August 1905, HM38509, Huntington MSS.
28. Yone Noguchi, Tokyo, Japan, to Frank Putnam, February 1903 or 1904, Yone Noguchi Letters, BANC MSS 82/130, BSC; Yone Noguchi, Tokyo, Japan, to Frank Putnam, 10 October 1904, Yone Noguchi Letters, BANC MSS 82/130, BSC; Yone Noguchi, Tokyo, Japan, to Frank Putnam, 27 January 1905, Yone Noguchi Letters, BANC MSS 82/130, BSC.

29. Elizabeth to Ethel Armes, 23 March 1905, Charles Warren Stoddard Papers, BANC MSS C-H 53, BSC; Elizabeth to Ethel Armes, n.d., Charles Warren Stoddard Papers, BANC MSS C-H 53, BSC.
30. Ethel Armes, Birmingham, AL, to Alice Wiggins, Franklin, MA, 12 June 1905, Dobbs Collection.
31. Yone Noguchi, Tokyo, to Charles Warren Stoddard, 25 April 1905, CEL, no. 367.
32. In a brief postscript he added, "Léonie, if you could come without feeling any trouble and pain, come to Japan. If Japan will not suit you and baby, in a year or so you can go back." Yone Noguchi to Léonie Gilmour, 6 April 1905, CEL, no. 366.
33. Yone Noguchi, Tokyo, to Léonie Gilmour, 28 January 1906, CEL, no. 371.
34. Ethel Armes, Birmingham, AL, to Alice Wiggins, Franklin, MA, 16 July 1905, Dobbs Collection.
35. C. M. Stanley, "An Alabama Romance and Its Painful End," *Montgomery Advertiser*, 2 July 1950.
36. Ethel Armes, Birmingham, AL, to Alice Wiggins, Franklin, MA, 31 October 1906 (postmarked), Dobbs Collection.
37. Ethel Armes, Birmingham, AL, to Alice Wiggins, Franklin, MA, 1 July 1911, Dobbs Collection.
38. Of the twenty-four recovered letters between Alice and Ethel that followed through 1914, none demonstrated the remarkable affection from the earlier period. For examples see Ethel Armes, Boston, MA, to Alice Wiggins, Franklin, MA, ? November 1905, Dobbs Collection; Ethel Armes, Boston, MA, to Alice Wiggins, Franklin, MA, 19 November 1905, Dobbs Collection; Ethel Armes, Birmingham, AL, to Alice Wiggins, Franklin, MA, 9 July 1906 [1906 on the postmark, 1905 written in letter], Dobbs Collection; Ethel Armes, Birmingham, AL, to Alice Wiggins, Franklin, MA, 31 October 1906 [postmarked], Dobbs Collection; Ethel Armes, Birmingham, AL, to Alice Wiggins, Franklin, MA, 12 April 1907, Dobbs Collection; Ethel Armes, Birmingham, AL, to Alice Wiggins, Franklin, MA, 6 September 1909, Dobbs Collection.
39. Ethel Armes, Birmingham, AL, to Alice Wiggins, Franklin, MA, 3 October 1905, Dobbs Collection. For more affectionate letters see Ethel Armes, Boston, MA, to Alice Wiggins, Franklin, MA, 17 October 1905, Dobbs Collection; Ethel Armes, Boston, MA, to Alice Wiggins, Franklin, MA, 9 November 1905, Dobbs Collection.
40. Ethel Armes, Birmingham, AL, to Alice Wiggins, Franklin, MA, 16 November 1907, Dobbs Collection.

41. Ethel Armes, Birmingham, AL, to Alice Wiggins, Franklin, MA, 19 December 1907, Dobbs Collection.
42. Five recovered letters from Alice to her mother and her sister Annie in 1910 exhibited little if no affection. These letters not only vary drastically from the ones Ethel wrote to Alice but also from Smith-Rosenberg's observation that mothers and daughters, and sisters wrote letters of affection and intimacy to one another. Alice did not express the sort of familial intimacy that may have seemed normal during this time period. For letters to Alice's mother, see Alice Wiggins, Venice, Italy, to G. W. Wiggins, Franklin, MA, 24 June 1910, Dobbs Collection; Alice Wiggins, Rome, Italy, to G. W. Wiggins, Franklin, MA, 3 August 1910, Dobbs Collection. For letters to Alice's sister, see Alice Wiggins, U.S.M.S. St. Paul, to A. H. Wiggins, Franklin, MA, "Sunday" n.d., around 2 July 1910, Dobbs Collection; Alice Wiggins, Naples, Italy, to A. H. Wiggins, Franklin, MA, 11 August 1910, Dobbs Collection; Alice Wiggins, Florence, Italy, to A. H. Wiggins, Franklin, MA, 29 July 1910, Dobbs Collection.
43. Yone Noguchi to Charles Warren Stoddard, 20 October 1905, CEL, no. 370.
44. Ibid.
45. In lengthy passages, Charlie revealed a contested masculinity as well as a vague sexuality in his protagonist Paul. Relationships with Foxlair and Roscius, two men whom Paul befriended, held homoerotic qualities. The one woman who became close to Paul lacked "woman[ly]" traits, taking on a male persona as "Jack." Their intense intimacy heightened around the fact that "Jack" was so unlike a woman. Charles Warren Stoddard, *For the Pleasure of His Company: An Affair of the Misty City* (San Francisco: A. M. Robertson, 1903). For more on Charles Warren Stoddard's life and works, see Austen, *Genteel Pagan*.
46. Yone Noguchi to Charles Warren Stoddard, 20 October 1905, CEL, no. 370.
47. Yonejirō Noguchi, "Jyūrokunen ato no kyōri," *Yomiuri Shimbun*, 30 October 1904, p. 1.
48. Noguchi, *Kichō no ki*, 62.
49. Ibid., 10.
50. Ibid., 32–33. For Poe's original poem see Edgar Allen Poe, *The Works of Edgar Allan Poe in One Volume: Tales and Poems* (Roslyn, NY: Black's Readers Service, 1971), 12.
51. Noguchi, *Kichō no ki*, 11–12, 20.
52. Ibid., 57.

53. Ibid., 62.
54. Ibid., 68–69.
55. While Japanese scholars have connected Yone's references to Annabel with Ethel, Annabel may more likely have been Léonie. As Yone recounted the letters from Annabel, the letters carried the more serious and straightforward tone of Léonie's writing rather than the relatively flirtatious and circuitous writing style of Ethel. Moreover, Annabel appears to have personally tasted Yone's affection only to find him emotionally unavailable for a committed relationship. As she grasped at his love, a "faint shadow" difficult to hold, she realized the futility of her actions, as if building a castle each day that would always self-destruct at the end of the day. Yone also teased Annabel that she appeared to be at least 110 years old. These two characterizations aptly depict Léonie's relationship with Yone. In fact, it would make little literary sense for Yone to create a pseudonym for Ethel when he recounts his love for her explicitly later in his book. Annabel likely pointed to Léonie, burned by Yone and with his child, well aware of his personality flaws and quick to point them out with little reserve as evidenced in her recovered letters to Yone. For Noguchi experts such as Atsumi who have asserted that Annabel Lee was in fact Ethel, see Atsumi Ikuko, "Yone Noguchi 'Waga Ananberu Li' Eseru Āmusu ni tsuite," *Ippan kyōiku bukai ronshu* 17 (1996): 87.
56. *Yomiuri Shimbun*, 13 November 1904, p. 1.
57. Miller and Noguchi, *Japan of Sword and Love*, 25–26. For additional examples see pages 27 and 35.
58. Instead Yone chose to profile Father Damien's work on Molokai treating individuals afflicted with Hansen's disease and only briefly mentioned Stoddard along with Stevenson as writers who introduced Damien's great achievement to the world. Ibid., 35. Stoddard's book titled *The Lepers of Molokai* is noted as the critical work that brought public attention to Father Damien's work. So famous is Stoddard's work on Father Damien that the National Park Service chose to open their web page on Father Damien with a quotation from the western writer. See http://www.newadvent.org/cathen/14298b.htm, http://www.answers.com/topic/charles-warren-stoddard, and http://www.nps.gov/kala/docs/damien.htm (accessed 1 July 2005).
59. Yonejirō Noguchi, "Shijin Mirā Rōbo o kokusu," *Yomiuri Shimbun*, 22 April 1906, p. 2; Yonejirō Noguchi, "Shijin Hoittoman," *Yomiuri Shimbun*, 17 March 1907, p. 3.
60. The longest string of sentences on Stoddard appear in a single paragraph that precedes Yone's reprinted "In the Bungalow with Charles Warren Stoddard." Noguchi, *Eibei no jūsannen*, 187.

61. Moreover, in his English-language essay on Edwin Markham, he expressed additional delight in his physical affection with another man. Yone wrote, "What a tender largeness in his heart? I felt a happy sensation from his hand—what a warm hand with sure grasp!—the sensation of meeting the dove-eyed Truth running through his blood. I was glad to leave my hand buried in his safe hand." Ibid., 157.
62. Noguchi, *The Story of Yone Noguchi Told by Himself*, 10.
63. Ibid., 23.
64. Ibid., 27–28.
65. Ibid. On his trek to Southern California as well, he encountered a "Spanish" town full of beautiful girls in San Luis Obispo. They held a "sweet atmosphere which only belongs to a Latin race." According to Yone, the women sat on balconies and sang serenades, and when he appealed to one household for assistance with his hunger and tired feet, they stopped their singing and rushed into the kitchen to cook something especially for him. Yone remarked, "How those young girls with such large black eyes and olive-skinned oval faces, sympathized with me when I told them I had walked so many miles that day!" Ibid., 53.
66. Ibid., 86.
67. Yone admired the blue eyes of the men of San Francisco as well as the women and perceived them to be more "handsome" than the men in Chicago. He declared, "Chicago boys are not handsome enough to stand exposing their vain faces with the air of the perfectly superior lady killer." Ibid., 89, 108.
68. Ibid., 85.
69. Ibid., 89, 245–247.
70. Michael S. Foldy, *The Trials of Oscar Wilde: Deviance, Morality, and Late-Victorian Society* (New Haven, CT: Yale University Press, 1997).
71. Yonejirō Noguchi, "Osukā Wairudo," *Yomiuri Shimbun*, 4 October 1908; Yonejirō Noguchi, "Osukā Wairudo," *Yomiuri Shimbun*, 11 October 1908.
72. Tsuneo Watanabe and Jun'ichi Iwata, *The Love of the Samurai: A Thousand Years of Japanese Homosexuality*, trans. D. R. Roberts (London: GMP Publishers Ltd., 1989); Paul Gordon Schalow, "Kūkai and the Tradition of Male Love in Japanese Buddhism," in *Buddhism, Sexuality, and Gender*, ed. José Ignacio Cabezón (Albany, NY: State University of New York Press, 1992), 215–230; Bernard Fauvre, *The Red Thread: Buddhist Approaches to Sexuality* (Princeton, NJ: Princeton University Press, 1998); Pflugfelder, *Cartographies of Desire*. See also Mark J. McLelland, *Male Homosexuality in Modern Japan: Cultural Myths and Social Realities* (Richmond, Surrey: Curzon Press, 2000). In Japanese see Ujie Mikito, *Bushidō to erosu* (Tokyo: Kōdansha, 1995); Komine Shigeyuki and Minami Takao, *Dōseiai to dōseishinjū no kenkyū*

(Tokyo: Komine Kenkyūjo, 1985); Iwata Jun'ichi, *Honchō danshokukō: danshoku bunken shoshi* (Tokyo: Hara Shobō, 2002).

73. Inazo Nitobe, *Bushido: The Soul of Japan* (Rutland, VT: Charles E. Tuttle Company, 1969).
74. *Bushido* was widely read in both the United States and Europe. Theodore Roosevelt reportedly bought sixty copies to distribute to friends and family. John F. Howes, ed., *Nitobe Inazō: Japan's Bridge across the Pacific* (Boulder: Westview Press, 1995); F. G. Notehelfer, "Review of Nitobe Inazō, ed., John F. Howes," *Journal of Japanese Studies* 22, no. 2 (1996): 450–453. Writer and Congregational preacher William Elliot Griffis declared in the introduction that *Bushido* served as a notable contribution to solving "this century's grandest problem—the reconciliation and unity of the east and west." Nitobe, *Bushido*, xxi. Within five years of *Bushido*'s publication date, Charmian London, Blanche Partington, and Léonie Gilmour had all read Nitobe's "wonderful" and "precious" publication. Léonie Gilmour, Pasadena, CA, to Yone Noguchi, 24 February 1906, Isamu Noguchi Museum; Charmian London, Glen Ellen, CA, to Blanche Partington, 15 February 1910, Partington Family Papers, BANC MSS C-H 84, BSC.
75. McLelland, *Male Homosexuality in Modern Japan*, 27.
76. Matsuzawa Goichi, *Ero no hon* (Tokyo: Wani no Ana, 1997).
77. Pflugfelder explains the increasing restrictions to be a result of a combination of "Confucian propriety" and "Victorian prudery." Pflugfleder, *Cartographies of Desire*, 147.
78. Ibid., 285.
79. For examples of more or less neutral if not positive articles, see "Chūgi budō harimaishi," *Yomiuri Shimbun*, 21 April 1891; "Nanshoku taiheiki," *Yomiuri Shimbun*, 15 May 1891; "Nanshoku taiheiki," *Yomiuri Shimbun*, 17 May 1891; and "Koan ban," *Yomiuri Shimbun*, 29 July 1894. For examples of negative articles, see "Chidorigabuchi kōen no bussō," *Yomiuri Shimbun*, 21 October 1898; "Inazumagidan no kenkyo," *Yomiuri Shimbun*, 3 September 1909; and "Jūdō dōjō no himitsu," *Yomiuri Shimbun*, 31 December 1909.
80. Articles on these tragic same-sex affairs, or *doseiai*, appeared through the 1930s. For examples see "Horaana ni sumu akkan," *Yomiuri Shimbun*, 13 June 1912, 3; "Shibusawadan o uttō," 6 September 1913, 3; "Kangokunai hitogoroshi," 6 May 1914, 7, "Dōsei no koi," *Yomiuri Shimbun*, 8 July 1914, 7; "Futari ga shihogama de shinjū," *Yomiuri Shimbun*, 29 January 1921, 5; "Dakiai shinjū," 26 November 1927, 7; "Ichimoku seken," *Yomiuri Shimbun*, 16 May 1929, 7; "Onnanashi no chō eroguro jigoku," *Yomiuri Shimbun*, 23 November 1933, 2; "Nishōnen tsuredatte shino iede," *Yomiuri Shimbun*, 12

March 1934, 7; "Yadode Dōseiai Shinjū," 30 May 1934; "Onnadōshi no sankaku renai," *Yomiuri Shimbun*, 13 June 1934; "Kaiki! shi no seiyaku," *Yomiuri Shimbun*, 23 February 1937; "Shiei basu onna shashō ga dousei shinjū," *Yomiuri Shimbun*, 4 Aprl 1937, 1 "Atooi shinju," *Yomiuri Shimbun*, 19 May 1937, 7; "Hentai jyokyū fukudoku," *Yomiuri Shimbun*, 10 January 1938, 2.

81. "Wairudo no bohi," *Yomiuri Shimbun*, 27 September 1912, 5.
82. Yasusaburo Sakaki, "Byōteki na ai," *Yomiuri Shimbun*, 21 August 1915, 4.
83. Yone Noguchi, "Gaka Biajiri," *Yomiuri Shimbun*, 16 April 1915, 6.
84. Scholars have long debated Yone's reason for leaving the United States. While some Noguchi experts have speculated it was his inability to marry Léonie because of California state antimiscegenation laws, others have described him as leaving to assist in Japan's war effort. One other scholar noted his departure as a deliberate escape from a pregnant Léonie. Duus, *The Life of Isamu Noguchi*, 39. Yone, in his own writing, however, appears to suggest that he had realized the limits of his literary success in America.
85. Noguchi, *Kichō no ki*, 1–2, 56.
86. Duus, *The Life of Isamu Noguchi*, 37.
87. Denbei Noguchi to Yone Noguchi, n.d., Yone Noguchi Scrapbook, Keio Special Collections.
88. Robert Maeda, "Isamu Noguchi and the Peking Drawing of 1930," *American Art* 13, no. 1 (Spring 1999): 84–93.
89. Yone wrote, "I am going to make out some short stories,—regular Japanese short stories, you know." "Don't Los Angeles papers pay for articles? If they do, I like to write a regular Japanese letter for them." Yone Noguchi, Tokyo, to Léonie Gilmour, 5 May 1906, CEL, no. 379.
90. I used the eleven selections of prose that Noguchi scholar Yoshinobu Hakutani deemed significant in his collected English writings of Yone Noguchi and counted seven works within those that blatantly played to images of exotic Japan both in its culture and its people. For examples see *The Spirit of Japanese Poetry* (London: John Murray, 1914); "What Is a Hokku Poem?" *Rhythm* 11 (January 1913): 354–359; "The Everlasting Sorrow: A Japanese Noh Play," *Egoist* 4 (1917): 141–42; "The Japanese Noh Play," *Egoist* 5, (1918): 99: *Through the Torii* (Boston: Four Seas, 1914); *The Spirit of Japanese Art* (New York: E. P. Dutton, 1915); *The Story of Yone Noguchi Told by Himself* (London: Chatto and Windus, 1914). For Hakutani's collection see Yoshinobu Hakutani, ed., *Selected English Writings of Yone Noguchi*, vol. 2: *An East-West Literary Assimilation* (Rutherford: Fairleigh Dickinson University Press, 1990).
91. Noguchi, *The Story of Yone Noguchi Told by Himself*, 12.

92. Noguchi, *Seen and Unseen*, n.p. In later submissions from Japan to *The Nation* as well, he unabashedly highlighted his Japanese ethnicity in a way that he never would have done in 1896. In a 1911 letter to the editor condemning anti-Japanese propaganda that depicted the country as attempting to take over the world, Yone underscored that Japan did successfully fight Russia with "two or three rice balls apiece and a few slices of pickled radishes." Moreover, for his 1915 essay on Robert Bridges Yone chose the title "A Japanese Impression of the Poet Laureate." He titled another letter to the editor in the same year "A Japanese Scholar on Western Civilization." Yone purposefully evoked Japan—an act he had loathed previously. Yone Noguchi, "The Pacific Ocean Associations," *The Nation* 93, no. 2407 (7 August 1911): 141; Yone Noguchi, "Robert Bridges: A Japanese Impression of the Poet Laureate," *The Nation* 101, no. 2624 (14 October 1915): 465–466; Yone Noguchi, "A Japanese Scholar on Western Civilization," *The Nation* 101, no. 2613 (29 July 1915): 145.
93. Yone Noguchi, Tokyo, to Léonie Gilmour, 28 January 1906, CEL, no. 371.
94. Ibid.; Yone Noguchi to Léonie Gilmour, 10 February 1906, CEL, no. 372; Yone Noguchi, Tokyo, to Léonie Gilmour, 28 January 1906, CEL, no. 371; Yone Noguchi, Tokyo, to Léonie Gilmour, n.d. [April, 1906?], CEL, no. 375.
95. Yone Noguchi, Tokyo, to Léonie Gilmour, 28 January 1906, CEL, no. 371.
96. Yone Noguchi to Léonie Gilmour, 10 February 1906, CEL, no. 372.
97. Nobuo Shiga, "Noguchi Yonejirō to Isamu Noguchi: futari no nijūkokusekisha," *Kaigai ijō* 592, (March 2000): 22. Yone and Matsuko together would have seven children. Yoshinobu Hakutani, "Noguchi, Yone," in *American National Biography*, ed. John A. Garraty and Mark C. Carnes (New York: Oxford University Press, 1999), 478; CEL, 13; Duus, *The Life of Isamu Noguchi*, 54; Wada, "Noguchi Yonejirō no Rondon: ayamekai no naifun," 14. Moreover, Takeda's background seems contested regarding whether she worked for Yone or posed as a nude model for Yone and his artist friends. Duus, *The Life of Isamu Noguchi*, 54.
98. Léonie Gilmour, Pasadena, to Yone Noguchi, Tokyo, 24 February 1906, CEL, no. 373.
99. Ibid. Yet as resolved as Léonie appeared in late February, one month earlier she may in fact have seriously considered a move to Japan. On January 20, 1906, Léonie informed Catherine that she had found a teaching position in Tokyo, and Yone had been making "all kinds of promises." She planned on crossing the Pacific with Baby on February 1. Léonie remained hopeful of

the future though the horizon appeared hazy. Léonie Gilmour, Los Angeles, to Catherine Burnell, 20 January 1906, Isamu Noguchi Museum.

100. Yone Noguchi, Tokyo, to Léonie Gilmour, 2 April 1906, CEL, no. 374; Yone Noguchi, Tokyo, to Léonie Gilmour, [April 1906?], CEL, no. 375.
101. Yone Noguchi, Tokyo, to Léonie Gilmour, 5 May 1906, CEL, no. 379.
102. Keio University paid Yone by the hour. He only worked five hours a week during the school year and had little hope of gaining more hours due to the university's financial constraints. Thus summer time, with no classes to teach would mean no income for Yone. Yone Noguchi, Tokyo to Léonie Gilmour, 5 May 1906, CEL, no. 379.
103. Yone Noguchi to Léonie Gilmour, 8 June 1906, CEL, no. 380; Yone Noguchi to Léonie Gilmour, 22 June 1906, CEL, no. 381.
104. Léonie Gilmour Noguchi to Charles Warren Stoddard, 6 December 1906, BSC.
105. From Charles Warren Stoddard, Monterey, CA, to Ina Coolbrith, San Francisco, 12 April 1907, HM38507, Huntington MSS.
106. In the early years of his Japanese career, Yone used katakana, a Japanese alphabet frequently used for non-Japanese words, in the spelling of his name.
107. "Koi no tabishi," *Yomiuri Shimbun*, 5 March 1907, 3.
108. Noguchi, *The Story of Yone Noguchi Told by Himself*, 188. For more details on their initial adjustment living in Japan together, see ibid., 189–199. See also Frank Putnam, "Isamu Comes Home," *Southwestern Farmer* (15 March 1911): 14–15.
109. Léonie described Iwamura further. "Brave, chivalrous, yes, also tall and fine looking from our western standpoint, given to every athletic sport—and a lover of poetry, perhaps versed in the ancient Chinese poetry." Léonie Gilmour, Tokyo, to Catherine Burnell, July 1907, Isamu Noguchi Museum.
110. Ibid.
111. Léonie Gilmour, Tokyo, to Catherine Burnell, 13 March 1909, Isamu Noguchi Museum.
112. Ibid.
113. Léonie Gilmour, Omori, to Catherine Burnell, n.d., Isamu Noguchi Museum. In an earlier letter she closed her note, "Goodbye my love." Léonie Gilmour, Tokyo, to Catherine Burnell, 13 June 1909, Isamu Noguchi Museum.
114. Yone Noguchi, Tokyo, to Charles Warren Stoddard, 19 May 1907, CEL, no. 384.
115. Yone Noguchi, Tokyo, to Charles Warren Stoddard, 26 July [1908?], CEL, no. 386.

116. Ibid. This second reference to Charlie's *For the Pleasure of His Company* further exemplifies how Yone may have continued to use Charlie's gayest works to express his own coded desire for Charlie's affections. One Sunday in April 1903, Yone spent the entire day with Stoddard's work as his "companion." Yone declared, "How I enjoyed it—from the reason that I felt as if I was with you, listening to you reminisce." From Yone Noguchi, Boston, to Charles Warren Stoddard, April 1903, HM37933, Huntington MSS.
117. Issio Kuge, "The Heights," to "Martin," 20 December 1905, Charles Warren Stoddard Papers, BANC MSS C-H 53, BSC; Issio Kuge, "The Heights," to Charles Warren Stoddard, 21 November 1905, Charles Warren Stoddard Papers, BANC MSS C-H 53, BSC; Issio Kuge, "The Heights," to Charles Warren Stoddard, Saratoga, CA, 19 July 1906, Charles Warren Stoddard Papers, BANC MSS C-H 53, BSC; Issio Kuge, Usuki, Japan, to Charles Warren Stoddard, 12 November 1906, Charles Warren Stoddard Papers, BANC MSS C-H 53, BSC; Issio Kuge, "The Heights," to Charles Warren Stoddard, 12 March 1909, Charles Warren Stoddard Papers, BANC MSS C-H 53, BSC.
118. Charles Warren Stoddard, "Island Heights: New Jersey" [1901–1907], Charles Warren Stoddard Papers, BANC MSS C-H 53, BSC.
119. Yone Noguchi, Tokyo, to Ina Coolbrith, 3 October 1906, CEL, no. 383.
120. Yone Noguchi, Kamakura, to Young, 16 May 1909, CEL, no. 388; Yone Noguchi, Kamakura, to Young, 12 October 1909, CEL, no. 389.
121. For Stoddard waiting for Yone's letter, see Charles Warren Stoddard, Monterey, CA, to Dewitt Miller, Philadelphia, 25 July 1907, HM38406, Huntington MSS. For Stoddard living in California and missing his belongings, see Charles Warren Stoddard, Monterey, CA, to Ina Coolbrith, San Francisco, 12 April 1907, HM38507, Huntington MSS; See also Austen, *Genteel Pagan*, 165.
122. Yoshinobu Hakutani, "Yone Noguchi's Poetry: From Whitman to Zen," *Comparative Literature Studies* 22 (1985): 75.
123. For Yone's quotation see Noguchi, *The Story of Yone Noguchi Told by Himself*, 242.
124. Yone Noguchi, New York, to Léonie Gilmour, [July 1901?], CEL, no. 85.
125. An additional Celtic folktale that Yone favored recounted a man who fell in love with a mermaid and proposed marriage. When she cautioned him that life with her would always be upon the restless waves, the man retorted that a woman who lives in that fashion was not woman. The mermaid smiled and swam into the ocean, leaving the man by himself. Though the man would eventually marry a human woman upon the suggestion from a god

that humans should choose humans for spouses, their children and their grandchildren would be forever possessed by the ocean. Yone stated that he also felt a part of this family and a child of the ocean—restless and perhaps possessed by a force of desire and a life course that he chose to relinquish. Yonejirō Noguchi, "Ritararī ramburu," *Yomiuri Shimbun*, 13 December 1908, 1.

126. Austen, *Genteel Pagan*, 167.

Epilogue

1. Marx, " 'A Different Mode of Speech,' " 288–306; Noguchi, *American Diary of a Japanese Girl*, 144.
2. Hosea Hirata, "Ezra Pound and Japan: Letters and Essays," *Monumenta Nipponica* 44, no. 4 (Winter 1989): 499; Wada Keiko, "Noguchi Yonejiro no Rondon (1)—shijin debyu ichizenya," *Ōsaka Gakuin Daigaku gaikokugo ronshū* 33 (March 1996), 118.
3. Hiroko Sumi, "The Isamu Noguchi Garden Museum," *Tansei*, June 2001, http://www.tansei.net/overseas/ny2/no1.htm (accessed 3 May 2010); Hiroshi Unno, "Uesuto kōsuto no Bohemia: San Furanshisuko no shiteki fūdo," *Gendaishi techō* 44, no. 2 (February 2001): 32–35.
4. Noguchi first began teaching at Keio in 1906 and later became the chair of the newly formed English Literature department. Yoshinobu Hakutani, "Noguchi, Yone," in *American National Biography*, ed. John A. Garraty and Mark C. Carnes (New York: Oxford University Press, 1999), 478.
5. For the reviews from *The Globe and Commercial Advertiser* and the *Critic*, see Miller and Noguchi, *Japan of Sword and Love*, 73, 74. For the parallel drawn between Noguchi and Shakespeare, see Iza Duffus Hardy, London, England to Charles Warren Stoddard, Monterey, CA, 28 July 1905, IC349, Huntington MSS.
6. Yone Noguchi, "The Death of Baron Takasaki," *The Nation* 95, no. 2453 (4 July 1912): 10–11; Yone Noguchi, "The Japanese Mask Play," *The Nation* 95, no. 2463 (12 September 1912): 231–232; Yone Noguchi, "On the Suicide of Gen. Nogi," *The Nation* 95, no. 2468 (17 October 1912): 352–353; Yone Noguchi, "Western Plays in Japan," *The Nation* 97, no. 2508 (19 June 1913): 84–85; Yone Noguchi, "The Downfall of the Western Civilization," *The Nation* 99, no. 2571 (8 October 1914): 432; Yone Noguchi, "The Future of Japanese Shintoism," *The Nation* 102, no. 2654 (11 May 1916): 512–513; Yone Noguchi, "Shakespeare in Japan," *The Nation* 103, no. 2665 (11 May 1916): 90–91. I thank Greg Robinson for pointing me to these articles.

7. W. G. C., "Hiroshige," *The Burlington Magazine for Connoisseurs* 40, no. 226 (January 1922): 43; Charles Holmes, "Hiroshige," *The Burlington Magazine for Connoisseurs* 65, no. 378 (September 1934): 137; S. P. "Utamaro, Hokusai," *The Burlington Magazine for Connoisseurs* 50, no. 290 (May 1927): 282; W. H. B., "The Ukiyoye Primitives," *The Burlington Magazine for Connoisseurs* 64, no. 373 (April 1934): 194; Hans Müller, "Harunobu," *Monumenta Nipponica* 3, no. 2 (July 1940): 679–680; B. Gray, "Harunobu," *The Burlington Magazine for Connoisseurs* 78, no. 457 (April 1941): 135.
8. *Rafu Shimpo* and *Kashu Mainichi*, Los Angeles' Japanese American newspapers, reported on Yone Noguchi's accomplishments and referred to him as a lyrical poet as well as a model of intermarriage. For examples see "Yone Noguchi to Speak in India," *Rafu Shimpo*, 23 August 1935; "Book Review: Hiroshige by Yone Noguchi," *Kashu Mainichi*, 28 June 1934; Larry Tajiri, "Village Augaries," *Kashu Mainichi*, 19 June 1934; Tamotsu Murayama, "Here Lives Art!" *Kashu Mainichi*, 8 April 1934; Eiji Tanabe, "She Was Just a Chow Mein Girl," *Kashu Mainichi*, 14 October 1934. I thank Stacey Hirose for pointing me to articles in the Japanese American press in the 1930s.
9. Yone Noguchi, *From the Eastern Sea*, 4th edition (Tokyo: Fuzanbō, 1905), 3.
10. Even Noguchi's son Isamu, a prominent sculptor, had few supportive words for his father's later writings on art. Isamu stated: "I've found it difficult to read [them] because he tried to be a poet or literary man discussing something else. I'm therefore, not much interested in his writing on art in the descriptive sense." Sato, "Yone Noguchi: Accomplishments and Roles," 4, 7, 8.
11. Sato further delegitimized Kaneko's statement by revealing his likely bias as Noguchi's former student. Ibid., 4, 6.
12. Ibid., 4, 7; Susan Napier, "Selected English Writings of Yone Noguchi: An East-West Literary Assimilation," *Bulletin of the School of Oriental and African Studies* 54, no. 3 (1991): 627–628.
13. Yoshinobu Hakutani, "Yone Noguchi's Poetry: From Whitman to Zen," *Comparative Literature Studies* 22 (1985): 67; Marx, " 'A Different Mode of Speech.' " 289.
14. http://www.temple.edu/tempress/titles/1765_reg.html (accessed 22 October 2006).
15. Juliana Chang, Benzi Zhang, and Carlos Bulosan have all recognized Yone Noguchi as one of Asian America's earliest poets. However, few scholars of Asian American studies have embarked on an analysis of his work

that goes beyond noting that Noguchi's work dates the origins of Asian American writing to as early as the 1890s. Juliana Chang, "Reading Asian American Poetry," *MELUS* 21, no. 1 (Spring 1996): 83; Benzi Zhang, "Mapping Carnivalistic Discourse in Japanese-American Writing," *MELUS* 24, no. 4 (Winter 1999): 22; Shirley Geok-Lin Lim, "Assaying the Gold: Or, Contesting the Ground of Asian American Literature," *New Literary History* 24, no. 1 (Winter 1993): 153.

16. Sui Sin Far's decision to identify with the Chinese American community becomes even more interesting in juxtaposition with her sister, Winnifred Eaton, a writer who passed as having a Japanese mother and wrote essays on Japan to ride the tide of Japonisme. Unlike her sister Far, Winnifred Eaton, who authored her work as Onoto Watanna, notably remains largely unclaimed by Asian Americanists in literature and history. Far wrote in popular journals such as *Overland Monthly* during the late 1890s and early 1900s. See Annette White-Parks, *Sui Sin Far/Edith Maude Eaton* (Chicago: University of Illinois Press, 1995), and Xiao-huang Yin, *Chinese American Literature since the 1850s* (Chicago: University of Illinois Press, 2000).
17. Carlos Bulosan, *America Is in the Heart: A Personal History* (New York: Harcourt, Brace, and Company, 1946). In 1989 controversy arose around whether the incidents in his memoir truly belonged to Bulosan alone. Regardless of whether Bulosan pieced together the experiences of others or not, I use his work here as an example of a protest piece that pointed to a brutally racist America. For more on the controversy, see Marilyn Alquizola, "Subversion or Affirmation: The Text and Subtext of *America Is in the Heart*," in *Asian Americans: Comparative and Global Perspectives*, ed. Shirley Hune et al. (Pullman: Washington State Univeristy Press, 1991), 199–209.
18. Yonejirō Noguchi, *Ware Nihonjin nari* (Tokyo: Takemura Shobō, 1938); Wada, "Noguchi Yonejirō no Rondon: ayamekai no naifun," 14.
19. Wada, "Noguchi Yonejirō no Rondon: ayamekai no naifun," 16.
20. Yoshinobu Hakutani estimated that one-quarter of Noguchi's books were written in English. Hakutani, "Noguchi, Noguchi," 478. Shiga Nobuo counted over 150 publications. Shiga, "Noguchi Yonejirō to Isamu Noguchi," 23.
21. Inderpal Grewal and Caren Kaplan underscore the original political valence of the term "transnational" as signifying the asymmetries of the globalization process rather than simply being displaced. Grewal and Kaplan, "Global Identities," 664. See also Inderpal Grewal and Caren Kaplan, "Introduction: Transnational Feminist Practices and Questions of Postmodernity," in

Scattered Hegemonies: Postmodernity and Transnational Feminist Practices, ed. Inderpal Grewal and Caren Kaplan (Minneapolis: University of Minnesota Press, 1994), 1–33.

22. The term "compulsory heterosexuality" comes from Adrienne Rich, who has argued that heterosexuality was a violent institution imposed, organized, and maintained by society to chain women's sexuality and well-being to male patriarchy. Here I extend Rich's original use of the term to include men with same-sex desires and to describe how they too experience violence when forced to comply with directives of mandated heterosexuality. Adrienne Rich, *Blood, Bread and Poetry: Selected Prose, 1979–1986* (New York: Norton, 1986).
23. Charles Warren Stoddard, Washington, DC, to Dewitt Miller, Philadelphia, 15 October 1901, HM38383, Huntington MSS; Joseph Dwight Strong to Charles Warren Stoddard, 20 April 1897, HM38140, Huntington MSS. For Stoddard's exoticization of Pacific Islanders, see A. Grove Day and Carl Stroven, eds., *Best South Sea Stories* (New York: Appleton-Century, 1964); Charles Warren Stoddard, *Cruising the South Seas*, ed. Winston Leyland (San Francisco: Gay Sunshine Press, 1987); Austen, *Genteel Pagan*, 27–30, 45.
24. Belle, the stepdaughter of Robert Louis Stevenson, was in fact divorced from the aforementioned Joseph Dwight Strong. Joseph harbored deep feelings of love for Belle long after their divorce. As he prepared to remarry in 1898, he would come face to face with Belle as he exited the San Francisco Bohemian Club. He wrote to Stoddard, "I was a little surprised to find her fat and dumpy, but [she] still has pretty eyes." Joseph Dwight Strong, San Francisco, to Charles Warren Stoddard, 31 January 1898, HM38152, Huntington MSS.
25. Isobel Osbourne Field, Vailima, Samoa, to Charles Warren Stoddard, December 1896, HM38001, Huntington MSS. For more on Belle's exotification of Samoa and its people, see Isobel Osbourne Field, Vailima, Samoa, to Charles Warren Stoddard, 24 February 1897, HM38002, Huntington MSS; From Isobel Osbourne Field, Vailima, Samoa, to Charles Warren Stoddard, March 1897, HM38003, Huntington MSS; Isobel Strong and Lloyd Osbourne, *Memories of Vailima* (New York: Charles Scribner's Sons, 1902).
26. Isobel Osbourne Field, Vailima, Samoa, to Charles Warren Stoddard, December 1896, HM38001, Huntington MSS; Isobel [Osbourne] Field, Sydney, Australia, to Charles Warren Stoddard, June 1891?, HM37993, Huntington MSS.
27. Unna, *The Coppa Murals*, 52–54.

28. The San Francisco Bohemian Club became increasingly "stuffy" after its first decade of existence. Millionaires at first took simple harmless pleasure in being closer to clever chaps who painted or wrote for a living. Soon after, though, they began to make organizational changes. Members had to behave themselves. Scribbling on the tablecloths and getting sloshed no longer stood as acceptable behavior. Newer members maintained dignity as part of bourgeois San Francisco. Parry, *Garrets and Pretenders*, 228; Emily Hahn, *Romantic Rebels: An Informal History of Bohemianism* (Boston: Houghton Mifflin Company, 1967).
29. Names of other writers with whom Noguchi interacted appeared on the list, such as Joaquin Miller, Ina Coolbrith, Ambrose Bierce, Gelett Burgess, Porter Garnett, Charles Augustus Keeler, Edwin Markham, and Charles Warren Stoddard. San Francisco Bohemian Club, *Bohemian Club Authors: A Brief Catalog of Their Published Works 1937* (San Francisco: Grabhorn Press, 1937). For the official history see Bohemian Club, *The Annals of the Bohemian Club*, vols. 1–8 (San Francisco: Press of Hicks-Judd Co., 1898–1909).
30. As problematic as an essential notion of race based on phenotype or last name might prove, I found these admittedly crude indicators useful in at least making a preliminary analysis regarding the racial diversity among the club members without documents that would otherwise detail the genealogy or racial background of each individual.
31. Bohemian Club, *Constitution and By-Law of the Bohemian Club of San Francisco* (1895). Elsie Whitaker Martinez, interviewed by Willa K. Baum and Franklin Dickerson Walker, San Francisco Bay Area Writers and Artists: Oral History Transcript/Elsie Martinez, Bancroft Library, University of California at Berkeley, 1962–1969.
32. Frank Putnam, "Yone Noguchi," *Boston Transcript*, 8 April 1903, n.p.
33. Iza Duffus Hardy was the daughter of Sir Thomas Hardy and Lady Hardy. A novelist in her own right, Iza published more than twenty novels. In the 1870s Jack London believed she would marry Joaquin Miller, yet the engagement was broken, and Iza never married. Charles Warren Stoddard, Washington, DC, to Yone Noguchi, London, England, 3 November 1902, CEL, no. 123.
34. Elizabeth Wilson, *Bohemians: The Glamorous Outcasts* (New Brunswick, NJ: Rutgers University Press, 2000), 39.
35. San Francisco Bohemians frequented Luna's, a Mexican restaurant, in the early 1890s. Frank Norris and other "thunderers" considered the place "headquarters" to seek sordid realism without forgetting good food. Joaquin Miller reportedly met Alice Oliver at Luna's, after which he invited her to live at the "Heights" with him. Later the more famous center of the group

became the Italian restaurant Coppa's. Clarence E. Edwords, *Bohemian San Francisco* (San Francisco: Paul Elder and Company, 1914); Jean White, "A Landmark of San Francisco's Bohemia," *Overland Monthly* 62, no. 3 (March 1916): 186–188; Albert Parry, *Garrets and Pretenders.*

36. Immigration historian Donna Gabaccia suggests Americans' incorporation of foreign food into their diet signals how the nation has accepted cultural diversity as a part of what defines America. Donna Gabaccia, *We Are What We Eat: Ethnic Food and the Making of Americans* (Cambridge, MA: Harvard University Press, 1998).
37. Elsie's first "beau" would visit with "reams of beautiful eucalyptus bark on which were inscribed his poems in exquisite Japanese characters." Her brothers would promptly burn them as fire starters. Elsie referred to the poet's name as "Kugi," which very well could have been Kuge Issio, who stayed on the Hights around 1905. Elsie Whitaker Martinez, interviewed by Willa K. Baum and Franklin Dickerson Walker, San Francisco Bay Area Writers and Artists: Oral History Transcript/Elsie Martinez, Bancroft Library, University of California at Berkeley, 1962–1969.
38. Ibid.
39. Albert Sherwood Bierce to Blanche Partington, 3 September n.d., Partington Family Papers, BANC MSS C-H 84, BSC. For one online account of the history of the Chutes, see http://www.historysmith.com/Chutes.html (accessed 8 April 2010). For Native Americans speaking out against the Wild West Show, see Black Elk, *Black Elk Speaks: Being the Life Story of a Holy Man of the Oglala Sioux*, ed. John G. Neihardt, foreword by Vine Deloria, Jr. (Lincoln: University of Nebraska Press, 2004).
40. Wilson, *Bohemians*, 39.
41. Bohemians engaged with Italians and Jews of Lower East Side, finding them animating and interesting. Though a few lingered in African American saloons and honky tonks, bohemians associated African Americans with the music and entertainment industry rather than with any social revolution. Stansell, *American Moderns*, 24–26.
42. Charmian London, Glen Ellen, CA, to Blanche Partington, 3 September 1909, Partington Family Papers, BANC MSS C-H 84, BSC.
43. Photographs of Phyllis and Blanche Partington, Carrie Sterling, and others in Northern California, photCL492, Huntington Rare Books, Huntington Library, San Marino, CA. For the "Black Mammy" as offensive, see Patricia A. Turner, *Ceramic Uncles and Celluloid Mammies: Black Images and Their Influence on Culture* (New York: Anchor, 1994).
44. Léonie Gilmour, Los Angeles, to Catherine Burnell, 20 January 1906, Isamu Noguchi Museum.

45. Jack attributed Manyoungi's sudden change in behavior to his not wanting to go on a voyage on the "Seven Seas" on an "inconsequential shallop," the *Snark*, as the Londons had planned to do. Charmian Kittredge London, *The Book of Jack London* (New York: The Century Company, 1921), 154–155.
46. Austen, *Genteel Pagan*, 92.
47. Strong and Osbourne, *Memories of Vailima*, 178, 193–194, 200–201.
48. The South Sea exhibit consisted of a Samoan house and a theater where performances took place. Joseph Dwight Strong, Chicago, to Charles Warren Stoddard, 10–11 June 1893, HM38039, Huntington MSS; Joseph Dwight Strong, Sacramento, to Charles Warren Stoddard, 14 November 1893, HM38057, Huntington MSS.
49. Not until the 1920s would New York's bohemian circles more actively include African Americans. Stansell, *American Moderns*, 67.
50. Noguchi, *Story of Yone Noguchi Told by Himself*, 73.
51. Austen, *Genteel Pagan*, 24.
52. Joseph Dwight Strong, Munich, Germany, to Charles Warren Stoddard, 22 September 1876, HM38023, Huntington MSS.
53. Austen, *Genteel Pagan*, xxvi, 159.
54. Explicit same-sex sexuality, if elliptically allowed, did not signify in the new sexuality of more carefree and companionate, and romantic, heterosexuality. Ibid., 251.
55. Helen Bridyman, Brooklyn, to Yone Noguchi, New York, 19 July [1904], CEL, no. 345.
56. Diary, October 23, 1898, Partington Family Papers, BANC MSS C-H 84, BSC. As noted in Chapter 1, Noguchi was fairly typical of other "houseboys" who came from middling class backgrounds to pursue education and opportunity in America while living and working in a white family as a domestic. The "nobility" that Blanche perceived likely came from her own physical attraction to the "handsome boy" whom she hoped would kiss her in 1898, as described in Chapter 2.
57. Ambrose Gwinnett Bierce, Bristol, England, to Charles Warren Stoddard, 29 December 1872, HM10102, Huntington MSS.
58. Wilson, *Bohemians*, 148–149, 153.
59. According to Austen, as the medical community published statements stigmatizing same-sex relationships as sexual perversion, Stoddard increasingly lived to hide his secret world. Austen, *Genteel Pagan*, 57.
60. Ibid., xxxiii.
61. Ikuko Atsumi, e-mail message to author, 16 May 2003.
62. Atsumi, "Yone Noguchi 'Waga Ananberu Li' Eseru Āmusu ni tsuite," 83.

63. Yone Noguchi to Charles Warren Stoddard, 19 March 1900, Yone Noguchi Collection, BANC MSS 82/130, BSC; Yone Noguchi to Léonie Gilmour, July 1901, CEL, no. 84; Yone Noguchi, Avon, NY, to Blanche Partington, Oakland, CA, 17 August 1900, CEL, no. 58; Ethel Armes, Birmingham, AL, to Alice Wiggins, Franklin, MA, 6 November 1902, Private Collection of Gary Dobbs.
64. Takayuki Yokota-Murakami, *Don Juan East/West: On the Problematics of Comparative Literature* (Albany: State University of New York, 1998).
65. In 1999 Karen Kelsky anticipated announcing Noguchi's bisexuality at the annual meeting of the Association for Asian Studies. Abstracts of the 1999 AAS Annual Meeting, 11–14 March 1999, Boston, MA, session 166: "Capital Offenses: Erotics and Desire in Twentieth-Century Japan"; Karen Kelsky, "Seen and Unseen: The American Diary of Yone Noguchi," http://www.aasianst.org/absts/1999abst/japan/j-166.htm. For a more recent proclamation of his bisexuality, see also Yone Noguchi, *American Diary of a Japanese Girl, an Annotated Edition*, ed. Edward Marx and Laura E. Franey (Philadelphia: Temple University Press, 2007).
66. Chauncey, *Gay New York*, 96; Marvin Zuckerman, "Physiological Measures of Sexual Arousal in the Human," *Psychological Bulletin* 75, no. 5 (May 1971): 297–329; Phillip M. Sarrel and William H. Masters, "Sexual Molestation of Men by Women," *Archives of Sexual Behavior* 11, no. 2 (1982): 117–131.
67. For more on how bisexuality has been ignored as a legitimate field of inquiry into sexual identities, see see Steven Angelides, *History of Bisexuality* (Chicago: University of Chicago Press, 2001).
68. I thank Don Romesburg, who underscored Noguchi's identity as heterosexual during an invited talk at Sonoma State University in February 2009.
69. Historian Mark McClelland has written of how Japan's use of the West historically has been both "strategic" and "rhetorical." Noguchi's intimate life sheds light on how this interaction may have played out in individual Japanese lives immersed in Western culture as well. McLelland, *Queer Japan from the Pacific War to the Internet Age*, 3. See also Sabine Frühstück, *Colonizing Sex: Sexology and Social Control in Modern Japan* (Berkeley: University of California Press, 2003).
70. Theorist Jeffrey Weeks posed sexuality as a culturally mediated category signifying social relations and norms. Jeffrey Weeks, *Sexuality and Its Discontents: Meanings, Myths, and Modern Sexualities* (London: Routledge and Kegan Paul, 1985).
71. The closeting of Noguchi's individual life thus holds significance as it reflects and contributes to Japan's move increasingly to perceive acts such as

same-sex male affection and coed bathing, which were once not considered necessarily sexual, as sexual in a distinctly perverse way. For more on the interrogation and historical evolution of the meaning of sexuality in Japan, see Yokota-Murakami, *Don Juan East/West*.

72. For more on debates around the sociopolitical value of "outing," particularly of public figures, see Timothy F. Murphy, ed., *Gay Ethics: Controversies in Outing, Civil Rights and Sexual Science* (New York: Haworth Press, 1994).
73. For the phrase "dime museum spectacle" see Miss Morning Glory, *American Letters of a Japanese Parlor-Maid*, 116. For Noguchi downplaying his intimacy with Stoddard, see Yone Noguchi, Bayonne, NJ, to Léonie Gilmour, 22 October 1901, CEL, no. 99.
74. According to sociologist Mary Waters, newer West Indian immigrants to the United States are more optimistic about opportunities than their counterparts who have lived longer in America and faced persistent blatant racial discrimination. Mary C. Waters, *Black Identities: West Indian Immigrant Dreams and Immigrant Realities* (New York: Russell Sage Foundation; Cambridge, MA : Harvard University Press, 1999).
75. For articles in Japanese on Ethel's literary success, see Atsumi, "Yone Noguchi 'Waga Ananberu Ri' Eseru Āmusu ni tsuite," 81–87. For Ethel's most famous work, originally published in 1910, which defined her as Alabama's first historian, see Armes, *The Story of Coal and Iron in Alabama*.
76. C. M. Stanley, "Ethel Armes Didn't Look Like a Historian," *Montgomery Advertiser—Alabama Journal*, 6 November 1949, n.p.
77. Léonie Gilmour, Chigasaki, to Catherine Burnell, 23 September [no year], Isamu Noguchi Museum. See also Duus, *The Life of Isamu Noguchi*,53.
78. For an excellent history of Noguchi's, Léonie's, and Isamu's lives, see Duus, *The Life of Isamu Noguchi*.
79. For Noguchi's involvement in the Japanese Patriotic League, see Wada Keiko, "Noguchi Yonejirō no Rondon: aikokushin to kokusuishugi," *Ōsaka Gakuin Daigaku gaikokugo ronshu* 45 (March 2002): 41–59. Noguchi once stated, "My pro-Japan stance was borne from my international experiences." Nakanishi Yoshie, "Noguchi Yonejirō no shīkaron," *Tsudajuku Daigaku kiyō* 9 (1977): 18.
80. Yone Noguchi, "The Downfall of the Western Civilization," *The Nation* 99, no. 2571 (8 October 1914): 432. In 1919 Noguchi seemed more hopeful that America had resolved its issues around race. Noguchi Yonejirō, "Beikoku de no ware ga koen," *Yomiuri Shimbun*, 13 October 1919, p. 6; 14 October 1919, p. 7.

81. After his homecoming Noguchi became well known for his political position as a nationalist in support of Japan's imperial aspirations. Noguchi's call to arms was all the more ironic since he had deliberately stayed in the United States to avoid the mandatory draft in Japan. Though he wrote of "our swords impatient[ly] stir[ring] in the[ir] scabbards" as trumpets called to arms, his own sword had hardly made a move to be drawn when military duty called him in his younger years. "Fight, fight, fight," Noguchi commanded the Japanese soldier as he outlined the glory of a warrior's life. Now exempt from serving, he took pride in a war in which his own life seemed to be no longer at stake. Several years later in articles in *The Nation* from 1911 to 1917 Noguchi positioned himself as an advocate for peace. See Yone Noguchi, "The Pacific Ocean Associations," *The Nation* 93, no. 2407 (7 August 1911): 141; Yone Noguchi, "The Downfall of the Western Civilization," *The Nation* 99, no. 2571 (8 October 1914): 432; Yone Noguchi, "On the Suicide of Gen. Nogi," *The Nation* 95, no. 2468 (17 October 1912): 352–353. Shortly before Noguchi died in 1947, he confessed that he had made a mistake in supporting Japanese nationalism. Miller and Noguchi, *Japan of Sword and Love*, 5, 7; Sato, "Yone Noguchi: Accomplishments and Roles"; Marx, " 'A Different Mode of Speech.' "
82. Sato, "Yone Noguchi: Accomplishments and Roles," 8. For more on Noguchi's philosophy of Orientalism, or *Nihonshugi*, see Hazumi Fuitsu, *Rondon no kirikaki: Makino Yoshio to Noguchi Yonejirō ni miru ushinawareta Nihon no geijutsu seishin* (Kasugai-shi: Rokuyukan, 1992). For a critique of Orientalism, see Said, *Orientalism*.
83. Theorists of queers of color have illuminated how prevailing notions of race, gender, and sexuality implicate marginalized people both as victims of inequality and as agents of resistance. David Eng, *Racial Castration: Managing Masculinity in Asian America* (Durham: Duke University Press, 2001); Dwight McBride, *Why I Hate Abercrombie and Fitch: Essays on Race and Sexuality* (New York: New York University Press, 2005); Siobahn Somerville, *Queering the Color Line: Race and the Invention of Homosexuality in American Culture* (Durham: Duke University Press, 2000); and José Muñoz, *Disidentifications: Queers of Color and the Performance of Politics* (Minneapolis: University of Minnesota Press, 1999).
84. In his memoir he noted, "I often ask myself how much of Japanese life is reality; it may not be altogether orientalism to say that there is nothing real except the fact of love between mother and son." Noguchi, *The Story of Yone Noguchi Told by Himself*, 202.

85. The winking black and white portrait of the young Noguchi might simply be "campy," an ironic move on Marx' part that has nothing to do with his same-sex affairs. Home page of Edward Marx, http://www.h.ehime-u.ac.jp/~marx/ (accessed 4 June 2005).
86. Noguchi, *Eibei no jūsannen*, 133.
87. Noguchi Yonejirō, "Gojussai no shokan," *Yomiuri Shimbun*, 8 February 1926, p. 4.

Selected Bibliography

Aldrich, Robert. *Colonialism and Homosexuality.* New York: Routledge, 2003.

Almaguer, Tomás. *Racial Faultlines: The Historical Origins of White Supremacy in California.* Berkeley: University of California Press, 1994.

Angelides, Steven. *History of Bisexuality.* Chicago: University of Chicago Press, 2001.

Armes, Ethel. *The Story of Coal and Iron in Alabama.* New York: Arno Press, 1973.

Asbury, Herbert. *Barbary Coast: An Informal History of the San Francisco Underworld.* New York: A. A. Knopf, 1933.

Atsumi, Ikuko. *Yone Noguchi Collected English Letters.* Tokyo: The Yone Noguchi Society, 1975.

———. "Yone Noguchi kankei eibun shokan ni tsuite—eibei bungakusha tachi tono kōryū to jyosei." In *Shijin Yone Noguchi kenkyū*, vol. 3, edited by Toyama Ūsaburō. Tokyo: Zōkei Bijutsu Kyōkai Shuppanbō, 1975.

———. "Yone Noguchi 'Waga Ananberu Li' Eseru Āmusu ni tsuite." *Ippan kyōiku bukai ronshu* 17 (1996): 81–87.

Austen, Roger. *Genteel Pagan. The Double Life of Charles Warren Stoddard.* Edited by John W. Crowley. Amherst, MA: University of Massachusetts Press, 1991.

———. *Playing the Game: The Homosexual Novel in America.* New York: The Bobbs-Merrill Company, 1977.

Ayers, Edward L. *The Promise of the New South: Life after Reconstruction.* New York: Oxford University Press, 1992.

Azuma, Eiichiro. *Between Two Empires: Race, History, and Transnationalism in Japanese America.* New York: Oxford University Press, 2005.

Bederman, Gail. *Manliness and Civilization: A Cultural History of Gender and Race in the United States, 1880–1917.* Chicago: University of Chicago Press, 1995.

Black Elk. *Black Elk Speaks: Being the Life Story of a Holy Man of the Oglala Sioux*. Edited by John G. Neihardt. Foreword by Vine Deloria, Jr. Lincoln: University of Nebraska Press, 2004.
Bohemian Club, *Annals of the Bohemian Club*. Vol 1. San Francisco: Press of Hicks-Judd Co., 1898.
———. *Annals of the Bohemian Club*. Vol. 2. San Francisco: Press of the Hicks-Judd Co., 1900.
———. *Annals of the Bohemian Club*. Vol. 3. San Francisco: Press of Hicks-Judd Co., 1909.
———. *Bohemian Club, 1872: A Chronicle of Our Years: Commemorating the Seventy-Fifth Anniversary of the Founding of the Bohemian Club of San Francisco*. San Francisco: Grabhorn Press, 1947.
———. *Christmas Jinks: December 1891*. San Francisco: C. A. Murdock and Company, Printers, 1891.
Boudinot, Elias. *An Address to Whites*. Philadelphia: Geddes, 1926.
Boyd, Nan Alamilla. "Who Is the Subject? Queer Theory Meets Oral History." *Journal of the History of Sexuality* 17, no. 2 (May 2008): 177–189.
———. *Wide-Open Town: A History of Queer San Francisco to 1965*. Berkeley: University of California Press, 2003.
Boyer, David. *Kings and Queens: Queers at the Prom*. Brooklyn, NY: Soft Skull Press, 2004.
Bray, Alan. *Homosexuality in Renaissance England*. London: Gay Men's Press, 1982.
Bredbenner, Candice Lewis. *A Nationality of Her Own: Women, Marriage, and the Law of Citizenship*. Berkeley: University California Press, 1998.
Brundage, W. Fitzhugh. *Lynching in the New South: Georgia and Virginia, 1880–1930*. Urbana, IL: University of Illinois Press, 1993.
Bulosan, Carlos. *America Is in the Heart: A Personal History*. New York: Harcourt, Brace, and Company, 1946.
Chan, Sucheng. *Asian Americans: An Interpretive History*. New York: Twayne Publishers, 1991.
Chang, Juliana. "Reading Asian American Poetry." *MELUS* 21, no. 1 (Spring 1996): 81–98.
Chauncey, George. *Gay New York: Gender, Urban Culture, and the Making of a Gay Male World, 1890–1940*. New York: Basic Books, 1994.
Cleto, Fabio, ed. *Camp: Queer Aesthetics and the Performing Subject*. Ann Arbor, MI: University of Michigan Press, 1999.
Dale, Alan. *A Marriage below Zero*. New York: G. W. Dillingham, 1889.
Dancer, Peter L., Peggy J. Kleinplatz, and Charles Moser, "24/7 SM Slavery." *Journal of Homosexuality* 50, nos. 2/3 (2006): 81–101.

Daniels, Roger. *Politics of Prejudice: The Anti-Japanese Movement in California and the Struggle for Japanese Exclusion*. Berkeley: University of California Press, 1962.

Darlington, W. A. *The World of Gilbert and Sullivan*. New York: Thomas Y. Crowell Company, 1950.

Day, A. Grove, and Carl Stroven, eds. *Best South Sea Stories*. New York: Appleton-Century, 1964.

D'Emilio, John, and Estelle Freedman, *Intimate Matters: A History of Sexuality in America*. Chicago: University of Chicago Press, 1997.

Dikötter, Frank. *Sex, Culture, and Modernity in China*. Honolulu: University of Hawai'i Press, 1995.

Dowd Hall, Jacquelyn. "The Mind That Burns in Each Body: Women, Rape and Racial Violence." In *Powers of Desire: The Politics of Sexuality*, edited by Ann Snitow, Christine Stansell, and Sharon Thompson, 328–349. New York: Monthly Review Press, 1983.

———. *Revolt against Chivalry: Jessie Daniel Ames and the Women's Campaign against Lynching*. New York: Columbia University Press, 1979.

Duberman, Martin Bauml, Martha Vicinus, and George Chauncey, Jr., eds. *Hidden from History: Reclaiming the Gay and Lesbian Past*. New York: New American Library, 1989.

Dubois, W. E. B. *The Oxford W. E. B. Dubois Reader*. Edited by Eric J. Sundquist. New York: Oxford University Press, 1996.

Duus, Masayo. *The Life of Isamu Noguchi: Journey without Borders*. Translated by Peter Duus. Princeton, NJ: Princeton University Press, 2004.

Edwords, Clarence E. *Bohemian San Francisco*. San Francisco: Paul Elder and Company, 1914.

Ellinghaus, Katherine. "Margins of Acceptability: Class, Education and Interracial Marriage in Australia and America." *Frontiers: A Journal of Women Studies* 3, no. 3 (2002): 55–75.

———. *Taking Assimilation to Heart: Marriages of White Women and Indigenous Men in Australia and the United States, 1887–1937*. Lincoln: University of Nebraska Press, 2006.

Eng, David L. *Racial Castration: Managing Masculinity in Asian America*. Durham: Duke University Press, 2001.

Espiritu, Yen Le. *Asian American Women and Men: Labor, Laws and Love*. Thousand Oaks, CA: Sage Publications, 1997.

Esquibel, Catrióna Rueda. *With Her Machete in Her Hand: Reading Chicana Lesbians*. Austin: University of Texas Press, 2006.

Faderman, Lillian. *Surpassing the Love of Men: Romantic Friendship and Love between Women from the Renaissance to the Present*. New York: Perennial, 2001.

Fauvre, Bernard. *The Red Thread: Buddhist Approaches to Sexuality*. Princeton, NJ: Princeton University Press, 1998.

Foldy, Michael S. *The Trials of Oscar Wilde: Deviance, Morality, and Late-Victorian Society*. New Haven, CT: Yale University Press, 1997.

Frühstück, Sabine. *Colonizing Sex: Sexology and Social Control in Modern Japan*. Berkeley: University of California Press, 2003.

Fukai Akiko. *Japonisumu in fasshion: umi o wattata kimono*. Tokyo: Heibonsha, 1994.

Gabaccia, Donna. *We Are What We Eat: Ethnic Food and the Making of Americans*. Cambridge, MA: Harvard University Press, 1998.

Garnett, Porter. *The Bohemian Jinks: A Treatise*. San Francisco: Hicks-Judd Co., 1906.

Gay, Peter. *The Tender Passion*. New York: Oxford University Press, 1986.

Gilbert, W. S. *The Mikado*. New York: Boni and Liveright Inc., 1917.

Gordon, Lynn. "The Gibson Girl Goes to College: Popular Culture and Women's Higher Education in the Progressive Era, 1890–1920." *American Quarterly* 39, no. 2 (Summer 1987): 211–230.

Green, Rayna. "The Pocahontas Perplex: The Image of Indian Women in American Culture." *Massachusetts Review* 16, no. 4 (1975): 698–714.

Grewal, Inderpal, and Caren Kaplan. "Global Identities: Theorizing Transnational Studies of Sexuality." *GLQ: Gay and Lesbian Quarterly* 7, no. 4 (2001): 663–679.

Hahn, Emily. *Romantic Rebels: An Informal History of Bohemianism*. Boston: Houghton Mifflin Company, 1967.

Hakutani, Yoshinobu."Noguchi, Yone." In *American National Biography*, edited by John A. Garraty and Mark C. Carnes, 478. New York: Oxford University Press, 1999.

———. *Selected English Writings of Yone Noguchi*. 2 vols. Rutherford: Fairleigh Dickinson University Press, 1990.

———. "Yone Noguchi's Poetry: From Whitman to Zen." *Comparative Literature Studies* 22 (1985): 67–79.

Hale, C. Jacob. "Leatherdyke Boys and Their Daddies: How to Have Sex without Women or Men." *Social Text* 52/53 (Autumn–Winter 1997): 223–236.

Hall, Owen. *The Geisha*. London: Ascherberg, Hopwood and Crew, 1896.

Halperin, David M. "How to Do the History of Homosexuality." *Gay and Lesbian Quarterly* 6, no. 1 (2000): 87–124.

Halverson, Cathryn. " 'Typical Tokio Smile': Bad American Books and Bewitching Japanese Girls." *Arizona Quarterly* 63, no. 1 (Spring 2007): 49–80.

Haritaworn, Jin, Chin-ju Lin, and Christian Klesse. "Poly/Logue: A Critical Introduction to Polyamory." *Sexualities* 9, no. 5 (2006): 515–529.

Hazumi Fuitsu. *Rondon no kirikaki: Makino Yoshio to Noguchi Yonejirō ni miru ushinawareta Nihon no geijutsu seishin*. Kasugai-shi : Rokuyukan, 1992.

Hing, Bill Ong. *Making and Remaking Asian America through Immigration Policy: 1850–1990*. Stanford, CA: Stanford University Press, 1993.

Hirata, Lucie Cheng. "Free, Indentured, Enslaved: Chinese Prostitutes in Nineteenth-Century America." *Signs: Journal of Women in Culture and Society* 5, no. 1 (1979): 3–29.

Hodes, Martha, ed. *Sex, Love, Race: Crossing Boundaries in North American History*. New York: New York University Press, 1999.

———. "The Sexualization of Reconstruction Politics: White Women and Black Men in the South after the Civil War." *Journal of History of Sexuality* 3, no. 3 (January 1993): 402–417.

———. *White Women, Black Men: Illicit Sex in the American South*. New Haven, CT: Yale University Press, 1997.

hooks, bell. *Black Looks: Race and Representation*. Boston: South End Press, 1992.

———. *Killing Rage: Ending Racism*. New York: Henry Holt, 1995.

Hosley, William. *The Japan Idea: Art and Life in Victorian America*. Hartford, CT: Wadsworth Athenaeum, 1990.

Howard, John. *Concentration Camps on the Home Front: Japanese Americans in the House of Jim Crow*. Chicago: University of Chicago Press, 2008.

Howes, John F., ed. *Nitobe Inazo: Japan's Bridge across the Pacific*. Boulder: Westview Press, 1995.

Hsu, Madeline Y. "Unwrapping Orientalism, Unwrapping Orientalist Constraints: Restoring Homosocial Normativity to Chinese American History." *Amerasia Journal* 29, no. 2 (2003): 230–253.

Hubbard, Elbert. *So Here Then Is a Little Journey to the Home of Joaquin Miller*. East Aurora, NY: The Roycrofters, 1903.

Hurtado, Albert L. *Intimate Frontiers: Sex, Gender, and Culture in Old California*. Albuquerque: University of New Mexico Press, 1999.

Ichioka, Yuji. "Ameyuki-san: Japanese Prostitutes in Nineteenth Century America." *Amerasia* 4, no. 1 (1977): 1–21.

———. *The Issei: The World of the First Generation Japanese Immigrants, 1885–1924*. New York: The Free Press, 1988.

Iwata Jun'ichi. *Honchō danshokukō: danshoku bunken shoshi*. Tokyo: Hara Shobō, 2002.

Johnson, Susan. " 'My Own Private Life': Toward a History of Desire in Gold Rush California." In *Rooted in Barbarous Soil: People, Culture, and Community in Gold Rush California*, edited by Kevin Starr and Richard Orsi, 316–346. Berkeley: University of California Press for the California Historical Society, 2000.

Kelly, Brian. *Race, Class and Power in the Alabama Coalfields, 1908–1921*. Urbana: University of Illinois Press, 2001.
Kiyama, Henry. *Four Immigrants Manga: A Japanese Experience in San Francisco*. Translated by Frederick L. Schodt. Berkeley: Stone Bridge Press, 1999.
Kodama Sanehide. *Amerika no Japonisumu*. Tokyo: Chūokōronsha, 1995.
Komine Shigeyuki and Minami Takao. *Dōseiai to dōseishinjū no kenkyū*. Tokyo: Komine Kenkyūjo, 1985.
Lee, Robert G. *Orientals: Asian Americans in Popular Culture*. Philadelphia: Temple University Press, 1999.
Letwin, Daniel. *The Challenge of Interracial Unionism: Alabama Coal Miners, 1878–1921*. Chapel Hill, NC: University of North Carolina Press, 1998.
Levin, James. *The Gay Novel in America*. New York: Garland Publishing, 1991.
Lim, Eng-Beng. "Glocalqueering in New Asia: The Politics of Performing Gay in Singapore." *Theatre Journal* 57 (2005): 383–405
Lim, Shirley Geok-Lin. "Assaying the Gold: Or, Contesting the Ground of Asian American Literature." New Literary History 24, no. 1 (Winter 1993): 147–169.
Loewen, James. *The Mississippi Chinese: Between Black and White*. 2nd ed. Prospect Heights, IL: Waveland Press, 1988.
London, Charmian Kittredge. *The Book of Jack London*. New York: The Century Company, 1921.
Lovaas, Karen E., John P. Elia, and Gust A. Yep. "Shifting Ground(s): Surveying the Contested Terrain of LGBT Studies." *Journal of Homosexuality* 52, nos. 1/2 (2006): 1–18.
Maeda, Robert J. "From Shape and Shadow: The Mother and Father of Isamu Noguchi." *Amerasia Journal* 22, no. 3 (1996): 104–120.
———. "Isamu Noguchi and the Peking Drawing of 1930." *American Art* 13, no. 1 (Spring 1999): 84–93.
Marberry, M. M. *Splendid Poseur: Joaquin Miller—American Poet*. New York: Crowell, 1953.
Markino, Yoshio. *A Japanese Artist in London*. Philadelphia: George W. Jacobs and Company, 1910.
Marx, Edward. " 'A Different Mode of Speech': Yone Noguchi in Meiji America." In *Recollecting Early Asian America: Essays in Cultural History*, edited by Josephine Lee, Imogene L. Lim, and Yuko Matsukawa, 288–306. Philadelphia: Temple University Press, 2002.
Massad, Joseph. "Re-Orienting Desire: The Gay International and the Arab World." *Public Culture* 14, no. 2 (Spring 2002): 361–385.
Matsuzawa Goichi. *Ero no hon*. Tokyo: Wani no Ana, 1997.

McBride, Dwight. *Why I Hate Abercrombie and Fitch: Essays on Race and Sexuality*. New York: New York University Press, 2005.

McClintock, Ann. *Imperial Leather: Race, Gender, and Sexuality in the Colonial Contest*. New York: Routledge, 1995.

McGrath, Ann. "White Brides: Images of Marriage across Colonizing Boundaries." *Frontiers: A Journal of Women Studies* 23, no. 3 (2002): 76–108.

McLelland, Mark J. *Male Homosexuality in Modern Japan: Cultural Myths and Social Realities*. Richmond, Surrey: Curzon Press, 2000.

———. *Queer Japan: From the Pacific War to the Internet Age*. New York: Rowman and Littlefield Publishers, 2005.

Meech, Julia, and Gabriel P. Weisberg. *Japonisme Comes to America: The Japanese Impact on the Graphic Arts, 1876–1925*. New York: Harryn Abrams, 1990.

Mihashi Osamu. *Meiji no sekushuariti: sabetsu no shinseishi*. Tokyo: Nihon Editā Sukūru, 1999.

Miller, Joaquin. *Complete Poetical Works*. San Francisco: The Whitaker and Ray Company, 1902.

Miller, Joaquin, and Yone Noguchi. *Japan of Sword and Love*. Tokyo: Kanao Bunyendō Publishers, 1905.

Miss Morning Glory [Yone Noguchi]. *American Diary of a Japanese Girl*. New York: Fredrick A. Stokes Publishing House, 1901.

———. *American Letters of a Japanese Parlor-Maid*. Tokyo: Fuzanbō, 1905.

Moran, Rachel F. *Interracial Intimacy: The Regulation of Race and Romance*. Chicago: University of Chicago Press, 2001.

Morgan, Tracy D. "Pages of Whiteness: Race, Physique Magazines, and the Emergence of Public Gay Culture." In *Queer Studies: A Lesbian, Gay, Bisexual, and Transgender Anthology*, edited by Brett Beemyn and Mickey Eliason, 282–290. New York: New York University Press, 1996.

Muñoz, José. *Disidentifications: Queers of Color and the Performance of Politics*. Minneapolis: University of Minnesota Press, 1999.

Murphy, Timothy F., ed. *Gay Ethics: Controversies in Outing, Civil Rights and Sexual Science*. New York: Haworth Press, 1994.

Nakazawa Kazutoshi. "Meiji kikō no kangeki." *Shinchō 45* 6, no.7 (1987): 176–196.

Napier, Susan. "Selected English Writings of Yone Noguchi: An East-West Literary Assimilation." *Bulletin of the School of Oriental and African Studies* 54, no. 3 (1991): 627–628.

Neary, Ian. "Burakumin at the End of History—History of Social Class in Japan." *Social Research: An International Quarterly of the Social Sciences* 70, no. 1 (Spring 2003): 269–296.

Niiya, Brian, ed. *Japanese American History: An A-to-Z Reference from 1868 to the Present*. New York: Facts on File, 1993.

Nitobe, Inazo. *Bushido: The Soul of Japan*. Rutland, VT: Charles E. Tuttle Company, 1969.

Noguchi, Yone [Noguchi Yonejirō]. *American Diary of a Japanese Girl, an Annotated Edition*. Edited by Edward Marx and Laura E. Franey. Philadelphia: Temple University Press, 2007.

———. *Collected Poems*. Edited by Usaburo Toyama. Tokyo: Yone Noguchi Society, 1965.

———. *Eibei no jūsannen*. Tokyo: Shunyōdō, 1905.

———. *From the Eastern Sea*. London: Unicorn Press, 1903.

———. "In the Bungalow with Charles Warren Stoddard: A Protest against Modernism," *National Magazine*, December 1904, 304–307.

———. *Kichō no ki*. Tokyo: Shunyōdō, 1904.

———. *Seen and Unseen: Monologues of a Homeless Snail*. San Francisco: Gelett Burgess and Porter Garnett, 1897.

———. *The Story of Yone Noguchi Told by Himself*. Philadelphia: George W. Jacobs and Company, 1915.

———. *Suwaru Ningen no Hyōron*. Tokyo: Kaizōsha, 1925.

———. *Voice of the Valley*. San Francisco: William Doxey, 1897.

———. *Ware Nihonjin nari*. Tokyo: Takemura Shobō, 1938.

———. *Yonejirō Noguchi senshū: 3 kaigai bungaku shiron*. Tokyo: Kabushikigaisha Kuresu Shuppan, 1998.

Notehelfer, F. G. "Review of Nitobe Inazō, ed., John F. Howes." *Journal of Japanese Studies* 22, no. 2 (1996): 450–453.

Novkov, Julie. "Racial Constructions: The Legal Regulation of Miscegenation in Alabama, 1890–1934." *Law and History Review* 20, no. 2 (Summer 2002): 225–277.

Ong, Aihwa. *Flexible Citizenship: The Cultural Logics of Transnationality*. Durham, NC: Duke University Press, 1999.

Osumi, Megumi Dick. "Asians and California's Anti-Miscegenation Laws." In *Asian and Pacific American Experiences: Women's Perspectives*, edited by Nobuya Tsuchida, 1–37. Minneapolis, MN: Asian/Pacific Learning Resource Center and General College University of Minnesota Minneapolis, 1982.

Painter, Nell Irvin. " 'Social Equality,' Miscegenation, Labor, and Power." In *The Evolution of Southern Culture*, edited by Numan Bartley, 47–67. Athens, GA: University of Georgia Press, 1988.

Parry, Albert. *Garrets and Pretenders*. New York: Covici Friede Publishers, 1933.

Pascoe, Peggy. "Miscegenation Law, Court Cases, and Ideologies of 'Race' in Twentieth-Century America." *Journal of American History* 83 (1996): 44–69.

———. "Race, Gender, and Intercultural Relations: The Case of Interracial Marriage." *Frontiers: A Journal of Women Studies* 12, no. 1 (1991): 5–19.

Pflugfelder, Gregory M. *Cartographies of Desire: Male-Male Sexuality in Japanese Discourse, 1600–1950.* Berkeley and Los Angeles: University of California Press, 1999.

Poe, Edgar Allan. *The Works of Edgar Allan Poe in One Volume: Tales and Poems.* Roslyn, NY: Black's Readers Service, 1971.

Putnam, Frank. "Yone Noguchi," *Boston Transcript*, 8 April 1902.

Rich, Adrienne. *Blood, Bread and Poetry: Selected Prose, 1979–1986.* New York: Norton, 1986.

Robertson, Pamela. *Guilty Pleasures: Feminist Camp from Mae West to Madonna.* Durham, NC: Duke University Press, 1996.

Rubin, Gayle. "Thinking Sex." In *The Lesbian and Gay Studies Reader*, edited by Henry Abelove, Michèle Aina Barale, and David M. Halperin, 33–44. New York: Routledge, 1993.

Said, Edward. *Orientalism.* New York: Vintage Books, 2003.

San Francisco Bohemian Club. *Bohemian Club Authors: A Brief Catalog of Their Published Works 1937.* San Francisco: Grabhorn Press, 1937.

Sarrel, Phillip M., and William H. Masters. "Sexual Molestation of Men by Women." *Archives of Sexual Behavior* 11, no. 2 (1982): 117–131.

Sato, Hiroaki. "Yone Noguchi: Accomplishments and Roles." *Journal of American and Canadian Studies* 13 (1995). http://www.info.sophia.ac.jp/amecana/Journal/13–5.htm (accessed 4 October 2002).

Saxton, Alexander. *Indispensable Enemy: Labor and Anti-Chinese Movement in California.* Berkeley: University of California Press, 1971.

Schalow, Paul Gordon. "Kūkai and the Tradition of Male Love in Japanese Buddhism." In *Buddhism, Sexuality, and Gender*, edited by José Ignacio Cabezón, 215–230. Albany, NY: State University of New York Press, 1992.

Sedgwick, Eve Kosofsky. *Between Men: English Literature and Male Homosocial Desire.* New York: Columbia University Press, 1984.

Shah, Nayan. "Between 'Oriental Depravity' and 'Natural Degenerates': Spatial Borderlands and the Making of Ordinary Americans." *America Quarterly* 57, no. 3 (September 2005): 703–725.

Shiga Nobuo. "Noguchi Yonejirō to Isamu Noguchi: futari no nijūkokusekisha." *Kaigai ijō* 592 (March 2000): 22–25.

Shunsuke Kamei. *Nashonarizumu no bungaku.* Tokyo: Kodansha, 1988.

Sinfield, Alan. *The Wilde Century: Effeminacy, Oscar Wilde and the Queer Moment.* London: Cassell, 1994.

Smith-Rosenberg, Carroll. *Disorderly Conduct: Visions of Gender in Victorian America.* New York: Oxford University Press, 1986.

Somerville, Siobahn. *Queering the Color Line: Race and the Invention of Homosexuality in American Culture*. Durham, NC: Duke University Press, 2000.
Spickard, Paul R. *Mixed Blood: Intermarriage and Ethnic Identity in Twentieth-Century America*. Madison, WI: University of Wisconsin Press, 1989.
Stanley, C. M. "An Alabama Romance and Its Painful End." *Montgomery Advertiser*, 2 July 1950.
Stansell, Christine. *American Moderns: Bohemian New York and the Creation of a New Century*. New York: Henry Holt and Company, 2000.
Stein, Marc. "Theoretical Politics, Local Communities: The Making of a U.S. LGBT Historiography." *GLQ: Gay and Lesbian Quarterly* 11, no. 4 (2005): 605–625.
Stoddard, Charles Warren. *Cruising the South Seas*. Edited by Winston Leyland. San Francisco: Gay Sunshine Press, 1987.
———. *For the Pleasure of His Company: An Affair of the Misty City*. San Francisco: A. M. Robertson, 1903.
———. *Hawaiian Life, or Lazy Letters from Low Latitudes*. Chicago and New York: F. T. Neely Publisher, 1894.
———. *A Troubled Heart and How It Was Comforted at Last*. Notre Dame, IN: Joseph A. Lyons, 1885.
Stoler, Ann Laura. "Sexual Affronts and Racial Frontiers: European Identities and the Cultural Politics of Exclusion in Colonial Southeast Asia." In *Tensions of Empire: Colonial Cultures in a Bourgeois World*, edited by Frederick Cooper and Ann Laura Stoler, 198–237. Berkeley: University of California Press, 1997.
Strong, Isobel, and Lloyd Osbourne. *Memories of Vailima*. New York: Charles Scribner's Sons, 1902.
Sueyoshi, Amy. "Finding Fellatio: Friendship, History and Yone Noguchi." In *Embodying Asian American Sexualities*, edited by Gina Masequesmay and Sean Metzger, 157–172. Lanham, MD: Lexington Books, 2009.
———. "Mindful Masquerades: Que(e)rying Japanese Immigrant Dress in Turn-of-the-Century San Francisco." *Frontiers: A Journal of Women Studies* 26, no. 3 (2005): 67–100.
———. "Miss Morning Glory: Orientalism and Misogyny in the Queer Writings of Yone Noguchi." *Amerasia Journal—Special Issue: Further Desire* 37, no. 2 (2011): 2–27.
Takaki, Ronald. *Strangers from a Different Shore: A History of Asian Americans*. New York: Penguin Books, 1989.
Thompson, Mildred E. *Ida B. Wells Barnett: An Exploratory Study of an American Black Woman, 1893–1930*. Brooklyn, NY: Carlson, 1990.
Tilton, Robert S. *Pocahontas: The Evolution of an American Narrative*. New York: Cambridge University Press, 1994.

Ting, Jennifer. "Bachelor Society: Deviant Heterosexuality and Asian American Historiography." In *Privileging Positions: The Sites of Asian American Studies*, ed. Gary Y. Okihiro et al., 271–280. Pullman: Washington State University Press, 1995.

Toyama Usaburō, ed. *Shijin Yone Noguchi kenkyū*. Vol. 3. Tokyo: Zōkei Bijutsu Kyōkai Shuppanbō, 1975.

———. *Yone Noguchi kenkyū: ronbunshū*. 2 vols. Tokyo: Zōkei Bijutsu Kyōkai Shuppankyoku, 1963–1965.

Traub, Valerie. "Friendship's Loss: Alan Bray's Making of History." *GLQ: Gay and Lesbian Quarterly* 10, no. 3 (2004): 339–365.

Turner, Patricia A. *Ceramic Uncles and Celluloid Mammies: Black Images and Their Influence on Culture*. New York: Anchor, 1994.

Ujie Mikito. *Bushidō to erosu*. Tokyo: Kodansha, 1995.

Unna, Warren. *The Coppa Murals: A Pageant of Bohemian Life in San Francisco at the Turn of the Century*. San Francisco: The Book Club of California, 1952.

Unno Hiroshi. "Uesuto kōsuto no Bohemia: San Furanshisuko no shiteki fūdo." *Gendaishitechou* 44, no. 2 (February 2001): 32–35.

Vicinus, Martha. *Intimate Friends: Women Who Loved Women, 1778–1928*. Chicago: University of Chicago Press, 2004.

Wada Keiko. "Noguchi Yonejirō no Rondon: aikokushin to kokusuishugi," *Ōsaka Gakuin Daigaku gaikokugo ronshū* 45 (March 2002): 41–59.

———. "Noguchi Yonejirō no Rondon: ayamekai no naifun." *Ōsaka Gakuin Daigaku gaikokugo ronshū* 41 (March 2000): 13–32.

———. "Noguchi Yonejirō no Rondon: Japonizumu no arashi." *Ōsaka Gakuin Daigaku gaikokugo ronshū* 39 (March 1999): 41–60.

———. "Noguchi Yonejiro no Rondon (1)—shijin debyu ichizenya." *Ōsaka Gakuin Daigaku gaikokugo ronshū* 33 (March 1996), 118–131.

———. "Noguchi Yonejirō no Rondon (2)—hajimete no shishū." *Ōsaka Gakuin Daigaku gaikokugo ronshū* 34 (September 1996): 112–114.

Watanabe, Toshio. *High Victorian Japonisme*. New York: Peter Lang, 1991.

Watanabe, Tsuneo, and Jun'ichi Iwata. *The Love of the Samurai: A Thousand Years of Japanese Homosexuality*. Translated by D. R. Roberts. London: GMP Publishers Ltd., 1989.

Waters, Mary C. *Black Identities: West Indian Immigrant Dreams and Immigrant Realities*. Cambridge, MA: Harvard University Press, 2001.

———. *Ethnic Options: Choosing Identities in America*. Berkeley: University of California Press, 1990.

Weeks, Jeffrey. *Sexuality and Its Discontents: Meanings, Myths, and Modern Sexualities*. London: Routledge and Kegan Paul, 1985.

White-Parks, Annette. *Sui Sin Far/Edith Maude Eaton* (Chicago: University of Illinois Press, 1995.

Wilson, Elizabeth. *Bohemians: Glamorous Outcasts*. New Brunswick, NJ: Rutgers University Press, 2000.

Wu, Judy Tzu-chun. *Doctor Mom Chung of the Fair-Haired Bastards: The Life of a Wartime Celebrity*. Berkeley and Los Angeles: University of California Press, 2005.

Yin, Xiao-huang. *Chinese American Literature since the 1850s*. Chicago: University of Illinois Press, 2000.

Yokota Junya. "Noguchi Yonejirō to shin seiki." *Kosho wandārando*, 66 (May 2001): 76–79.

Yokota-Murakami, Takayuki. *Don Juan East/West: On the Problematics of Comparative Literature*. Albany: State University of New York, 1998.

Yoshihara, Mari. *Embracing the East: White Women and American Orientalism*. New York: Oxford University Press, 2003.

———. "The Flight of the Japanese Butterfly: Orientalism, Nationalism, and Performances of Japanese Womanhood." *American Quarterly* 56, no. 4 (2004): 975–1001.

Zhang, Benzi. "Mapping Carnivalistic Discourse in Japanese-American Writing." *MELUS* 24, no. 4 (Winter 1999): 19–41.

Zuckerman, Marvin. "Physiological Measures of Sexual Arousal in the Human." *Psychological Bulletin* 75, no. 5 (May 1971): 297–329.

Index

About the Author

Amy Sueyoshi is an associate professor with a joint appointment in race and resistance studies and sexuality studies at San Francisco State University. She has published on topics ranging from cross-dressing, same-sex marriage, romantic friendship, and Asian American pornography. Before her career in academia, she served as a U.S. Peace Corps volunteer and worked as a community organizer for Asian Americans for Equality in New York City. She is active in APIQWTC, Asian Pacific Islander Queer Women and Transgender Community, and is on the board of directors of the GLBT Historical Society.